Anti-Foundationalism
and Practical Reasoning

Anti-Foundationalism and Practical Reasoning

Conversations between Hermeneutics and Analysis

Edited by Evan Simpson

Published by
Academic Printing & Publishing
Edmonton, Alberta, Canada

Canadian Cataloguing in Publication Data

Main entry under title:
  Anti-foundationalism and practical reasoning

  Based on papers originally presented at a conference
held at McMaster University in September 1986.
  Includes bibliographical references and index.
  ISBN 0-920980-26-0 (bound) — ISBN 0-920980-27-9 (pbk.)

  1. Hermeneutics. 2. Analysis (Philosophy).
I. Simpson, Evan, 1940-
BD241.A58 1987   121'.68   C87-091375-1

© 1987 Academic Printing & Publishing
Cover art by Alasdair Gray
Printed by Art Design Printing Inc., Edmonton, Alberta, Canada

Table of Contents

Part III – Moral Reflection

Part IV – Legal Deliberation

Acknowledgements

The following papers originated in a conference on 'Anti-Foundationalist Views of Practical Reasoning' held at McMaster University in September, 1986. They respond to an invitation to engage in 'conversations between hermeneutics and analysis,' and thanks are owed to the contributors who courageously confronted the dangers of mixed conversation and now expose their words to a wider readership.

Acknowledgements are due to the British Council, the Social Sciences and Humanities Research Council of Canada, and McMaster University for financial support; to *Telos* for permission to reprint Rebecca Comay's contribution to this volume; to Manon Ames and Jacquie Collin of McMaster's Humanities Word Processing Center for helping to bring a diversity of scholarly styles into a common editorial format; and to Shari Mercer of the Department of Philosophy for the meticulous and flawless organization which enabled our discussions to proceed free from technical complications and interruptions.

Thanks are owed as well to the chairpersons of the four sessions, who have contributed brief orientations to each of the four groups of papers; to Robert Ezergailis for careful summaries of the proceedings and useful comments about the central themes; and to the members of the audience, whose questions and remarks gave sharp definition to the issues raised in the papers. These people are the real authors of much of the introductory essay to this volume.

E.S.

Evan Simpson

Colloquimur, ergo sumus

In essays on Vico and Herder, Isaiah Berlin observed:

> The notion that there exist eternal and unalterable truths, laws, rules
> of conduct which entail ends of life which any man might, in theory,
> have recognized in any time and in any place, and the discovery and
> pursuit of which is the sole and sufficient goal of all human behavior,
> is the central principle of the Enlightenment. Its rejection, with its ap-
> peal for a far wider psychological imagination, marks a decisive turning-
> point in the history of Western thought.[1]

For the most part, however, the posssibility of finding grounds for
our practices only in the history of our culture rather than in the recognition of eternal realities or principles has not become the dominant
opinion in modern philosophy. Whether it could ever do so is open
to question.

When Berlin was exploring the historicist tradition during the
1950s and 1960s the dominant issue about 'foundations' was a fairly
clearly and narrowly defined question in analytic philosophy about
the justification of belief.[2] Since then, the debate about foundations
has become much wider and more diffuse. It has been claimed repeatedly that the search for foundations of knowledge has been effectively discredited by thinkers as different as W.V. Quine and Ludwig
Wittgenstein on the one hand, Hans-Georg Gadamer and Martin
Heidegger on the other. It has also often been claimed that the broadly analytic philosophy prevailing in English-speaking countries and
the broadly hermeneutical philosophy generally associated with the
European continent share central interests.[3] Conjoining these claims
generates the third thesis that a primary point of convergence between
the two philosophical traditions is a revived and broadened 'anti-
foundationalism.'

Much of the new vigour of the debate on foundations stems from
Richard Rorty's success in establishing 'anti-foundationalism' as a slogan

1

for a complex cluster of ideas previously lacking resonant expression.[4] Suddenly 'anti-foundationalist' is a good thing to be. Of course, questions of abiding interest are as subject to the novelty of philosophical fashion as the utility of clothing is to the latest styles, but in philosophy the fashions may have their own utility, constituting new perspectives from which to revitalize voices which have been too weak.

Although the anti-foundationalist tendency first focused on epistemology, it has just as much application to practical matters — to questions in which the place of decision has always been evident, that is, to the questions which define political, moral, and legal philosophy. Together they constitute the areas in which the convergence of analytical and hermeneutical interests is most apparent. In the snapshot of contemporary debate constituted by this volume, it is clear that a dozen able philosophers speak a language which, for all its different idioms, accents, and professional jargons, is not difficult to understand and to appreciate. They engage the possibility of practical knowledge without foundations and the relationship between philosophy and change when there is no Archimedean point from which to understand human nature or society.

I The Concept of Foundations

One consequence of the recent liberation of the issue of foundations from technical philosophy is that the concept is often used in an untamed way. The word has become elastic, stretching easily to cover a variety of positions. As a result, the expressions 'anti-foundationalism,' 'post-foundationalism,' and the like have little descriptive usefulness until the main disagreements this flexibility harbours are clear.

Foundationalism and anti-foundationalism remain positions best understood by their relationship to epistemology. The one seeks, and the other dismisses the notion of, criteria defining conditions in which some beliefs are finally justified. Few deny that beliefs need foundations, that is, the more or less secure grounds which make the conclusions of argument as solid as they can be. Any pure foundationalism, however, supposes that genuine grounds for judgment are not merely confident assumptions but absolutely secure bases which are not subject to amendment, or are amendable only in the direction of greater accuracy. Only in this way could they serve as arbiters of rational judgment. This is the notion of a single, over-arching, ahistorical standard against which any claim can be tested, so that it is possible in principle to decide between rival points of view.

The strongest conception of foundations is that of criteria for unassailably certain beliefs. The corresponding anti-foundationalism is a rejection of all candidates for such certainties — intuitve self-evidence, analytical relations of ideas, sense-impressions, or whatever. Since intuitions, impressions, and other immediate encounters with reality no longer represent theories that are taken very seriously, almost all philosophers today are anti-foundationalists in this sense.

In place of such discoverable agreements between assertions and realities, it is tempting to understand justification as a matter of rational agreement amongst bodies of assertion. Kai Nielsen's defence of 'wide reflective equilibrium' as such a criterion is anti-foundationalist in the above sense. While foreswearing certainties, it is arguably foundationalist in another: seeking a general criterion which justifies a whole body of beliefs even though none of them is individually beyond question. A consensus which represents reflective equilibrium is that which justifies the whole. To be sure, any such equilibrium is tentative and probably temporary, but it remains possible to dispute whether the criterion of wide reflective equilibrium is itself tentative and temporary. If it is taken to be so, that suggests an anti-foundationalism which rejects any attempt to provide an irrevisable criterion of rational justification. Seen from this perspective, methodologies like wide reflective equilibrium may be very useful, but their value will be that of practical maxims rather than unquestionable principles. The maxim in this case is perhaps that anything may be relevant to anything else and should be taken into consideration. If this interpretation of the method deprives it of justifying power, the loss may be preferable to supposing that in order to resolve any problem we require a way of solving all problems.

To replace forms of justification which appropriate the notion of agreement with reality with appeals to consensus is not to make a foundationalist move if it does not demand that there be a privileged philosophical criterion for distinguishing a rational consensus from whatever agreements are reached through discussion. Such indifference to basic criteria of rationality can be expressed as a disclaimer of interest in fashioning a theory of truth or knowledge, although one may nevertheless seek to articulate what one means by the word 'true,' explain its connection with 'know' and other words, trace the history of the concept, etc. The problem of knowledge, seen in this way, is no longer a foundational one, or one which might have a theoretical answer of the sort sought by epistemology.

From the standpoint of epistemology this viewpoint is difficult to understand. It is natural to interpret expressions of the anti-foundationalist attitude as new versions of old debates, as just forms of scepticism or relativism. The attack on foundations does not see itself in this way, however, for while epistemological scepticism challenges our claims to knowledge, it accepts the notion that there is such a thing as knowledge only if there are foundations for it. By rejecting this conception of knowledge, the anti-foundationalist position distinguishes itself from scepticism in the traditional sense. Moreover, in contrast to relativism and the suggestion that languages and cultures have an inside and an outside, there is room in the anti-theoretical point of view only for meaningfulness or for failure of understanding. It is not that truth is 'relative' to a language or culture but that the only alternative to a capacity for agreement is incomprehension.

A philosophical position without foundations can be discomfiting. It seems scarcely more satisfying to the modern mind than the ancient cosmological picture of the earth resting on the backs of elephants with their feet firmly planted on a tortoise surrounded by a serpent whose mode of support is undefined. For philosophers accustomed to solid ground, the result can be a sort of vertigo or sea-sickness, fear of losing touch and going mad. The assault on foundations is not meant to satisfy the modern mind, however, but to dispense with its quest for a resting place. The best palliative for such uneasiness may be another set of pictures or metaphors, such as those which dot Wittgenstein's *On Certainty*. Beliefs need grounds, but these grounds are like a riverbed whose course changes with time. A system of beliefs must be stable, but this stability is like the axis of rotation of a spinning top rather than a permanently fixed point. Some beliefs are fundamental, acting as the hinges on which others presently turn, but the placement of the hinges need not be permanent.[5]

Metaphors are not arguments and need not be persuasive. The position they represent may seem flatly inconsistent, and a variety of arguments can be advanced to suggest that anti-foundationalism entails some form of foundationalism. Thus: anti-foundationalism purports to be anti-theoretical, but to reject a theory is to state a theoretical position, hence to be committed to (anti-anti-)foundationalism. It is not clear, though, that anyone need assent to the premise that to reject one theory is to be committed to another. It may instead be to insist that the questions the theory addresses are absurd or unanswerable.

Another common argument for the incoherence of anti-foundationalism is this: If the claim is that the only grounds for belief are located within an historical context, then this assertion too must be so located, and it therefore has limited validity and cannot command philosophical assent; but if the anti-foundationalist claim is not itself context-dependent we are back to absolutes and therefore to foundations. This familiar dilemma for historicism can be deflected by cheerful indifference to the ideal of universal asset. Instead of supposing that rationality has a nature and trying to explicate it theoretically, the point rather is to be sensitive to the fact that the intelligibility of social practices depends on taking them on their own terms, and that assessing other practices depends on the comparability of cultural contexts. Within Western society it makes sense to debate the respective desirability of a Christian and a secular way of life. By contrast, the corresponding question about Christianity and primitive witchcraft asked in the abstract makes little sense. There is not enough continuity between the traditions.

Still another argument uncovering the hidden foundations of anti-foundationalism is the following reflection. The identification of a problem indicates that something is not as it should be, and any such judgment requires a criterion for distinguishing when things have gone right from when they have gone wrong. Without such a criterion nothing can be identified as a problem, yet any such criterion entails a kind of foundationalism, since we can never know that the problem is a real one until it is appropriately integrated with all of our knowledge. It is far from clear, though, that we need an abstract or general criterion for distinguishing what is experienced as a problem from a 'real' problem. Without having accepted the foundationalist viewpoint in the first place, it would seem that the anxieties and tensions arising within local understandings of the good are sufficiently real.

Just as there is no relevant sense in which we can get 'inside' or 'outside' a system of belief, there is no valid view of life from 'above' or 'below.' With foundations of knowledge goes the notion that our practices can be rationalized by something transcending praxis. Anti-foundationalism accepts the precariousness of all projects. It sees no possibility of an ultimate criterion of what it is to be reasonable, of what it is for something to be a moral problem, or what it is to be a meaningful conversation. These are judgments made by members of an historical community, and historicity is the enemy of foundations.

II Philosophical Practices

The above disagreements put in issue the objectives of philosophy. If one thinks that the job of philosophy is to be the guardian of reason and to define basic reasons for beliefs and actions, then 'foundations' are required to make this possible. If one thinks that the job of philosophy is to contribute to the conversation of a culture or to engage in social criticism, then 'foundations' may constitute a distortion of or impediment to discussion.

In repudiating the project of epistemology and the conception of philosophy defined by this project, anti-foundationalism expresses the hope that the successor to modern philosophy may escape the academicism into which contemporary philosophy has settled and endorses an interest in practical matters. It strives to bring the 'human sciences' back into common discourse and purports to open up a political dimension in which a variety of post-foundationalist projects can be pursued. Sullivan's distinction between anti- and post-foundationalism enables philosophers to move from acceptance of the critique of epistemology to participation in contentious cultural debates. There is a strong tendency among post-foundationalists to view philosophy as including social criticism but to disagree in their critical judgments. Some echo Bertolt Brecht's claim that 'art is not a mirror held up to reality, but a hammer with which to shape it.' Others, while agreeing that philosophy is not a mirror of nature, do not believe that it has a significant role in shaping the future or in determining which shape would be most desirable.

Rorty is a strong defender of the political and social institutions of liberal democracies, so much so that (given the flexibility of 'foundationalism') he can be accused of a kind of 'foundationalism' himself. Comay finds in his writings a 'presentism,' a view of the present as providing our grounds of evaluation and as lacking impetus towards anything better. While her picture may promote an ambiguity – conflating the truism that rational judgments have grounds with the notion that grounds might be independent of an historical context – it does accurately represent a central feature of Rorty's anti-foundationalist viewpoint. By confining meaningful criteria of evaluation to cultural norms it tends, like other traditionalisms, to be deeply (although not necessarily uncritically) conservative, or or at least anti-utopian. This may also describe a limitation of the hermeneutical point of view. It is open to question whether philosophical hermeneutics, given the central role it ascribes to particular social understandings, can admit the possibility of radical political critique.

This conservative tendency is evident from Sullivan's observation that anti-foundationalism recognizes the cultural character of thought, while it has been the dream of modern philosophy to transcend that limitation by finding a single standard of value in terms of which to assess all cultures and purposes from a prior-to-society perspective. Post-foundationalism is a reflection of its failure and therefore a recognition that the customs of a community constitute the starting point of evaluation and the means of identifying problems. There being no external point of view from which social practices can ultimately be judged, they are as authoritative as anything could be. The primacy of the participants' point of view precludes judgments from 'above' or 'outside' and shows that the hope of finding a dependable way of resolving all disagreements rationally is misguided.

This is a peculiar conservatism, however, since it appears able to accommodate the whole spectrum of political possibilities. Some anti-foundationalists, including MacIntyre and possibly Gadamer, are anti-modernists in seeking to recover the traditions which they view as essential to a satisfactory sense of self and social unity. Others, like Rorty, view the way of life of liberal democracies as defining the most successful form of social solidarity human beings have yet achieved.

Still others, like Nielsen, seek to define new social possibilities, adjudicating between socialism and capitalism and solving the problem of the best society.

Given the anti-foundationalist denial of general criteria for distinguishing problems from non-problems, it is questionable whether philosophy can adjudicate successfully between alternative social possibilities or deal with large-scale social problems in any efficacious way. It is difficult to see how this could be done except from the standpoint of some conception of human nature or other standard to which certain social arrangements do not conform. In the absence of dependable foundations for human practices, the best we can do is to present novel arrangements for consideration and try to make them appealing. To urge their value in advance of their success in practice seems perilously close to foundationalist pretensions. The stronger the progressive urge, the more it may be necessary to beware these pretensions becoming assumptions.

The apparent sharpness of the distinction between epistemology and politics, as represented by the anti-foundationalist project and various post-foundationalist projects, might here come into question. Insofar as the matters can be kept distinct and we can resist substituting epistemological questions for political ones, then the rejection of theories of knowledge opens the doors wide to social criticism. At the same time it precludes any purely a priori critique of particular practices or policies. It constitutes a cautious approach to certainty in political philosophy, placing experience over speculation, conversation over revolution.

Certainty is always culturally located, residing only in practices. A practice — whether it be the law, morality, politics, or literature — can only proceed through a system of rules which determine what is a relevant consideration. Because the facts of the matter in these various cases are read through the rules and are not brute facts, deliberation is always an interpretative activity. The facts in question are often determinable, so that it is possible to make true claims with legal, moral, political, or literary certainty, but these truths cannot be compared to the objects of traditional epistemology. As MacCormick suggests, they have implications for what there is and what can be known, but these metaphysical and epistemological issues may perhaps be best seen as branches of practical activity rather than speculative thought. They are not 'first philosophy' but expressions of what is done rather than the normative grounds of our activity.

A foundationalist model of certainty in practical reasoning tends to represent decisions as inferences from a general claim and a particular instance of it: murder is always punishable, and this is murder, therefore this is punishable. It is not clear that the notion of deduction does any significant work here. The interesting part of such judgments is in the identification of an action as murder. This is a matter of interpretation rather than something that can be determined as the result of deductive argument alone. The importance we assign to deduction might therefore best be explained not as giving information about the nature of practical reasoning but as expressing commitment to the equality of all persons involved in a discussion. Just as the equality of citizens is expressed in treating actions subject to legal adjudication alike, bringing other practical decisions under universal conditions also expresses the equality of the decision-makers. Such expressions evidently constitute a conception of rational argument rather than define an independently rational criterion of argument.

III Utopian Tensions

Within a dialectical mode of inquiry many strains are to be expected: denials are ever-present and the urge to overcome these negations is endemic. The tendency to find foundational assumptions at the heart of the contrary position is a clear example of this urge. It pertains as well to the claims of convergence between once-isolated streams of philosophical inquiry, a generalization which seems to fall easy victim to any sensitivity for differences.

Parts of the dispute about convergence result from the fact that neither analytic nor Continental philosophy is an homogeneous movement. The hermeneutical trends in Continental philosophy can be characterized as 'conservative' and as having important affinities with the work of Rorty, Dworkin, and others. These commonalities and convergences of interest are far less evident in the case of members of the Frankfurt School before Habermas. Their Marxist assumptions would seem to presuppose the possibility of a standard against which to measure progress, to see the culture-centered tendencies of hermeneutics as naively idealist, or to surpass the limited perspective of philosophy which is concerned only to interpret the world.

Those, like Comay, who would save Continental philosophy from conservatives cannot easily be convicted of sneaking in the foundationalist assumptions their historicism rejects. By practicing only 'negative critique,' the earlier Frankfurt School could depict liberal society in terms contrary to the culture's own self-understanding, and the critics were not obliged to support this unflattering interpretation with a practical alternative. When it comes to Habermas the picture is more complicated. Rather as MacCormick tries to discern general conditions of practical reasoning, Habermas seeks to describe the conditions necessary for the possibility of any human dialogue and to provide an account of truth as the outcome of free and undistorted discussion. Success in the endeavour would give a criterion of progress as whatever conformed to the result of such conversation, rather than as something knowable in advance: but in trying to lay down once for all what a rational conversation is and what truth is, we seem to have here a clearly foundationalist idea. The proper resolution of this issue is unclear. One reason for seeking an account of truth and conversation is to protect ourselves from the socially powerful who can dominate social exchanges and get away with it unless there is such an account to set the rules. Seen in this way, Habermas's commitment to transcendental conditions, like the place suggested above for the role of deductivist reconstructions of legal reasoning, appears to express a political purpose rather than an epistemological one. The objective is to gain acceptance for a regulative ideal.

At this point, the practical equivalent of epistemological vertigo can no longer be forestalled. If there is no essence of reason, truth, and knowledge, then there is no infallible defense against anti-rationalist movements such as fascism and religious fanaticism. The hard-headed response is that there is no defense of the kind that philosophers have sought: the only defense is to keep talking. The final solution to anti-rationalism is the recognition that there are no final solutions. Understanding this, we are left with a practical problem: the limited willingness or capacity of people who see the world very differently to engage in productive conversation.

There could hardly be a more striking opposition than that between perceptions of our society as in the midst of crisis, moral incoherence, a breakdown of practical reasoning, and claims that, far from lacking shared values sufficient to sustain conversation, we enjoy the best form of solidarity to date. There is no accepted criterion of 'crisis' or 'coherence' but only conflicting interpretations of our social institutions and structures. Neither set of voices can silence the other if they adopt the unassailable positions afforded by the optionality of interpretation, in contrast to the compulsion of fact. This is not promising stuff for a conversation: the only appeals are to an audience or to patience. The limits of philosophical analysis and hermeneutics reside here, where dogma and history appear to supervene upon the decorum of discourse between parties interested in securing agreement, or at least continuing an argument.

The rejection of foundations means that philosophy cannot secure the rationality of conversation by some other means than conversation itself – and that conversation cannot be definitively distinguished from sophistical rhetoric. This does not mean that the ancient contest between philosophy and rhetoric is decided in favour of persuasion over reason. The following papers make a contrary case. They attest to the indefatigability of the critical and philosophical temperament in senses of 'philosophy' and 'criticism' which remain unbroken. They assert a continuing role for philosophy as the critical enterprise which reflects upon the assumptions of our discourses. Seeking the conditions of knowledge of self and nature, of moral and legal traditions, philosophy has tried to bring to discussions more than well-developed critical skills and a store of classical arguments. Even if it has not notably succeeded, the problems it addresses continue to assert their demands. The demands are unrelenting if only because our discourses do include assumptions about acceptable evidence and valid argument, hence about what there is and how we know it. These unsecured assumptions belong to the class of the most permanent objects of critical inquiry we can imagine.

When philosophy turns its critical attention to its own conditions, the outcome can always be predicted. The anti-foundationlist expression of the inevitable uncertainty yields conclusions which can scarcely be doubted. We are reminded that philosophers explore competing interpretations of the world, a point whose value lies in the fact that it is a reminder rather than a new and interesting discovery. We are provided with slogans – 'anti-foundationalism,' 'hermeneutics'

— which are valuable in reasserting a valid point of view but which like other slogans are likely to drop quickly into disuse. The present ones, while they last, are in the best tradition of self-examination. They restore realization of the deep connections between discussion and our understanding of our existence.[6]

NOTES

1 Isaiah Berlin, *Vico and Herder: Two Studies in the History of Ideas* (New York: Viking Press 1976), 140

2 The issue is reviewed by Ernest Sosa, 'The Raft and the Pyramid: Coherence versus Foundations in the Theory of Knowledge,' *Midwest Studies in Philosophy* **5** (1980) 3-25.

3 See, for example, Ronald Bruzina and Bruce Wilshire, eds., *Phenomenology: Dialogues and Bridges* (Albany: State University of New York Press 1982) and Richard Bernstein, *Beyond Objectivism and Relativism* (Philadelphia: University of Pennsylvania Press 1983), 1-7.

4 See Richard Rorty, *Philosophy and the Mirror of Nature* (Princeton, NJ: Princeton University Press 1979), along with many of his other works cited in the following discussions.

5 Ludwig Wittgenstein, *On Certainty* (Oxford: Blackwell 1969), sections 97, 152, 341

6 Thanks are due to Barry Allen, Stanley Clarke, and David Hitchcock for suggestions about this introduction.

I

Practical
Philosophy

Practical Philosophy

One of the most encouraging developments at the present time is the dialogue that has begun to take place in North America between those two worlds which hitherto were, quasi-axiomatically, held to be incommensurable: so-called Continental thought and analytic philosophy. The papers which follow should furnish ample proof that a genuine dialogue has indeed begun. As is the case with dialogues over fences, the papers by Sullivan, Grondin, and McCormick do not conclude in a grand statement of universal agreement. Instead they clarify issues and isolate possible areas of agreement and disagreement. In so doing they show that there remains a great deal for philosophy to do after the end of what Rorty has referred to as Philosophy.

As William Sullivan remarks in his paper, one of the great benefits of the movement away from philosophical foundationalism is that it allows philosophers to enter into meaningful conversations with non-philosophers. It has, as he says, 'brought academic philosophy back into the wider world of discourse.' Sullivan attempts to show how what he calls post-foundationalism is the first really new movement in Anglo-American philosophy since positivism, and he provides not only an historical background of the post-foundationalist movement in the Anglo-Saxon world but also a critical delineation of its main features. In this regard he discusses Habermas's objections to the post-modern aspects of post-foundationalism (e.g., its apparent denial of universal validity claims) and the kind of responses Rorty would make to these objections. This leads him to discuss some of the deep cultural divisions he perceives to exist between the Anglo-American and the Continental cultural traditions. Here Sullivan reveals quite clearly the moral-practical concerns of post-foundational thinking and shows that if discourse is to go forward what needs to be provided is 'not Reason, but reasons for minds and positions to change.' The conversational exchange is not a mere war of words.

Jean Grondin seeks to show how the hermeneutical notion of truth provides a possible bridge between analytic philosophy and hermeneutics. This reflection by a 'Continentalist' on the current North American scene links the hermeneutical position with its wider European background and, in particular, with the key notion of 'truth' in Gadamer's philosophizing. This is a notion which Gadamer himself has not fully thematized, and Grondin sets out some of its main features. The principal question he confronts is: How does a hermeneutical philosophy, one which stresses the historicity of all validity claims, approach the problem of truth and show that it remains a valid notion in a post-metaphysical age? Like Sullivan, he seeks to underline the ultimately moral-practical nature of a post-foundationalist notion of truth. The issue is not a moralistic one; it is a question of *ethos*. Precisely because there are no definite, or definitely groundable, norms for human comportment, ethos is a supremely important issue. It is, as Grondin says, 'the only way to cope without foundations.' While being strongly opposed to all forms of foundationalism, however, he explicitly rejects relativism as a viable moral option. Conversation or dialogue, properly conceived, is not a recipe for relativism but for a possible universal human community.

If anyone has sought over the years to create the basis for a conversation between 'Continentalists' and analysts, it is Peter McCormick. It is quite understandable, therefore, that, over the years as well, he has been attacked by analysts for being too 'Continental' and criticized by 'Continentalists' for catering too much to analysts. This does not stop him from entering once again into a dialogue. His paper is a discussion of human agency which seeks to balance analytic claims about the nature of action with more recent hermeneutical accounts, finding fault in the process with both of them. McCormick presents a text by T.S. Eliot, shows the seemingly insuperable difficulties it poses for philosophical exegesis, and explores the positions that a hypothetical analytic philosopher and a hypothetical hermeneutical philosopher might take towards them. By considering such 'anomalies' as non-intentional acts, ineffectual causes, fruitless actions, and inconsequential results, McCormick exposes some of the difficulties for self-understanding and agency that lie ahead for philosophy.

McCormick deliberately sets his 'non-foundationalist' analysis of intentional action in opposition to both a 'naturalized analytic causal account' and a 'dialectical hermeneutical volitional account.' What he says is needed is a new idiom which is neither just naturalistic and causal nor just volitional and reflexive. He opposes a certain post-modern conception of philosophy which views it as 'the play of the mind with itself, since no representation of the world is genuine and no talk about the world is more than a text about the world' – in other words, a view of philosophy as a kind of mere word play de-void of any claim to 'truth' (a view which McCormick imputes to Rorty). The overriding purpose of his analysis of action is 'to work against the grain of this particular kind of anti-foundationalism.' McCormick is in effect attempting to outline a non-foundationalist view of human understanding which avoids the linguistic relativism which characterizes, or is thought to characterize, many forms of post-modern *anti*-foundationalism.

This attempt points to what is perhaps the underlying, common thread tying together the three papers in this section and making of them parts of the long-to-be-protracted conversation over the 'end of philosophy.' It is significant from this point of view that Sullivan prefers to speak of *post*-foundationalism rather than *anti*-foundationalism. The issue is 'making sense after foundationalism.' What Sullivan is at pains to indicate is that the abandonment of foundationalism does not neces-sarily entail – as foundationalist critics maintain – an abandonment pure and simple of meaning or sense, i.e., rationality. What it does entail or call for is a redefinition or reconceptualization of rationali-ty. As Sullivan remarks, such a reorientation points inescapably toward a reconception of the role of philosophy. 'The "death of philosophy" after foundationalism is in fact better conceived as a transfiguration.'

Sullivan refers to 'the post-foundationalist understanding of reason-giving' as 'interpretive dialectics.' Its principal characteristic is that it is non-instrumental, being instead 'an effort to build solidarity by discovering new commonplaces among diverse cultural traditions.' It is moral-practical in nature and thus does not admit of undeniable or even rigorously defined premises. Like Grondin, who emphasizes the rhetorical dimensions of post-foundational reason, Sullivan main-tains that 'rationality is always argumentative or dialogical.'

If the issue of rationality stands out as the common, underlying concern of these three discourses, one could also characterize their *locus communis* as an attempt to arrive at a revised notion of *truth*.

Indeed, it could well be said that what principally serves to characterize non- or post-foundational thinking and distinguishes it from mere 'anti-foundationalism' is its attempt not simply to break with the traditional epistemological conception of truth as correspondence but, over and above this, to articulate in a positive way a decidedly non-foundationalist notion of truth. It views truth in an anti-metaphysical fashion as essentially historical and emphasizes its relation to praxis. 'For hermeneutics truth isn't primarily a matter of correspondence,' Grondin writes, 'but of "meaningfulness."' That is true which enables us to order our experience in a meaningful way, which enables us to 'cope' with that which we hold to be real.

Hermeneutics, Grondin reminds us, views the quest for methodological certainty as an attempt to flee, if not to ignore, the finitude of the human condition. 'Hermeneutics is dedicated to what truth means for finite beings.' In its attempt to think through in a rigorous yet non-foundational way such central notions in the philosophical tradition as intelligibility, rationality, and truth, post-foundational philosophy could justifiably be said to be the first really serious attempt on the part of human beings to conceptualize that finitude which is the essence of our being and of all of our works.

Pierre Aubenque once remarked: 'Les hommes ne dialoguent que dans la mesure où ils ne voient pas l'être dont ils parlent et ne se résignent pourtant pas à le réduire à l'expérience unilateral qu'ils en ont.'[1] As these papers show us, dialogue is the attempt to reach common agreements in the absence of metaphysical certainty. A dialogical philosophy is as much opposed to anti-rationalist proclamations of cultural relativity and incommensurability, which amount to a reduction of being to our unilateral experience of it, as it is to all forms of foundational reasoning which seek to determine being in a methodologically indubitable and univocal way and whose net result would be the cessation of dialogue altogether, the end of 'the conversation of mankind.'

G.B. Madison

NOTES

1 Pierre Aubenque, 'Évolution et constantes de la pensée dialectique,' *Les Études philosophiques* (juillet-septembre 1970) 289-301, 301

William M. Sullivan

After Foundationalism:
The Return To Practical Philosophy

I From Anti- to Post-Foundationalism

Perhaps the best effect of the philosophical controversy about what
has come to be called foundationalism is that it has brought academic
philosophy back into the wider world of discourse. Philosophical arguments and debates suddenly seem relevant to a variety of intellectual endeavors in the humanities as well as the social sciences.
Practitioners in those fields are, for the first time in a long time, now
genuinely interested in 'what's going on in philosophy.' Of course,
the foundationalist controversy is not the only area of lively contact
between academic philosophy and the environing cultural worlds. For
some time, the life sciences and health professions have been engaged
in dialogue with philosophical ethics. But while ethics has long been
viewed by much of the philosophical profession as a peripheral field,
the controversy over foundationalism is taking place in the very heart-
land of the empire of analytic philosophy, in philosophy of language,
philosophy of science, and philosophy of mind. Moreover, the arguments have found echoes and powerful resonances in the formerly
very distant realm of Continental philosophy as well, so that Hans-
Georg Gadamer, Jürgen Habermas, and Paul Ricœur now share many
concerns with Alasdair MacIntyre, Charles Taylor, and Richard Rorty.

What then is foundationalism, and what is at issue in the conflict? The figure who has probably done most to put the term 'foundationalism' in the contemporary lexicon and the controversy on the
intellectual map is Richard Rorty. In his seminal book of 1979,
Philosophy and the Mirror of Nature, Rorty retold the story of modern
philosophy as a recovery from the devastating shock the new science

21

of the seventeenth century had dealt to metaphysics as the most profound and general knowledge of reality. Drawing on antecedent figures
such as Descartes, Kant was able to give philosophy a new and, in
principle, commanding role in the new age of science, defining
philosophy as the 'most basic discipline.' Philosophy 'became "primary"
no longer in the sense of "highest" but in the sense of "underlying,"'
and so in a cultural sense *the* foundational discipline, a kind of methodology of methodologies which would define and secure the rational
basis of all claims to valid knowledge.[1]

Rorty did not then proceed as most philosophers of either Anglo-
American 'analytical' or Continental persuasion would have: he did
not marshall arguments for and against the Kantian, foundationalist
thesis, though he did survey recent analytic critiques of the thesis. In
other words, Rorty did not continue to argue from within standard
modern philosophy; he did not continue the game or topic but literally changed the subject. To have marshalled arguments pro and con
with the aim of providing a dialectical resolution would have been
to continue looking for the norms of commensurability which Kant
proclaimed as the goal and basis of epistemology: 'a set of rational rules
which will tell us how rational agreement can be reached on what
would settle the issue on every point where statements seem to conflict ... to find the maximum amount of common ground with others.'[2]
Rorty's intention was neither to praise nor blame epistemological
philosophy but to bury it, by writing its history as an epitaph for
an historical formation in Western culture that is now passing.

His purpose was 'therapeutic rather than constructive ... designed
to make the reader question his own motives for philosophizing.'[3] The
shock effect of this 'therapy' has derived in large part from its explicit
embrace of a strategy that, while not rejecting the value of argument,
shifts the focus away from the search for timeless rules of thought
and conditions of intelligibility toward the insight of Thomas Kuhn
that all uses of the term 'rational,' like uses of 'science,' must be qualified by noting the historical context of discourse within which their
use makes sense. Just as there is today less talk about an unqualified
science than about 'seventeenth-century' or 'Newtonian' or 'post-
Darwinian' science, Rorty has been urging that we can abandon a
provincial absorption in the historically specific forms of argument
we have been calling 'philosophy.'

Rorty's heroes are Wittgenstein, Heidegger, and Dewey. Each was a philosopher who, in three different twentieth-century contexts, came to see that, since science was getting on very well without philosophical support, it was possible to glimpse a 'post-Kantian culture.' In such a culture there is no longer any need for an 'all-encompassing discipline which legitimizes or grounds the others,' a role philosophy had taken over from Christian theology and its ancillary metaphysics.[4] It is the vision of such an Emersonian culture, which Rorty calls 'transcendentalist through and through, whose center is everywhere and circumference nowhere,' that his history is designed to make plausible and appealing.

As philosophers, or rather former philosophers, move toward recognizing that all of us are linked by neither a common ground nor a mutual concern with a common end but more casually by civility, the appropriate form of intellectual discourse is more like literary or cultural criticism than traditional philosophy. The social role and identity of the 'philosopher' as we have known it likewise fades away. Rorty's history, then, is not simply a story of mistaken methodology. If his anti-foundationalism is not an argument in the traditional philosophical sense, neither is it a value-neutral academic history. It is instead a rhetorically powerful narrative whose purpose is to persuade us that foundationalism is a cultural project we would do well to leave behind.[5]

This argument is not unique. A similar case has been pressed in the fields of moral and political philosophy by Alasdair MacIntyre. But while MacIntyre shares Rorty's emphasis upon the historically-conditioned character of the categories of thought, he presents a very different, even a conflicting view of what it means to abandon foundationalism.

MacIntyre's *After Virtue: A Study in Moral Theory* appeared in 1981. In it, MacIntyre made the failure of the foundationalist project a central diagnostic tool for grasping what he takes to be the pathology of modernity. 'The central feature of contemporary moral utterance is that so much of it is used to express disagreements,' wrote MacIntyre, driving home the point that the resulting debates are, 'interminable ... There seems to be no rational way of securing moral agreement in our culture.'[6] The tone of this assessment is, of course, precisely the opposite of Rorty's celebration of the free-wheeling secular, pluralistic, post-Kantian culture of liberal societies. For MacIntyre, we live in the aftermath of a cultural 'catastrophe' which has robbed moral discourse of rationality and us of the possibility of an uncoerced, reasoned consensus.

After Virtue was not arguing that this loss of rationality in practical life was somehow the result of the failure to provide moral judgments with adequate conceptual foundations. Rather, the search by philosophers since Kant to 'found' moral principle in some necessary aspects of reason or speech was taken by MacIntyre to be as much a result of the catastrophic loss of moral rationality as the interminable moral debates of our time.

A key feature of moral philosophy since Kant has been the distinction between pure, or theoretical, and practical reason. This distinction is closely tied to and supported by the epistemological philosophy Rorty has termed foundationalism. The theoretical/practical contrast has worked in modern philosophy to give the perspective of the spectator, who reasons theoretically, a logical priority over the perspective of the actor, who reasons practically from within a context of interaction. The logical conditions for establishing claims of fact have been identified exclusively with theoretical reasoning, making it impossible to judge or discuss the truth of evaluative claims put forward from the perspective of action. This distinction provided a separate sphere for moral reasoning with its own internal norms for validity, but it also made the whole realm of practical reasoning peripheral to efforts to establish the truth about human affairs. It left discourse about 'values' unrelated to claims of 'fact.'

Viewed historically, the theoretical/practical distinction was a response to a situation of profound cultural conflict. Modern philosophy grew up in an age of clashing religious and political views, each claiming to speak the truth about human nature and its moral ends. At the same time the new natural sciences disputed much of the traditional theology and metaphysics that undergirded various moralities. By separating questions of value from those of truth, Kantian philosophy hoped to justify normative principles in the realm of practical reason so as to avoid the problem of upholding the claim that traditional Western Christian morality had a foundation in the nature of things. Thus, the project of modern moral philosophy was to establish a rational core of moral reasoning independent of claims about nature or history. Indeed, modern moral philosophy began as a response to the loss of confidence in historical tradition and a coherent social order. But for MacIntyre it was that social order which had provided the actual basis for moral reasoning in the form of generally held, 'objective' norms for interpreting action and motivation.

Moral reasoning was grounded in social practices rather than the other way around. The culture before the 'catastrophe' was guided by what MacIntyre terms the tradition of the virtues, which in a general way he identifies with Aristotle's conception of ethics and practical philosophy. Moral ideas were interwoven with and grounded in the particular social contexts of ancient and medieval life. It is MacIntyre's project to show that only a reconstitution of this broadly Aristotelian conception of practical reason can retrieve moral coherence or, finally, even intelligibility in contemporary life. His 'disquieting suggestion' is that the social dislocation and cultural incoherence is so far advanced that we no longer have the necessary practical basis for such a retrieval. This is particularly disquieting for academic philosophy, both analytic and Continental, since *After Virtue* argued that neither tradition has been able even to recognize the problem.[7]

The problem with modern philosophy has been precisely its effort to ground claims to moral validity in putatively universal and ahistorical standards of reasoning. Philosophers have thought, reasonably enough, that a society shaped by mutual discourse and persuasion is preferable to one ruled mostly by coercion and manipulation. However, having already largely lost the social basis of moral coherence, together with a language of the virtues and human ends which could describe it, they have sought to find common standards which would have universal appeal, which make no reference to actual social practice. They have constructed ingenious methods of doing so in the utilitarian and deontological traditions of ethics. But the efforts to 'found' moral norms on some presumably neutral and universal basis which could compel rational agreement have consistently failed. In describing this failure, MacIntyre mounted an anti-foundationalist argument, though he did not use the term. *Afer Virtue* began a project of explicating a post-foundationalist conception of rationality for which 'foundations' are superceded by a kind of socially-located, historical reconstruction.[8]

MacIntyre's movement to his post-foundational positon began with the question: why, after two centuries of labor, has the foundational project for moral philosophy failed? The answer he gave in *After Virtue* is intricate and complex, but, very roughly, it proceeds this way. The consistent undoing of modern moral philosophy has been its Kantian adherence to the infamous fact-value dichotomy. This principle, that one cannot validly derive an 'ought' from any factual statement, was first advanced as a question by Hume in the *Treatise*, then taken over as an assertion by Kant.[9] The difficulty is that this assertion, once accepted dogmatically, places any effort to ground ethical norms rationally in an impossible position. For a moral norm to be asserted as having universal force, it must be free, in Kant's usage, of any conception about human happiness, nature, or God's will. It must be a pure imperative of reason, unconnected with any factual account of things. But every claim to have discovered such a postulate of what Kant called 'pure practical reason' has, at least to date, failed in one of two opposing ways.

Every candidate for the position of an objective moral principle that would carry authority by the sheer force of its logical power has either wrecked on the Charybdis of unsupported belief, as in intuitionism, or been drawn into the Scylla of the 'naturalistic fallacy.' 'Naturalism' is the admission into ethical theory of moral norms drawn from factual statements, such as the existing moral practice or ideals of a given society. It violates the Kantian proscription of any but those imperatives derived from purely formal or analytical concepts of practical reason, such as the ideas of rational agency and responsibility. The wreck of intuitionism took place around the turn of the century when philosophers followed Sidgwick in conceding that the moral imperatives of utilitarianism, such as the priority of the greatest happiness of the greatest number, could not be derived from that theory's psychology and had to be acknowledged as 'intuitions,' for which no further reason could be given. This undercut the effort to 'found' these moral beliefs in something other than mere assertion.

On the other side, MacIntyre himself played Scylla to Alan Gewirth's recent revival of the Kantian effort to show that something like the categorical imperative is an inherent constraint on all moral reasoning. Here the key issue was a kind of equality that Kantians call universalizability: the notion that each rational person must, under pain of self-contradiction, extend to all other persons the same consideration his or her purposes receive. In *Reason and Morality*,[10] Gewirth began his case for the categorical imperative by arguing that it is evidently good to exercise rational agency and that the prerequisites for its exercise are a measure of freedom and well-being. He went on to say that if one acknowledged the necessity of freedom and well-being for rational agency, one must also acknowledge that one has a right to such goods, and he concluded that the notion of a right claimed in virtue of the characteristic of rational agency entails acknowledging that this right also belongs to anyone else having those characteristics. Notice, however, that the property of universalizability inheres not in the concept of rational agency (the Kantian starting point), but in the notion of right. To this MacIntyre responded, 'the latter [rights] in fact presuppose, as the former [characteristics of agency] do not, the existence of a socially established set of rules ... Thus Gewirth has illicitly smuggled into his argument a conception which does not in any way belong, as it must do if his case is to succeed, to the minimal characterization of a rational agent.'[11]

For MacIntyre, the point of this anti-foundationalist sparring is more than to show that the emperor has no clothes. Rather, he has attempted to redirect the attention of those in modern culture concerned about our capacity to be moral agents in something like Gewirth's sense away from a fruitless enterprise. The stakes in this intellectual effort are very high. He would have us consider what the contemporary incommensurability in moral discourse means, namely: 'the obliteration of any genuine distinction between manipulative and non-manipulative social relations.'[12]

Through the nineteenth century social factors such as continuing religious beliefs in duty prevented Western people from experiencing the full import of the breakdown of this distinction between moral argument as appeal to impersonal and mutually held criteria and as manipulative self-assertion. However, the extension in our own century of totalitarian politics, the bureaucratic management of interpersonal relations, and of intrapsychic relations by psychotherapy, have made Nietzsche's once prophetic statement that all moral claims are guises of the will to power a description of everyday practice. In a sense the belief in foundationalism, while it has always been an unredeemed claim, acted socially to check the spread of Nietzsche's discovery of our moral groundlessness. Yet, for MacIntyre, Nietzsche's diagnosis was correct, though overgeneralized. Not *all* morality is unable to generalize its standards in a rationally defensible way, as Nietzsche asserted, though modern Western morality, for reasons that are at once social and intellectual, clearly cannot. In this affirmation of Nietzsche's insight, MacIntyre is accepting a kind of historicism.

Yet, MacIntyre's substantive project is explicitly an argument against, not for, Nietzsche's way of thinking about how to live. Nietzsche's error was to move from the historically accurate characterization of modern moral thinking, as founded on nothing more than individual or collective assertion, to an explanation for this fact which relied on a version of nineteenth-century psychology. For that psychology, culture was a rarefied or sublimated expression of physiological drives. The individual or group was finally a vehicle of those drives, whose only end was their own assertion. Nietzsche's famous characterization of this biologically-rooted tendency was the will to power. In this view, cultural forms, including morality, became subject to essentially psychological judgments of their capacity to promote or inhibit self-assertion, a view familiar enough today in its sociobiological variant.[13] Nietzsche's view also had much in common with both the more humanistic pragmatism of William James and the darker literary vision of his brother, Henry.[14] Given the tendency of modern socio-cultural evolution, for MacIntyre all foundationalist efforts to ground moral language can at best be only temporary footholds on the slippery slope toward a Nietzschean declension.

It is in this way that MacIntyre's rejection of the Kantian and Utilitarian projects for grounding moral philosophy in some atemporal and universal principles leads him, like Rorty, toward a kind of historicism. Yet, MacIntyre's historicism is unlike Rorty's in its insistence that because historical judgments are a species of moral judgment, they therefore proceed from the standpoint of practices which have normative status for the interpreter. For MacIntyre, it is only when a society has rejected the rootedness of its discourse in the 'institutionalized theories' of normative practices that intellectuals feel the need to 'construct a morality from reason-as-such or with Rorty seek to come to terms with a fragmented status quo.'[15] Thus, while MacIntyre and Rorty can be seen as sharing a critique of philosophy as the guarantor of rationality in a timeles sense, it is only from the perspective of that 'foundationalist' enterprise of modern philosophy that their positions appear similar, as 'anti-foundationalist.'

Both Rorty and MacIntyre would bring philosophy into the general discourse of modern culture, but as to what purpose they are much at odds. To the degree that these issues, rather than the question of foundationalism itself, begin to focus attention, philosophy has become post-foundational.

II Why Post-Foundationalism Seems Puzzling

To recapitulate: for both the contemporary path-breaking anti-foundationalists in Anglo-American philosophy, Rorty and MacIntyre, rejection of the project of grounding all thinking in an epistemology or theory of language or representation was only a way station toward a post-foundational position. The new perspective this position opens up has affinities with what from a traditional philosophical point of view was called historicism. For the post-foundationalists, historicism is neither irrational nor necessarily sceptical. Rather it is an aspect of an essentially pragmatic conception of thinking, one in which there is no final difference to be found between facts, as determined by application of a formalized method, and values, or between theoretical and practical rationality. The usual dichotomy of facts and values is here reconceived on the analogy of action within a situation: thinking is no longer detached nor fully detachable from the situation and must inevitably carry within it some stance toward or interpretation of the situation.

The 'death of philosophy' after foundationalism is in fact better conceived as a transfiguration. MacIntyre and Rorty both see themselves as driven by implications of their own previous work to take up the mantle of forbears who struck off from the post-Kantian mainstream in new directions. For MacIntyre the pathfinders are Hegel and Collingwood. Rorty continually refers to the later Wittgenstein, the later Heidegger, and Dewey: a fallen-away logical positivist, a lapsed phenomenologist, and a pragmatist.[16] For all of these thinkers, abandoning foundational philosophy meant that thought is necessarily tied to history, culture, and practical life, and finds its point in contributing in some way toward orienting, criticizing, and comprehending human culture. Yet these figures represented minority positions in their own times.

Throughout the nineteenth and early twentieth centuries Western societies lived a cultural life in which philosophy, as champion of science, guarantor of truth and the arbiter of secular meaning, played a widely accepted role, particularly as the role of the churches as public teachers of meaning declined. If the days of foundationalism are numbered, it must be because that earlier culture of secular middle-class liberalism no longer holds hegemony. With its own place no longer secure in a changing culture, philosophy must follow the lead of Hegel, Collingwood, Dewey, Wittgenstein, and Heidegger and seek to reorient itself. That requires rejoining the effort to understand — and to shape — the movement of culture and history.

Post-foundationalism is the first new movement to sweep the Anglo-American philosophical scene since the logical positivists' announcement of their 'breakthrough' to a truly scientific philosophy. The current movement seems to signal the final retreat of the positivists' empire. In that way, post-foundationalism draws upon and succeeds the struggles of hermeneutics and critical theory against positivistic rationalism in Germany during the 1960s and 1970s, the opposition of hermeneutical phenomenologists like Paul Ricœur, and the later revolt against structuralism in France. Yet, the cultural 'tone' of post-foundationalism differs drastically from the heady optimism of logical positivism in its youth. Rather than a dramatic leap beyond history on the basis of a better theory, the new movement shares with postwar European existentialism a distrust of theory in particular and formalism more generally. Along with Rorty and MacIntyre, figures such as Taylor and Kuhn share with Gadamer and Ricœur a concern with context, history, and practical reasoning. Perhaps their closest analogues were the turn-of-the-century philosophers of process such as James, Bergson, Dewey and others whose work embodied a spirit Morton White characterized as the 'revolt against formalism,' thinkers who 'all protest their anxiety to come to grips with reality, their attachment to the moving and vital social life.'[17]

What is most striking, and at least initially puzzling, about this movement, particularly in its British and North American representatives, is that it is not coming from a professed anti-modernist position such as Heidegger's, but from within logical positivism's academic successor, analytical philosophy. This seems a reversal of the usual and expected valences of theoretical positions. Historically, anti-formalism has generally been hostile to the prestige and cultural centrality of modern science, accepting the link which Edmund Burke emphasized between the 'rationalism' of Enlightenment science and the revolutionary attempt to engineer the transformation of society. So, for example, Nietzsche's anti-foundationalist hermeneutics of suspicion became a weapon to be used against socialism and democracy, which he denounced as corrupt offspring of a decadent age. By contrast, Rorty's post-foundationalism is benignly Whiggish in its embrace of the cultural pluralism of the liberal capitalist order of the West, and his adoption of Michael Oakeshott's phrase, 'conversation of mankind,' suggests the accommodating British conservatism of Burke's later inheritors.

However, to a sympathetic European critic such as Habermas, there is real danger in post-foundationalism. For Habermas, the turn away from the effort to secure unconditionally good reasons for our convictions, as opposed to reasons relative to our practices, has immediate moral and political implications. As heir to both the intellectual legacy of German Neo-Kantian liberalism and Marxism, as well as Germany's historic twentieth-century tragedy, Habermas reads the abandonment of the ideal of criteria of truth as creating an opening for irrationalist social movements of group chauvinism. But he also argues that post-foundationalism of Rorty's stripe tends to lose any fulcrum for cultural criticism. It can slide toward a simple endorsement of the status quo. In an age of advertising and propaganda, arguing that our social practices are all we have may not be so innocent as it sounds. Drawing on Max Weber's sociological vision, Habermas's assessment of modern pluralism is less benign than Rorty's, noting that genuine pluralism of goals and understanding puts great pressure on citizens of modern democracies to decide among competing ideologies and commitments. As Habermas puts it, because 'the gaps between competing convictions reach deep into the domain of "questions that admit of truth," there exists, contrary to Rorty, a philosophical interest "to see social practices of justification as more than just such practices."'[18]

III The Salience of Cultural Stance

As Habermas sees it, Rorty's work is a criticism of philosophical foundationalism at the methodological level, conjoined with a largely uncritical stance toward the practices of modern society. Habermas thinks that this odd mixture results from what he calls Rorty's absolutizing of the perspective of the observer.[19] This is an odd charge to be levelled at a critic of the 'spectator theory of knowing'! Yet it resonates with Habermas's other criticism that post-foundationalism is naive about its own cultural location. In essence, Habermas's argument is that no one can actually live in accord with Rorty's description. Acting in the first person, each of us confronts serious choices − 'live options,' in James's phrase − and when we do we reach toward an 'unconditioned' moment in which we search for the best reason available. Rorty would have us replace the implicitly normative and unconditioned conception of 'valid reasons' with the description, 'held to be valid for us at this time.' Habermas objects that, as participants if not as observers, we are always acting as if we could argumentatively transcend the conventions currently described, as from time to time by Rorty's admission and example, we do.[20]

One could argue that claims for universal validity implicit in our actual practice of communication are indeed never finally redeemable. These claims make our descriptions of ourselves (our theories and interpretations) always dependent upon a communicative, practical situation we participate in but cannot exhaustively describe. Indeed, to be able in principle to locate all validity claims as we make them and debate them as relative to a context would require a position outside the practical situation: a position resembling the spectator legacy of Cartesian philosophy. Rorty refuses, however, to be drawn into a dialectial argument about the formal implications of how 'reason' may function in what Habermas calls communicative interaction. Instead of dialectics, Rorty gives a Wittgensteinian or Nietzschean riposte to the effect that his intent is simply to call attention to the relativity of reason-giving to efforts at defining and coping with practical situations. Meta-theoretical discussions are simply beside the point here.

Still, Habermas's critique is substantive as well as formal. He objects to the instrumental and utilitarian quality of Rorty's style of pragmatism. It is this aspect of his thinking that in the end counts most in setting it off within a post-foundationalist context. He fears that Rorty's kind of pragmatism retains the positivists' enthusiasm for getting out from under the weight of the past — an effort Habermas agrees is not necessarily bad — so as to get the future under better control. This poses the danger that technocratic management may stifle genuine politics and ethical debate. While this is hardly Rorty's intention, his conscious conflation of scientific investigation with moral deliberation, and of politics with social engineering[21] could work at cross-purposes with his celebration of 'solidarity' as the 'ground' of language. There is at least ambiguity in this vocabulary. Finally, it seems to be Rorty's dogmatic optimism which worries Habermas: 'But does it not remain an open question whether or not the social integrative powers of the religious tradition shaken by enlightenment can find an equivalent in the unifying, consensus-creating power of reason?'[22]

Rorty counters Habermas's criticism. Societies rarely if ever develop by deliberation and the formation of a new consensus through argument aiming at some higher synthesis. On the contrary, new cultural vocabularies are best analogized to tools which make possible an intelligible formulation of an emerging social or individual purpose. The upshot of what Rorty calls his 'Nietzschean history of culture' is that we should see culture and language 'as we now see evolution, as new forms of life constantly killing off old forms — not to accomplish a higher purpose, but blindly.'[23]

Of course, Rorty does not want to preclude the possibility of persuasion toward change, nor to deny that cultural revolutions usually do give their new 'tools' a grand and noble purpose (just as logical positivism did). However, for Rorty, as for Nietzsche, it is the revolutionary, creative bursts in culture which are interesting, in large part because they are self-justifying and so need no foundation. So, 'once we found out what could be done with a Galilean vocabulary, nobody was interested in doing the things which could be done with an Aristotelian vocabulary.'[24] Modernity, then, is to be celebrated because it represents a great acceleration of these creative formulations of new tools and the first time that humanity has glimpsed the heady truth that it can be its own point and purpose.

The key contrast in this view is between the way communication and thinking go on within an established vocabulary that has been in place, and the limit-situation of groping toward a new 'tool' to accomplish an as yet only dimly felt new purpose. The contrast is Rorty's gloss on Kuhn's distinction between ordinary or paradigmatic science and the 'revolutionary' gestation of a new scientific description of things. As Richard Bernstein has shown, Kuhn's *Structure of Scientific Revolutions* was the starting point for Anglo-American antifoundationalism.[25] Kuhn argued that in science new vocabularies rarely win many converts among adherents of established paradigms; rather, the new succeed the old as the superannuated adherents of the old die off. From another angle, Kuhn's and Rorty's use of the selection metaphor could be taken as an example of the political naivety of North American academic thought which concerns Habermas. One suspects that a 'Nietzschean history of culture' as construed by analogy to natural selection carries a very different cultural resonance in Germany or Europe than it does in North America. To paraphrase Mark Twain, American innocence does not necessarily strike the right note abroad.

It is at this point that the arguments among the post-foundationalists reveal a deep cultural divide between the philosophical heirs of Anglo-American analysis and the Continental proponents of a hermeneutics of practice. A thinker such as Rorty opposes foundationalism largely for methodological or metaphilosophical reasons: it contributes nothing to the progress of science and impedes the expansion of modernity, understood as the victory of the culture of human self-assertion.[26] The superior 'truth' of Western modernity is vouched for in Nietzschean style by its selective success, and so self-assertion in scientific, artistic, political, technological, and military arenas is pretty much all there is in human affairs, for good or ill.

In sharp contrast, the European hermeneutical tradition descending from Hegel through Dilthey, the later Husserl, and Heidegger to Gadamer has been deeply ambivalent about the cultural legacy of the scientific Enlightenment. Thus, Gadamer has warned that the tendency of modern technical thinking is to institute in machines, institutions, and habits of life the objectifying attitudes of Cartesian science, and to forget that human beings remain dependent upon and interconnected with the natural and social worlds they try to control.[27]

The hermeneutical tradition has worried that triumphant technical reasoning could overwhelm the social bonds needed to limit the manipulative capabilities opened up by our technological and organizational powers. Thus, Gadamer's own critique of foundationalism is fundamentally a strategy for making the rationality of Aristotelian *phronesis*, or practical wisdom, intelligible and legitimate. For Gadamer, the appeal to practice is at once an appeal to continuity, to the survival of non-instrumental forms of rationality, and an effort to build solidarity by discovering new commonplaces among diverse cultural traditions.[28] Not surprisingly, while Rorty celebrates the early romantic poets as prophets of active human self-assertion, Gadamer looks to the later romantics with their concern for connecting history and social community with individual freedom and harmonious personal development.

Gadamer's post-foundational hermeneutics shares with Nietzsche the sense that history is contingent, but understands this contingency in a different way. Gadamer interprets hermeneutics to mean the replacement of the foundational project by self-interpretation within a practical context. The infatuation with method that has characterized philosophy since Descartes and Bacon has propelled the effort to define truth and reality as what is revealed by the application of formal systems of reasoning. So understood, exalting method means to exalt the superior and detached stance of the outside observer, or of theory in the modern sense of the term. By contrast, to reject the hegemonic claims of method means opening up to the complexity and diversity of the contexts of human living, so that the rigidity of formalism can give way to the flexibility of a topical understanding that recognizes that various subject matters require diverse approaches.

The implication of this position is the turn toward practice. For Gadamer, we find ourselves already formed by the practices of our society and the implicit cultural understandings they bear. This is his use of Heidegger's famous 'hermeneutical circle.' We are able to construe and understand only because we begin with habits of gesture and language, prejudices or pre-judgments which give us both our starting point and our interest in understanding our context. The circle is, of course, not a closed one, but neither can our engagement in the new ever completely leave behind our formation within a tradition and a history. For this reason, practice and culture are never transparent from within or entirely graspable from without. We can simply never wholly disengage ourselves from the context of practice.[29]

Gadamer's hermeneutics of practice, then, stands as a postfoundational alternative to the claim of a Nietzschean attempt to leap

beyond cultural location. Even if one takes Nietzsche's historical geneal-
ogies as ironic rhetorical gambits rather than claimants for propositional truth status, one is still left with a peculiar set of alternatives.
On the one hand Nietzsche may have been trying to create a new,
heroic myth to move Europe beyond its decadent traditions. In this
case the practical implication would be to ignore solidarity with past
generations and do something new (another idea which plays better
today in North American than Europe). On the other hand Nietzsche
may have been offering a more moderate therapy. Perhaps his aim
was to force Europeans obsessed by schemes of inevitable progress
to confront the fundamental contingency of their own development.
If so, then it is hard to see how awareness of the contingency of our
history does not bring us immediately to the paradoxical question posed
by Gadamer: how to make moral sense of a contingency in which
we necessarily find ourselves. After all, modernity as the culture of
revolutions and new beginnings has become a long and established
tradition. We all ineradicably bear its formative marks. The issue is
what stance we will take up toward this situation, and in what perspective we will come to place the several formative traditions that
have contributed to modern Western identity.

IV Making Sense After Foundationalism: A Practical Task

If the foregoing account of some central debates in the post-
foundationalist genre is a reasonable one, MacIntyre's thesis turns out
to be correct: the fundamental issue *is* Nietzsche or Aristotle, that
is, two understandings of practice and two divergent attitudes toward
the past and its meaning for the present. The contrast seems apposite.
Nietzsche is '*the* moral philosopher of the present age,' who first an-
nounced that after the failure of Enlightenment foundationalism the
moral project must be to 'make ourselves into autonomous moral subjects by some gigantic and heroic act of will ... to construct in an entirely original way, how to invent a new table of what is good and
a new law.' This has become 'a problem for each individual.'[30] By contrast, Aristotle stands for the 'philosophically most powerful of pre-
modern modes of moral thought' which, unlike modern moral
philosophy, but like Nietzsche, poses directly the question 'what sort

of person am I to become?'[31] — very much still the central question of practice.

Thus, as Richard Bernstein has argued, the topic which has to occupy the center of post-foundational philosophical attention is the nature of modernity and our response to it. By which traditions and what balances among them are we to live?[32] It is noteworthy that, unlike the questions which preoccupied most Atlantic philosophers of all persuasions in this century, the topic is substantive rather than methodological, and at once both moral-practical and historical-interpretive.

If this discourse is to go forward, it will require that we pay attention to the conditions that could make some resolution possible, that could provide not Reason, but reasons for minds and positions to change, rather than leaving natural selection to settle the matter. Here MacIntyre's argument about history and moral philosophy bears very closely on the wider issue, for his claim is that rationality develops by the weaving of narrative and counter-narrative. This story-telling process seeks at first antagonistically, but with an ultimate possibility of mutuality, to compel self-recognition by producing a convincing interpretation of the past which can show us how we got to our present state. This practice of narrative is unlike ordinary academic history in an important respect. Taking his bearings from Hegel and Collingwood, MacIntyre insists that the starting point of the narrative must be explicitly evaluative, not value-free, presupposing 'standards of achievement and failure, of order and disorder.'[33] The 'new' kind of history can incorporate all the critical work of modern scholarship, while it rejects the modern pretense of the purely detached point of view and takes its stand self-consciously in the commitments of a specific practical context that is the source of the history's evaluative standards.

The conception of argument at work here is very close to Taylor's notion of 'interpretive dialectics.' As opposed to a 'strict dialectics' which begins from apparently undeniable premises, interpretive or hermeneutical dialectics are reconstructions of the way ideas or events have developed 'which convince us by the overall plausibility of the interpretation they give.'[34] The specific problem for MacIntyre's story is that the objects of inquiry and criticism are practices and ideas long-established and central to modern life. MacIntyre's task is to make

Nietzsche's now commonplace, even obvious, characterization of moral discourse, as 'a set of rationalizations which conceal the fundamentally non-rational phenomena of the will,'[35] appear not as a necessary truth but as an historically contingent, if challenging, formulation. To do this, MacIntyre has to somehow retrieve what Nietzsche's formulation had closed off: Aristotle's very different description of moral action together with the practical context in which that description made sense.

In his argument on behalf of Aristotle against Nietzsche, MacIntyre's account can serve as paradigmatic for philosophical discourse after foundationalism, even or precisely because the specifics of his interpretation call out challenge and counterclaim. The first half of *After Virtue* presents MacIntyre's attempt to free us from what Taylor calls the 'presumption of uniqueness' that attaches to ideas embedded in current practice, in this case Nietzsche's account of moral language as assertion.

He tells a story of how the Enlightenment came to be so hard put to find 'foundations' for the moral norms and ideals it inherited from the medieval past. 'If the deontological character of moral judgments is the ghost of conceptions of divine law which are alien to the metaphysics of modernity,' meaning the mechanist view of Enlightenment sciences, '... we should expect the problems of understanding and assigning an intelligible status to moral judgments both continually to arise and as continually to prove inhospitable to philosophical solutions.'[36] Note that MacIntyre is not simply presenting us with Aristotelian morality as an alternative to the Nietzschean account or the Enlightenment's, but showing that this evolution began at a point where a new picture came to take the place of an older one.

The older picture was Aristotelian teleology, which viewed moral virtue as the means by which human capacities were developed toward their fulfilment in full human flourishing. In that older view, human action, because it is teleologically conceived, 'not only can but must be characterized with reference to the hierarchy of goods which provide the ends of human action,' so that facts about action necessarily include facts about what is valuable for humans. However, once, for perfectly good reasons of their own, the pioneers of the new science of the seventeenth century moved away from teleological accounts of natural phenomena toward wholly mechanical-causal explanations, the new science of human nature and politics followed suit. But in this new view, there could be 'no facts about what is valuable' and fact became 'value-free.'[37] Thus, the inherited conceptions of human excellence became impossible to 'derive' from a human nature mechanically construed. The virtues came to be thought of as either representing some 'non-natural' properties or imperatives, or appeared as arbitrary conventions. This was the intellectual impasse which made possible Nietzsche's radical reinterpretation of 'values' as blindly determined by a psychology of non-teleological drives. Here MacIntyre's argument converges with Gadamer's critique of science discussed above.

In MacIntyre's narrative we are brought to see that terrible conceit lurked behind the Enlightenment's claims to have at last stripped off of human nature the teleological interpretations anthropomorphically projected by the ancients and medievals. It was a claim made again more forcefully by Nietzsche: that he had at last, in all humility, seen human nature just as it is! MacIntyre thus redescribes Nietzsche's description of morality as the historical result of a kind of amnesia. Modern culture has been unable to see that the interpretive change inaugurated by modern science, while it has conferred real benefits in vastly improving our mastery of nature, when extended to the realm of human action has exacted great costs through its simplified and impoverished instrumental conception of action. The Enlightenment's particular conception of itself as contrasted to the Dark Ages contained a singularly naive vainglory.[38] The great critical advances of modern culture have given us a misleading self-conception which is embodied in the Nietzschean legacy. Breaking with tradition as illusion is the primordial step of the modern anti-traditional tradition. Only this tradition does not imagine that it remains heavily determined by the prejudices it aims to leave behind. Yet, those twentieth-century movements that have sought to follow Nietzsche's counsel and take heroic leaps into the future have tragically demonstrated not so much self-overcoming as a brutal return of repressed prejudices.

By contrast, the therapeutic aim of MacIntyre's history is to remind us that we need to take the past seriously, to reconstruct it so as to see ourselves in a new way, as formed by the past but not determined by it. Freedom thereby appears within the interpretive argument, only it is a freedom fully located within ongoing social life.

Unlike the freedom of Kant and later idealists, who located autonomy in 'mind' beyond physical nature to rescue it from being undermined by a mechanistic psychology, MacIntyre's account presupposes a subjectivity which is, in Taylor's phrase, 'situated' within a bodily, social, historical context.[39]

This conception of situated subjectivity as neither outside physical nature and culture (as in the idealist view) nor completely dissolved into lines of physical causation (as in the most common accounts of positivistic science) is a key connecting link between Continental and Anglo-American post-foundationalists. In both traditions, the shift of focus from logic to language after World War II laid the basis for the discovery – or recovery – of the location of meaning in history and the social world. That discovery has brought post-foundationalists in North America and Europe into increasing conversation with those in other fields who have been rediscovering many of the same commonplaces and a similar history. Rorty has moved his professional affiliation to literary studies, while Gadamer has had a lifelong interest in philology. MacIntyre and Taylor have long united social scientific concerns with their philosophical work. Taylor could be describing MacIntyre's efforts along with his own when he writes that the kind of historical retrieval which is made possible by 'creative redescriptions' of taken-for-granted conceptions aims to 'transfer what has sunk to the level of an organizing principle for present practices and hence is beyond examination, into a view for which there can be *reasons*, either for or against.'[40] Interpretation, then, becomes an exemplary practice of situated freedom.

The post-foundationalist understanding of reason-giving escapes the stance of mere assertion by making its own evaluative premises explicit in the process of argument. So, MacIntyre's defense of his reconstructive history has led him to make explicit the dependency of his categories of teleological development and corresponding models of moral order and disorder upon a particular historical-cultural formation. He has progressively clarified that set of standards and forms from a relatively vague 'quest for a meaningful life' in an Aristotelian spirit toward a more explicit engagement with theistic Aristotelianism.[41] In this way, MacIntyre's project of 'interpretive dialectics' has been becoming clearer about the practical context and interpretive tradition within which his redescriptions take on plausibility. This particularizing of the place from which he argues has not reduced his claims to a vacuous relativism. On the contrary, *After Virtue* shows how a self-critical location in a specific tradition makes possible the sort of argument about the good of different practices, the giving of reasons, which has always been the hope of philosophy. The casting of interpretive accounts as argumentative discourse draws upon and makes vivid the insight of post-Wittgensteinian philosophers that the meaning of words only becomes finally clear in the context of socially ordered practical contexts of 'forms of life.'

By emphasizing that rationality is always argumentative or dialogical, MacIntyre is also highlighting the rhetorical dimensions of discourse which Stephen Toulmin has rescued from near-oblivion in a philosophical context obsessed by formal thinking.[42] By this reasoning, the power of one's account lies in its capacity to persuade one's interlocutors, even opponents, to recognize themselves and their position as effectively revealed in one's argument. Only by providing such an account can one hope to vindicate the plausibility of one's premises and their context. The superiority of one account or tradition over another is always a contingent matter. It depends on whether the argument has 'provided generally more cogent accounts of its rivals' defects and weaknesses and of its own than those rivals have been able to supply.'[43] As it is repeatedly encountered, this very contingency can give rise to that rage for certitude which has often in the past made a practical, rhetorical understanding of discourse seem insufficient. Yet, it might also produce an insight akin to irony. By intimating the partiality and uncertainties of even our bedrock convictions, the ironic spirit opens a glimpse of a larger, more complex human drama, to which our struggles for clarity are related but which they never fully encompass or exhaust. Irony can also act as a reminder of our need to continue the conversation.

Yet our arguments are serious. The struggle to establish an intepretation is a search for our own identity which irony may lighten but cannot substitute for in the final analysis. But the tradition of humanistic rhetoric descending from Cicero reminds us that argument is not simply a defense of established positions. It is a way toward new findings, to invention, as well. Its agonistic quality may serve a destructive end, but it may also make it possible to establish a new common place which could enable us and others to see ourselves and our histories as contributors to a previously unimagined future. Something like this aim is implicit in the practice of interpretive dialectics as argument. Its rhetorical strategy is simple, and as old as Socrates's precarious and difficult discourse with Callicles in Plato's *Gorgias*. In the exchange and mutual scrutiny, both have begun to search out together the truth about 'how one should live,' as Socrates put it. It is in this way that the return to practice in post-foundationalist philosophy gives reason for hope.

NOTES

1 Richard Rorty, *Philosophy and the Mirror of Nature* (Princeton, NJ: Princeton University Press 1979), 132

2 Ibid., 316

3 Ibid., 5

4 Ibid., 6

5 Richard Rorty, *Consequences of Pragmatism* (Minneapolis: University of Minnesota Press 1982), 70

6 Alasdair MacIntyre, *After Virtue: A Study of Moral Theory* (Notre Dame, IN: University of Notre Dame Press 1981), 6

7 Ibid., 5-6

8 This conception is developed most clearly in the 'Postscript to the Second Edition' of *After Virtue*, 1984, 264-78.

9 Ibid., 56

10 Alan Gewirth, *Reason and Morality* (Chicago: University of Chicago Press 1978)

11 MacIntyre, 67-8

12 Ibid., 23

13 See Mary Midgley, *Evolution As a Religion* (New York: Methuen 1985).

14 See MacIntyre, 24-5; Rorty, *Consequences*, 150-8.

15 Alasdair MacIntyre, 'Moral Arguments and Social Contexts: A Response to Rorty,' in Robert Hollinger, ed., *Hermeneutics and Praxis* (Notre Dame, IN: Notre Dame University Press 1985), 223

16 See the 'Preface' to *After Virtue*, ix-xi, and the 'Introduction' to *Philosophy and the Mirror of Nature*, 3-13.

17 Morton White, *Social Thought in America: The Revolt Against Formalism* (Boston: Beacon Press 1957), 6

18 Jürgen Habermas, 'Questions and Counterquestions,' in R.J. Bernstein, ed., *Habermas and Modernity* (Cambridge, MA: MIT Press 1985), 195

19 Ibid.

20 Ibid., 194

21 See Rorty's essay, 'Habermas and Lyotard on Postmodernity,' in *Habermas and Modernity*, esp. pp. 170-5.

22 Ibid., 197

23 Richard Rorty, 'The Contingency of Language,' *London Review of Books* **8**, 7 (April 17, 1986), 6

24 Ibid.

25 Richard J. Bernstein, *Beyond Objectivism and Relativism: Science, Hermeneutics and Praxis* (Philadelphia: University of Pennsylvania Press 1983), 20-5; 51-93

26 See Hans Blumenberg, *The Legitimacy of the Modern Age* (Cambridge, MA: MIT Press 1983).

27 Hans-Georg Gadamer, 'What is Practice?', in *Reason in the Age of Science*; trans. Frederick G. Lawrence (Cambridge, MA: MIT Press 1981), 84-5

28 Ibid., 86-7

29 See Hans-Georg Gadamer, *Truth and Method* (New York: Seabury 1975), 153-344.

30 MacIntyre, *After Virtue*, 114

31 Ibid., 118

32 See Bernstein, *Beyond Objectivism*, 171-231.

33 MacIntyre, *After Virtue*, 3

34 Charles Taylor, *Hegel* (Cambridge: Cambridge University Press 1975), 218

35 MacIntyre, *After Virtue*, 117

36 Ibid., 111

37 Ibid., 84

38 Ibid., 81

39 See Taylor's discussion of 'situated freedom' in the final section of *Hegel*.

40 Charles Taylor, 'Philosophy and its History,' in Richard Rorty, J.B. Schneewind, and Quentin Skinner, eds., *Philosophy in History: Essays in the Historiography of Philosophy* (Cambridge: Cambridge University Press 1984), 28

41 See MacIntyre, *After Virtue*, Chapter 15, and 'Postscript to the Second Edition,' 268.

42 See Stephen Toulmin, *The Uses of Argument* (Cambridge: Cambridge University Press 1958). See also his *Human Understanding* (Princeton, NJ: Princeton University Pres 1972).

43 MacIntyre, *After Virtue*, 277

Jean Grondin

Hermeneutical Truth and its Historical Presuppositions: A Possible Bridge between Analysis and Hermeneutics

A convergence of analytical and Continental philosophy has undoubtedly taken place in the last few decades, but philosophers are just beginning to become aware of it. This paper suggests, from a
hermeneutical point of view, that the internal development of ana-
·lytic and continental thought in the twentieth century has followed
paths towards coalescence. These paths are the pragmatization of analytic philosophy and the hermeneutization of Continental philosophy.
They share essential methodological as well as ethical positions: an
anti-foundationalist stance coupled with a sometimes too uncritical
confidence in common sense. In as far as hermeneutics and analysis
abandon seemingly metaphysical speculation on foundations and stress
the importance of pragmatical *phronēsis* and contextualism, they can
also claim to bridge the classical gap between theory and practice. It
appears that the goal of *prima philosophia*, the symbiosis of theory
and praxis, could only be reached by getting rid of *prima philosophia*
in the foundationalist sense. This virtue or aporia is common to hermeneutics and pragmatism.

The pragmatic turn of analytical philosophy was exemplified,
if not initiated, by Quine's attack on the dogmas of empiricism.[1] The
very fact that empiricism was being labelled 'dogmatic' from the inside was in itself a rather bold undertaking. Empiricism had always
considered itself to be in sheer opposition to the dogmatism of rationalism or metaphysics. Kant, for instance, constantly identified dogmatism with metaphysical rationalism and empiricism with scepticism.
Quine, however, undermined these understandings by questioning the
distinction between analytic and synthetic truths and the dogma of
reductionism, that is, the belief in the reducibility of meaningful statements to terms which refer immediately to experience. The history

45

of this pragmatic turn has been instructively narrated by Richard Rorty.[2] As this reconstruction in Rorty's works is well known, I will focus on the increasing hermeneutization of Continental philosophy, whose somewhat more complicated history has yet to be written.

In conducting this examination it may be useful to point out that in analytic philosophy there has been a certain change of focus *from language to reason*, in Continental philosophy a movement *from reason to language*. On the analytical side, following the pragmatic turn just alluded to, language is no longer seen as rooted in logic alone but as a matter of social practices which are particular to communities. The main question of rationality thus arises: how can a truth-claim be sustained if everything is a matter of cultures? While problems of the rationality of belief are vigorously and widely debated in the on-going analytical discussion, the problem of language itself, strangely enough, tends to fade away. Rorty, for instance, believes that language is but one topic of philosophical inquiry and by no means its privileged concern. Thus, it seems to me that the question of rationality has come to overshadow the former interest in language. On the Continental side, meanwhile, a strong interest in reason has been inherited from Descartes, Kant and Hegel; but in the twentieth century, especially with Heidegger and Gadamer, reason has come to be seen as thoroughly embedded in language. Being that can be understood, says Gadamer, is language – a point tantamount to the claim that reason lies in language. Continental philosophy, in its hermeneutical accomplishment, thus culminates in a panlinguistic thesis. This is, to a certain extent, also true for Habermas, who believes that the traditional claim to rationality can only be grounded on the pragmatic presuppositions of language. *Prima philosophia* takes on the form of universal pragmatics. One cannot escape the conclusion that, with its hermeneutical turn, language has become the main subject of Continental philosophy.

The hermeneutization of Continental philosophy has been brought about by the introduction of history and historicity into philosophical theory. Traditional metaphysical philosophy had little to do with the realm of history. In fact, metaphysics can be defined as a study of the non-historical, that which escapes change, movement, mortality and opinion. The standard formula for this definition of metaphysics is to be found in the eleatic and platonic distinction between *epistēmē*, science, and *doxa*, mere opinion. Science deals with eternal truths, which Plato calls 'ideas.' The task of philosophy consists in liberating human beings from the shadows of experience in order to enable us to contemplate the 'ideal forms' which constitute a celestial realm. Preoccupied with truths that are stable, immutable, and thus serve as norms for human action and worldly order, metaphysics tends to discard the merely temporal, except to the extent that it partakes, by virtue of its symmetry and mathematical regularity (as demonstrated in the *Timaeus*), in the eternal world of ideas.

This conception was already criticized in Plato's time, especially by the sophist ancestors of our pragmatists; and it is well known that, oddly enough, Plato's Academy turned out to be the most outspoken advocate of scepticism in the hellenistic period. Nevertheless, Plato's conception of metaphysics established the structure of what would count as serious knowledge or science. From then on, true knowledge had to concern universals, formal laws, and the like. Anything else was irrational, solely historical. It is revealing that Kant, who himself delivered a serious blow to metaphysics on the grounds that it illegitimately transcends the field of experience, continues to oppose, in the Architectonic of pure reason, historical and rational knowledge, the a posteriori and the a priori.[3]

It was however in Kant's century that history became a central point of attention for philosophers. As Ernst Cassirer showed,[4] the philosophy of history, which has remained a main current of Continental philosophy ever since, was born during the century of the Enlightenment in the wake of Montesquieu, Voltaire, Herder and Kant (who tempered the historical optimism of Herder by reminding us that 'history is not a novel'). As it expanded its horizons and compared itself to other epochs and cultures, the eighteenth century discovered that social institutions and human culture had not remained the same throughout the ages. There had been change, even revolution, in human affairs, and for the Enlightenment that meant progress.

But if all human knowledge is subject to evolution, what happens to the traditional claim of philosophy to eternal truths? The problem of philosophical truth (or reason) and history became a central challenge to German Idealism at the beginning of the nineteenth century. How must truth be understood if it is to resist the relativization of history? As Rüdiger Bubner put it, the philosophy of German Idealism reacted to the historicization of thought by means of an intellectualization of history.[5] If history hinges on the perennial status of the philosophical idea, the only proper response had to be an idealization of history. A philosophical reconstruction of 'Reason in History,' the title of Hegel's lecture, prescribed the task of a whole century. One has to grant that Hegel's understanding of history is more subtle, yet a tension persists in his works between a stronger and a weaker conception of philosophy. On the one hand, philosophy focuses on the Absolute, the identity of subject and object, which synonymous terms like God, truth, and the infinite epitomize. On the other hand, philosophy more modestly views itself as the expression of its own time ('*ihre Zeit in Gedanken erfasst*').[6] Whereas the first conception seems to aim at something atemporal, the second is thoroughly temporal and conscious of its own historicity.

Contemporary hermeneutics can easily identify with this later conception and, indeed, it has contributed to its re-enactment, but the former was already largely rejected by nineteenth-century intellectuals (whether of Marxist, historicist, or positivistic obedience). Helmut Schnädelbach has ably discussed what happened to the self-understanding of philosophy in the course of the nineteenth century.[7] For some (neo-Kantians, positivists), philosophy had to content itself with being a reflection on science and its foundations; for others (left-Hegelians and Marxists), philosophy had to transform itself into a critique of society; yet others (Nietzsche, Kierkegaard, the *Lebensphilosophen* who led to existentialism) believed that philosophy had to be a theory of what escaped science altogether. However, Marxist thinkers were not generally considered as philosophers and the philosophers of life also remained marginal figures up to the twentieth century. Mainstream philosophy was represented by the epistemological movement.

At the beginning of our century, Husserl's phenomenology, the direct ancestor of contemporary hermeneutics, marked a turning point. Its catch-phrase '*Zu den Sachen selbst*' meant that philosophy could stop perceiving the methodology of science as its prime focus of attention. Philosophy could become once again, in its full right, a theory of fundamental phenomena. For Husserl, the main phenomenon was the constitution of intentionality in the realm of the transcendental ego. The rejection of this Archimedean point paved the way for the hermeneutics of Heidegger, Gadamer and their numerous followers.

Husserl's legacy for the hermeneutical tradition has scarcely been one of continuity. Though Husserl's vocabulary (*life-world, intentionality, perspectivism, intersubjectivity*, etc.) laid the groundwork for hermeneutics, by an amazing turn of events this terminology acquired a very un-Husserlian flavour, and indeed an anti-Husserlian import. Perspectivity no longer indicated the direction of seeing, but the projection that relativized the metaphor and the very possibility of 'raw seeing' that pervades Husserl's phenomenology. Intersubjectivity no longer had to be constituted by the ego; it became the instance that called into question the idea of constitution altogether. The life-world ceased to be the bedrock of science and rationality and became a mere cultural entity that precluded the idea of rigorous science and strict rationality. Consequently, the paradigm of science and rationality seemed to fade away in the transition from phenomenology to hermeneutics. Husserl saw this coming, not only in what he branded the anthropologism of his pupil Heidegger, but as early as 1913 in his impassioned *Logos* article, 'Philosophy as a Rigorous Science,' where he reacts to the relativistic consequences of psychologism and, most importantly, historicism. Although Husserl's rejection of historicism was total, this cannot be said of his followers. Considering his offspring, one might contend that Husserl lost his battle with historicism, just as he might be celebrating a belated victory in the more rational version of hermeneutics developed after Heidegger in the writings of Habermas, Apel and even Gadamer.[8] Interpretation supplanted intuition and constitution in the hermeneutical transformation of phenomenology. This is why Ricœur explains the rise of hermeneutics out of the foundering of the idealist presuppositions of Husserl's phenomenology.[9]

Gadamer underlines the pervasiveness of historicity in his work *Truth and Method*. One of the vital sections of this book, where the concepts of the hermeneutical circle and of *Wirkungsgeschichte* are elaborated, is given the provocative title: 'The elevation of the historicity of understanding to the status of hermeneutical principle.'[10] Historicity, the traditonal foe of any foundations, becomes ennobled with principled status. This has far-reaching implications. How can historicity, which relativizes every position, lay claim to the status of principle and function as the starting point of a philosophical endeavour? We will address this question by focussing on a central theme of traditional philosophy and hermeneutics, the problem of truth.

The problem of truth has been one of the most enduring in the whole philosophical tradition. Whereas many traditional notions of philosophy have become more or less obsolete (e.g., the concepts of being, God, representation), the problem of truth has managed to withstand the vicissitudes of time. The ontological meditation of Parmenides, the father of metaphysics, rests on the separation of truth from opinion, truth being the main and sole topic of *prima philosophia*, as Aristotle and Hegel also underline. Philosophers of the twentieth century like Heidegger and Habermas, both of whom are critical of metaphysics, have nevertheless elaborated two fundamentally original conceptions of truth (*Unverborgenheit* and consensus). Obviously, the notion of truth is essential to philosophy, and for many reasons. Not only does philosophy, as a meta-reflection on other theories, have to confront their claim to truth, it must also attempt to justify its own claim to validity. How those claims are to be understood or sustained is a vital matter to any philosophy.

How does a hermeneutical philosophy, one that stresses the historicity of all validity claims, approach the problem of truth? We naturally consult a book entitled *Truth and Method: Foundations for a Philosophical Hermeneutics* for an answer. In spite of its title, Gadamer's masterpiece does not have an explicit theory of truth to offer, and the fact that he does not develop a systematic theory is essential to his message.[11] A hermeneutical philosophy cannot construct a truth-theory *in abstracto*. It is content with describing the happening of truth in everyday life, in art, and in the human sciences as an event (*Geschehen*, *Ereignis*) that precedes the methodical bringing about of truth. An explicit theory of truth, in its inevitable distance from the concrete experience of truth, would consolidate the methodological approach which hermeneutics seeks to undermine. However, even if hermeneutics does not present a theory of truth, it lives on a conception of truth. Gadamer cautiously leaves it inexplicit, but it can be brought to a level of philosophical clarity sufficient for differentiating it from traditional and competing conceptions.

The classical understanding of truth is rooted in the idea of correspondence, between *intellectus* and *res*, idea and reality, sentences and facts. Hermeneutics maintains that this conception is both inescapable and insufficient. It is inescapable because true statements, ideally at least, are those that correspond to reality. For those who question the naivety of this claim, the simplest of examples will suffice to illustrate it. Suppose that one country claims that another has shot down a civilian airliner and the accused country denies it. In this case, *tertium non datur*, either the claim or the denial is true, i.e., corresponds to what really took place. So truth does have something to do with correspondence. Refusing to admit that would rob the idea of truth of much of its critical meaning. This conception remains insufficient however. A sentence like '2 + 2 = 4' is true, but doesn't necessarily 'correspond' to facts in the outside world. Rather, it is coherent with a specific set of axioms and definitions. Many philosophers draw the conclusion that truth is a matter of coherence, not of correspondence, but hermeneutics has more fundamental reasons to question the idea of correspondence or *adaequatio*. In many cases, correspondences are simply impossible to establish with any kind of definitiveness, but truth-claims are nevertheless made. To point out a field close to hermeneutical praxis, one only needs to think about the domain of text-interpretation. All interpretations lay claim to truth, but since many of them are competing and often contradictory, truth appears difficult to account for. We are also aware that in the course of history unanimously held views or interpretations have later been called into question and rejected. The parallel of text-interpretation can easily be extended to the realms of science and everyday life, where truth claims are also made without there being an identifiable and interpretation-free reality to which they would correspond. We don't need hermeneutics to realize that moral and political beliefs which are held to be cogent today might very well be rejected in another time and culture.

Without denying the critical import of the notions of correspondence and coherence, hermeneutics explores another approach to truth. For hermeneutics truth isn't primarily a matter of correspondence (a criterion that is not applicable everywhere), but of 'meaningfulness.' An experience of truth is an experience of something meaningful that helps us 'cope,' to use the central verb in the pragmatist vocabulary. Even if it may seem awkward, at first, to identify truth with meaningfulness, this characterization is a fair description of what is *held* to be true by human beings in the absence of a criterion of correspondence.

This conception of truth also has the support of two traditions, one biblical and one Greek. In the Bible, the word usually translated 'truth' is *emeth*, a word that doesn't connote the idea of correspondence but that of solidity, fidelity, something we can rely on. The symbol of truth is often the rock we can build upon.[12] When the psalms speak of God as being the truth, they mean that we can count on God, that God helps us through the adversities of life. When Jesus is quoted as saying that he is the way and the truth, he doesn't mean by truth that he 'corresponds' to something but simply that we can rely on him. Our goal is by no means to restore a biblical understanding of truth (which wouldn't be very philosophical), but to call attention to the fact that our tradition has room for an understanding of truth as meaningfulness, as something we can rely upon rather than as something whose correspondence to reality is the important thing.

This conception also finds an echo in Greek and platonic thought, provided that we read the word *alētheia* through Heidegger's suggestive translation as dis-closure.[13] Understood as *a-lētheia*, truth is viewed as a revelation of meaning, as some kind of un-concealment. Truth emerges as a disclosure of meaning that takes shape from the background of 'closure' which characterizes our being in the world. To use the metaphor of light, which is also anchored in the platonic tradition, truth for finite beings is experienced as a sort of illumination, casting light on some part of the darkness we encounter. This platonic conception of truth as an immediate illumination also occurs in the *Metaphysics* of Aristotle, where we can read that truth is something we 'grasp' (*thigein*) all of a sudden, the opposite of truth being 'not to grasp at all' (*mē thigganein*).[14] Finite beings have to rely on this kind of illumination, which has no possibility of being grounded. One might say that this Platonic conception stresses the evocative character of truth, but it is still part of what truth means to us. When we hear an acute saying or a witty joke, we might react by saying 'this is very true.' By that we do not mean that it corresponds to reality, but that it is highly suggestive or that it is to the point. The fact that it discloses the world in a meaningful and illuminating way is more decisive than the idea of correspondence. It is easy to think of examples. As Gadamer once said, the opposite of 'true' in this case is not 'false,' but 'empty.'[15]

Surely the inspiration for this evocative understanding of truth is not to be found in logic or scientific method but in art. It is of the utmost significance that the opening section of *Truth and Method* car-

ries the title 'The uncovering of the question of truth through the experience of art.'[16] One might be tempted to think that art replaces
logic, or method, as the organon of hermeneutical truth. Much of
Gadamer's efforts in the first section of his book are devoted to calling into question the 'aesthetic differentiation,' that is the belief that
art commands an autonomous aesthetic universe that scorns the pretensions of knowledge and truth. Gadamer replies to this alleged abstraction of truth claims in the realm of artistic experience by arguing that
art always has something to say and is therefore related to knowledge.
Art not only produces an aesthetic feeling, it reveals something that
can be integrated in our self-understanding and that definitely has its
Sitz im Leben. Art that didn't have anything meaningful to say would
be of no interest to us. We encounter, once again, the conception of
truth as concrete meaningfulness, as disclosure of sense.

It is obviously this paradigm of disclosure that governs the whole
hermeneutical endeavour, but art also possesses other features that por-
tend the hermeneutical awareness of truth. First of all, artistic truth
takes on the character of a happening (*Ereignis*), a revelation that literally strikes us as meaningful. This overwhelming aspect of artistic truth
entails a decisive desubjectivization of truth. Truth is not something
a subject can induce by following some method or logic of discovery.
It simply happens, falling upon the subject, so to speak. Gadamer uti-
lizes the notion of play to portray this truth happening exemplified
by art:

> What we mean by truth here can best be determined again in terms
> of the concept of play. The way in which the weight of the things
> that we encounter in our understanding disposes itself is itself a lin-
> guistic event, a game with words playing around and about what is
> meant ... The attitude of the player should not be seen as an attitude
> of subjectivity, since it is, rather, the game itself that plays, in that it
> draws the players into itself and thus itself becomes the actual subjec-
> tum of the playing.[17]

The happening of truth isn't a matter of methodological assurance;
it manifests itself as a play in which we are involved. The desubjectivization and demethodization of truth go hand in hand. Only a subject that knows itself to be the cornerstone of truth can attempt to

develop a method in order to ascertain truth. It is no coincidence that the father of the *cogito* also wrote a 'Discours de la méthode.'

Yet another feature of art important to the hermeneutical understanding of truth is the simple fact that art *appeals* to us and our senses. There is a particular gloss (*Schein*) that attracts us in any true experience of art. Thus the brightness of something meaningful becomes an intrinsic part of what hermeneutics understands under the notion of truth. At this point Gadamer links artistic truth with the rhetorical tradition that reflected on a truth that is plainly illuminating without being able to be definitely established. In our life-world we constantly rely on some obvious, illuminating truths that never can nor need to be founded. This illuminating aspect is part of their meaning, because

> what is illuminating (*einleuchtend*), is always something that is said, a proposal, a plan, a conjecture, an argument, or something of the sort. The idea is always that what is clear is not proved and not absolutely certain, but it asserts itself by reason of its own merit within the area of the possible and probable ... The hermeneutical experience belongs in this sphere because it is also the event of a genuine experience.
>
> That there is something illuminating about something that is said, without the implication that it is in every direction secured, judged and decided is, in fact, always the case when something speaks to us out of tradition.[18]

This artistic and rhetorical conception, destined to relativize the idea that truth might be definitely founded through method, is rooted in the finitude of human existence, the keystone of hermeneutical philosophy. One could feasibly argue, and I believe this is one of the points Gadamer wants to make, that the methodological craving for certainty and assurance all too often ignores the reality of human finitude. Hermeneutics is dedicated to what truth means for finite beings. It is therefore sceptical about any methodological claim to definitive truth and the very idea of methodological foundations.

Gadamer's motto on this issue is stated in the foreword to the second edition of *Wahrheit und Methode*: 'do we need a foundation for that which has always carried us?'[19] The recognition of human finitude precludes any claim to definite foundations. This post-foundationalist approach is based on the conviction that the life-world is carried by the community of language, that is by dialogue. Dialogue rebels against the idea of ultimate foundations because any such foundation can be called into question in the course of dialogue. Those who already have a definitive foundation do not really need communication. They have already found the answer. To put it in thesis-form, we have dialogue because we don't have any ultimate foundations. One could feasibly go further and assert that we also have ethics because we don't possess definite foundations. From this perspective, the search for an ultimate grounding of moral norms, a search that preoccupies many moral philosophers, reveals a deep misunderstanding of what ethos is all about. Ethics, as a reflection on ethos, has to do with human action and the orientation of human conduct in a given community. It is because there are no definitely foundable norms that there is an ethos, that we behave according to certain established patterns, follow the rules and values of some part of society. Ethos is the only way to cope without foundations. On this ground, the post-foundationalist approach is the only reasonable one for ethics.

This hermeneutical conception of truth as something entrenched in the experience of meaningfulness for finite beings, that is conquered on the basis of the rhetorical tradition and artistic experience, is open to fundamental doubts and criticism. Granted that the human predicament couldn't do without the experience of meaningfulness that resists foundation, does it follow that everything that makes sense has to count as true? One might just as well expel any critical analysis whatsoever from hermeneutics, as many commentators have feared. Those alarmist conclusions are far too hasty. One has to remember that the hermeneutical approach was critical to begin with: it was elaborated in order to rectify a scientistic and methodological distortion of truth that appears irreconcilable with the reality of human finitude. By no means does this rectification lead to relativism or some version of Feyerabend's 'anything goes.' Hermeneutics relies too much on the facticity of human reason to accept this. (No human really lives by the maxim that anything goes.) Contemporary philosophy has to be grateful to Rorty for recalling that relativism, understood as 'the view that every belief on a certain topic, or perhaps about *any* topic, is as good as every other,'[20] has never been held by anybody. Relativism is usually nothing but the bugbear of particularly fundamentalistic conceptions of what philosophy ought to look like. Rorty is also right in pointing out that 'the philosophers who get *called* "relativists" are those who say that the grounds for choosing between such [incompatible] opinions are less algorithmic than had been thought.'[21]

Hermeneutics generally agrees with such a view. It eschews the accusation of total relativism by taking into account the reliance of hermeneutical truth on communication. This openness to dialogue results from the recognition of human finitude. Conscious of the cultural and historical limitations of our beliefs, we engage in dialogue to share our experiences and, at times, to seek orientation. In the unfolding of conversation, some of our opinions can be put to the test. Dialogical arguing is a central feature of hermeneutical rationality. This rationality is the one founded on the binding force that accompanies the better argument on some issue. The rationality of beliefs lies in the fact that they *can* be dialogically founded and that they remain open to criticism.[22] We can and at times do reject some of our convictions if evidence shows that they are incoherent or inadequate and thus cease to be illuminating (even though the experience of dialogue often teaches that the partners in a dispute will stubbornly stick to obviously untenable views). By virtue of the rationality of dialogue, we do set aside some of what we once held to be true. It does not follow that what replaces old beliefs is grounded once and for all. We adopt new perspectives because they seem more appropriate, more appealing at the time, but they might very well turn out to be indefensible in the future. Dialogue is an inalienable part of the human quest for truth, but it does not provide the absolute orientation that would enable us to escape our finite limitations. Communication continues to function as a critical forum where arguments can be put forward to sustain some of our views, but those arguments are never free of rhetoric and human interests. What one accepts as a valid argument in the course of conversation remains hermeneutically rooted, that is, dependent on social practices and language games we identify with. This is why hermeneutical truth lays claim to universality.

NOTES

1 W.V.O. Quine, 'Two Dogmas of Empiricism,' *From a Logical Point of View*, 2nd ed. (Cambridge, MA: Harvard University Press 1961)

2 See Richard Rorty, *Philosophy and the Mirror of Nature* (Princeton, NJ: Princeton University Press 1979); *Consequences of Pragmatism* (Minneapolis: University of Minnesota Press 1982); 'Epistemological Behaviorism and the De-Transcendentalization of Analytic Philosophy,' in R. Hollinger, ed., *Hermeneutics and Praxis* (Notre Dame, IN: University of Notre Dame Press 1985).

3 Immanuel Kant, *Kritik der reinen Vernunft*, A835 = B863

4 See Chapter V, 'The conquest of the historical world,' of Ernst Cassirer, *The Philosophy of the Enlightenment*, 4th ed. (Boston: Beacon Press 1961).

5 Rüdiger Bubner, *Geschichtsprozesse und Handlungsnormen* (Frankfurt a.M.: Suhrkamp 1984), 78

6 This distinction roughly corresponds to Rorty's distinction between philosophy and capitalized Philosophy, *Consequences of Pragmatism*, xiv.

7 Helmut Schnädelbach, *Philosophie in Deutschland 1831-1933* (Frankfurt a.M.: Suhrkamp 1983)

8 See, for instance, Hans-Georg Gadamer, *Reason in the Age of Science* (Cambridge, MA: MIT Press 1982).

9 Paul Ricœur, 'Phénoménologie et herméneutique,' *Phänomenologische Forschungen* **1** (1975) 31-77

10 Hans-Georg Gadamer, *Wahrheit und Methode* [*WM*], 4.Aufl. (Tübingen: J.C.B. Mohr [Paul Siebeck] 1975), 250; *Truth and Method* [*TM*] (New York: The Seabury Press 1975), 235. Most quotations from the English version are modified in this paper.

11 See Jean Grondin, *Hermeneutische Wahrheit? Zum Wahrheitsbegriff Hans-Georg Gadamers* (Königstein: Forum Academicum 1982), 1-8. For an analytic parallel see Rorty's *Consequences of Pragmatism*, xiii, where he writes: 'The essays in this book are attempts to draw consequences from a pragmatist theory about truth. This theory says that truth is not the sort of thing one should expect to have a philosophically interesting theory about.' This opening statement has to be taken *cum*

grano salis for it strikes the eye that Rorty argues on the basis of a very definite theory of truth, namely James' definition of truth as 'whatever proves itself to be good in the way of belief' (*ibid.*, xxv). Post-foundationalist philosophies like hermeneutics and pragmatism have the tendency to open up fundamental philosophical perspectives and to deny doing it at the same time, as if *prima philosophia* would consist in rejecting *prima philosophia*.

12 See O. F. Bollnow, *Das Doppelgesicht der Wahrheit* (Stuttgart: Kohl-hammer 1975), 9.

13 Which might very well be etymologically correct. See my 'L'alētheia de Platon à Heidegger,' *Revue de Métaphysique et de Morale* **87** (1982) 551-6.

14 Aristotle, *Metaphysics* Θ 10, 1051b24-5

15 Hans-Georg Gadamer, *Kleine Schriften IV* (Tübingen: J.C.B. Mohr [Paul Siebeck] 1977), 248; see also my 'Zur Entfaltung eines hermeneutischen Wahrheitsbegriffs,' *Philosophisches Jahrbuch* **90** (1983) 145-53.

16 *WM* 1; *TM*, 3

17 *WM* 464; *TM*, 446

18 *WM*, 360; *TM*, 441-2

19 *WM*, xxv; *TM*, xxiv

20 Rorty, *Consequences of Pragmatism*, 166. On Rorty's qualified relativism see R.J. Bernstein, 'Philosophy in the Conversation of Mankind,' *Hermeneutics and Praxis*, 72.

21 Rorty, *Consequences of Pragmatism*, 166

22 On this communicative rationality see Jürgen Habermas, *Theorie des kommunikativen Handelns*, Bd. 1 (Frankfurt a.M.: Suhrkamp 1981), and my essays 'Rationalité et agir communicationnel chez Habermas,' *Critique*, 464-465 (1986) 40-59; 'De Heidegger à Habermas,' *Les Études philosophiques* (1986) 15-31.

Peter McCormick

After Foundationalism:
Interpreting Intentional Actions

Richard Rorty has remarked that 'nothing grounds our practices, nothing legitimizes them, nothing shows them to be in touch with the
way things really are.'[1] In all areas, human inquiry is not a matter of
bringing our beliefs and desires into conformity with something else
but of 'reweaving our fabric of belief and desire, our attitudes towards
various sentences of our language.'[2] And why, we may ask? Rorty
replies:

> There is no way to underwrite or criticize the ongoing, self-modifying
> know-how of the user of language by a philosophical account of the
> nature of the relation of his mind or his language to the object. There
> is no way to reach outside our language-game to an account of the re-
> lation between that language-game as scheme to "the world" as
> "context."[3]

Philosophy becomes what Schiller understood as the play of the mind
with itself, since no representation of the world is genuine and no
talk about the world is more than a text about the world. The only
game left to play is an Anglo-European game where analytic
philosophers and Continental ones recognize the greater importance
of their similarities to their differences.

In the spirit of William Sullivan's sympathy for the view that
neither analytic nor Continental philosophy has been able to recognize certain problems, I would like to work against the grain of this
particular kind of anti-foundationalism by putting on exhibit a case
study of certain conceptual inadequacies in both recent analytic and
hermeneutic philosophy. I begin with a puzzling representation of
a putative intentional action in a literary work, and then argue that
characteristic discussions of the nature of intentional action in contemporary analytic and hermeneutic accounts cannot accommodate

such central cases partly because of a shared foundationalist strategy. I conclude with a sketch of intentional action which an alternative non-foundationalist approach would need to address.

I

T.S. Eliot's poetic drama, *Murder in the Cathedral*, begins with a choral meditation on waiting. The old and poor women of Canterbury are discovered before the cathedral. 'Here let us stand, close by the Cathedral. Here let us wait,' go the play's first words.[4] Further on the women chant: 'For us, the poor, there is no action, but only to wait and to witness.' These opening words are doubly important. They announce one of the central themes of the play, waiting, and they exhibit the usual understanding of waiting which the course of the play will put into question. The traditional construal of waiting is something static and hence 'no action' at all; but the 'waiting' the play will dramatize is dynamic — more a course of events than a state of affairs. The first words Becket utters in the play are part of the justification for reading *Murder in the Cathedral* as a play about the nature of action:

> They know and do not know, what it is to act or suffer.
> They know and do not know, that action is suffering
> And suffering is action. Neither does the agent suffer
> Nor the patient act. But both are fixed
> In an eternal action, an eternal patience,
> To which all must consent that it may be willed
> And which all must suffer that they may will it,
> That the pattern may subsist, for the pattern is the action
> And the suffering, that the wheel may turn and still
> Be forever still. (22)

The themes of knowing and not knowing, a pattern in the in-tersection of time and eternity, and the image of the wheel moving at the rim and still at its centerpoint are relatively familiar. What is strange is the talk of a willing which is a consenting. For the passage seems to suggest some connection between an action which is passive, a willing which is not a wanting but a consenting, and a motionless waiting which is an action.

Becket must learn howher to save himself nor to sacrifice himself. He must neither try to escape, nor actively seek martyrdom; rather he must learn how to act in not acting, how to enact a kind of waiting. Both acting and suffering are fixed in an eternal action, a pattern to which all must consent. This is something Becket knows and does not know, says the Fourth Tempter, repeating to Becket his own words and thereby fulfilling his task of telling Becket only what he knows (39). Later, in the sermon Becket preaches on Christmas morning in the same year 1170, this acting and suffering are said to be involved in a larger reality. For the pattern comprises being born and dying, beginning and ending, the sorrowful reenactment of a death and the joyful celebration of a birth in the same mysterious action which is Becket's Mass (51). Becket must learn, in the words of 'Little Gidding,' 'to make an end.'

The sermon includes the key insight which enables Becket to resolve his dilemma, the insight which spells out the till now cryptic and repeated doctrine of consent to a pattern. A Christian martyrdom, Becket tells the people, is not

> the effect of a man's will to become a Saint, as a man by willing and contriving may become a ruler of men. A martyrdom is always the design of God ... never the design of man; for the true martyr is he who has become the instrument of God, who has lost his will in the will of God, and who no longer desires anything for himself, not even the glory of being a martyr. (53)

To win through to this insight Becket is shown as having understood that the last temptation is to do the right thing for the wrong reason. He thereby escapes from the fate that would otherwise have overtaken him, the terrifying loss Eliot describes in passages in the play and elsewhere about 'the void,' 'the horror of the effortless journey, to the empty land which is no land, only emptiness, absence, the Void' (88, cf. 20). The insight here seems to be the one formulated in Eliot's poetic pageant, *The Rock*, where the choruses repeat: '*Make perfect your will* ... make perfect your will.'[5] And, in Part II of *Murder in the Cathedral*, Becket will say, in trying to calm his frightened priests who want him to save himself and thereby to save them as well: 'All my life I have waited. Death will come only when I am worthy;/ And if I am worthy, there is no danger./ I have therefore only to make perfect my will' (75).

On Eliot's view the essence of tragedy is to be found in its ritualistic and communal dimension and thereby involves participation by a community and the recreation and reaffirmation of its identity.[6] The play ends with another choral ode which now, unlike the opening ode, is no longer an expression of a paralyzed inactivity, but is a psalm, a song of praise, thanks, and contrition. Becket's action has fructified in the lives of these women in opening their eyes to a spiritual vision of all experience. He has achieved a consummation of his life in a martyr's death, a consummation he has learned neither to forego through inaction, nor actively to avoid, nor actively to desire, but to affirm in an efficacious waiting, in the still movement of the dancer, in a moment of neither action nor inaction.

How are we to understand this waiting, this peculiar kind of active inaction or inactive action? The basic problem here is understanding the implicit claim throughout that Becket's waiting is an action, indeed an intentional action. In the light of this description of a puzzling kind of action in *Murder in the Cathedral*, I would like to inventory briefly two recent philosophical accounts of action, one analytic, the other hermeneutic. My point is not that Becket's action is a counterexample to these accounts. I want to suggest that many of the peculiarities in Becket's putative action are puzzling not because they are only incompletely describable in analytic or hermeneutic terms but because they can work such an effect on readers and audiences that the very terms in which both analytic and hermeneutic accounts present human action seem strongly inappropriate.

II

When we consider recent analytic accounts of action,[7] we find working definitions of action and intentional action together with descriptions of their complex cognitive and conative components. Action is to be defined not as a mere doing but as an event understandable in the context of a particular version of the causal theory. Thus, informally, an *action* is a type of event which results from some proximate and appropriate antecedent mental event which cannot be identified merely as a conjunction of believing and desiring. Similarly, an *intentional action* is an action whose mental antecedent consists of an immediate intending which involves both a complex cognitive and a complex conative element, and which proximately causes that action. *The cognitive complex* of immediate intention as the proximate cause of intentional action is taken as, first, the preconceived master representation of an activity in the form of an agent's plans, scripts, and scenes in which he ascribes to himself the primary role; and, second, the agent's guidance and monitoring through perceptual feedback and correction of that activity throughout its course to completion. *The conative complex* of intentional action as the proximate cause of intentional action is taken to involve, first, with respect to plan selection, a motivational system which initiates action by interaction with memory on the occasion of environmental stimuli; and, second, with respect to plan enactment, the operation of a production set (a series of procedural rules) interfacing with scripts and working memory to activiate motor schemata which guide bodily behavior.

Now even on its own terms, such an account raises at least five critical issues. First, the working definitions of action and intentional action here are arguably shortsighted in making too little room for some of those actions which an agent does not merely do or merely let happen but in some strong sense suffers. Second, the account of the cognitive complex is overly narrow in excluding some arguable construals of belief and desire as possible candidates for at least part of the role given to intention. Third, the computational model of the conative complex is both overly narrow – it provides no discussion of the key notion of a conscious subject – and overly speculative – it relies on generalization only from ethological analyses. We are left, if this is not unfair, with three black boxes: storied representations, motivational systems, and conscious agents. Fourth, the naturalistic aims of this account, while of great philosophical interest generally, lead to overlooking other available conceptual resources for a philosophical theory of human action. Since psychology does not yet have either a satisfactory cognitive (central processing) or conative (motivation) theory available, limiting oneself to a cognitive transformation of certain views is in part self-defeating. Finally, it remains highly questionable whether such an attempt at a naturalized philosophy of action is properly described as ontologically neutral. Moreover the understanding here, if not of causality at least of events, of intentions as attitudes having contents, and of intentional contents as properties requires critical scrutiny. Without such scrutiny the final choice of a terminology for action theory remains unjustified.

In this analytic account some of the peculiarities of important species of human actions, like those which include Becket's waiting, are seen obscurely if at all. When we return to the poetic representation of Becket's action, part of what we find does not seem to be appropriately described in terms of an exclusively naturalistic version of complex cognitive and conative components of the proximate causes of Becket's action.

Recall, first, that Becket's action arises out of an unusual dilemma — whether he acts or does not act Becket thinks that he will violate his own ideal of personal fulfillment. That is, if Becket acts in prudently avoiding mortal danger he loses the opportunity to witness before his community to certain values he holds to be transcendent, namely the primacy of the spiritual order. Yet if he does not act, he risks failing to witness before his community to other values he also holds to be transcendent, namely spiritual humility. In the first case he risks sacrificing the primacy of the spiritual to the interest of self-preservation, whereas in the second he risks sacrificing humility to the proud impulse to be a martyr. Whether he acts or not Becket can only fail. Yet Becket acts and succeeds. The first elusive feature then of Becket's action is that it arises unexpectedly from a spiritual dilemma which it succeeds in resolving.

Second, Becket's action here is neither the self-directed performance of an action, nor the self-serving forbearance to act, but the decision to wait on what is to happen. As such, this act is both an enactment of what has gone before, an instance of a ritual repetition through memory, and an anticipation of what is to come, a prophetic gesture in a charged social space. The gap between the antecedent mental event here and the actual effect in waiting is not to be characterized just in terms of a gap between remote and proximate causes in a causal process but must take into account such opaque elements as self-doubt, temptation, weakness, and so on — what Eliot calls 'the shadow between motive and act.' Describing the shadow as a causal gap is inappropriate because such a description leaves out too many relevant features. Thus the second elusive feature is the nature of the relation between proximate and remote antecedents to acts of a symbolic and ritual sort.

Further, Becket's act, at least on the evidence of the language of the play, seems to involve certain curious prerequisites if not conditions. In order to act in waiting Becket needs to attain what is described here and elsewhere as a state of personal dispossession, an emptiness, an attitude towards his own action — 'proferring one's deeds to oblivion' in the language of 'Ash Wednesday,' and 'seeking the good deeds that lead to obscurity' (SP 108), or 'the one right action that will fructify in the lives of others.' In short a prerequisite is detachment, but detachment understood in a special way. Accordingly, a third elusive feature of Becket's action is the nature of a prerequisite which a merely analytic account of causal antecedents whether remote or proximate leaves without comment.

But if this curious state of mind called detachment is a prerequisite for Becket's act, the features of that act seem just as puzzling. Thus Becket is represented as having to act in such a way as not to perform an action all the while being occupied in acting, and to renounce not the act but its fruits. Becket is to incorporate what Eliot's Harvard teacher Irving Babbitt called 'the will to refrain.' His act is to be a renunciation, a sacrificial act, an enactment which both reenacts what is past and creates a possibility for future acts of a community.

What follows on such an act of renunciation are not so much results as consequences — both at the individual and communal levels. Thus Becket's act is to yield a release not from a cyclic existence but from suffering, a reconciliation among those who are caught up in its circle, a fruitfulness in subsequent stages of communal activity. Here the public dimension of action is not to be understood by opposition to the private but as a communal feature of certain acts which allow a community to participate and thereby to recreate and to reaffirm its identity while opening itself outward through subsequent activity of its own towards world and cosmos.

Here then are four elusive features of actions like Becket's which do not seem to receive an appropriate description in terms of a representative analytic account of human action — their source in dilemmas rather than strategies; their peculiar links to past and future action through reenactment and prophetic witness; their dependence on self-less states of mind; and their promise of both individual and communal liberation. Such features however do not simply call for still further revisions in a naturalized causal theory of action but seem to put into question in different and still obscure ways the appropriateness of such an idiom as a whole.

III

If we now consider a recent hermeneutic account of action an importantly different view appears.[8] An *action* is what an agent both does and undergoes. As an activity, action is an exercise without any requisite prior knowledge of certain capacities which cannot be reduced either to their antecedent causes or to mere desires. As a passivity, action is the issue of certain dispositions and motivational fields which include motives, forces, and especially desires which arise out of the agent's lived experiences of his or her own body precisely as one's own, as a 'corps propre.' An *intentional action* is one which fulfils both essential and nonessential conditions for the agent to have an intention to act. Forming an intention to act involves imaginative selection from a repertoire of basic actions, and the propositional and discursive articulation of derived actions or action strategies in a project. In deciding to act intentionally the agent traverses degrees of deliberation before settling on the specific ends which the action project then incorporates. Acting intentionally involves not just a verbal but also a mental expression of the intention to act. The latter has the form of a first-person, self-addressed command to initiate, carry out, and to complete what is intended, and includes as well a voluntary component. Completing an intentional act involves making rather than letting things happen. The agent carries through the exercise of his capacity to act by intervening in natural courses of events and thereby setting in motion the operation of a closed system his activity has already isolated. *Representing* an intentional act involves a necessary symbolic articulation of action at the different levels of concepts, social practices, and cultural conventions. All action is mediated symbolically. The *explanation*, understanding, and interpretation of action must include the systematic articulation of the conceptual network in which the term 'action' is situated. It must also include the interpretive readings of the symbolic mediations of action, and metaphysical reflections on the 'existential' and not merely formal character of the temporal instant in which action takes place, a gathering of the past and the future in a lived now.

Now just as in the analytic account, we find here also at least five difficulties with this hermeneutic account. First, this account has the merit of insisting on the role not just of cognition and conation in intentional action but also of 'capacities' or 'powers.' This crucial element however, which could be taken as closing one of the important gaps in analytical theories, is left seriously undeveloped. Second, the hermeneutic account also leaves undeveloped the suggestion that desires and motives in some cases must be analyzed in other terms than merely those of a dichotomy between causes and reasons. A third difficulty arises from the numerous appeals to phenomenological doctrines such as eidetic description, noematic contents, intuition of essences, and especially the notion of the lived body, the body as a quasi-object. The problem here is the failure to push the parallels far enough. What a hermeneutic account needs is detailed attention to at least one general hypothesis, namely the idea of rearticulating a phenomenological psychology as a version of contemporary work in cognitive psychology and even as a critical extension of this work. A fourth difficulty lies in whether the account can be critically reconstructed in such a way as to preserve its genuine insights about the various roles of volitional phenomena, its phenomenology of the will, without falling prey to the serious objections which every volitional theory faces. Finally, at a more diagnostic level, it is important to realize that this hermeneutic account starts with a critical and speculative reinterpretation of Hegel. But the difficulty here is that this account is centered on a kind of action which is almost always the action represented in tragic drama, whether in Aristotle's analysis of generally Sophoclean action or in Hegel's analysis of the action in the *Antigone*. Thus, the suspicion arises that much of the focus in a hermeneutic account of action may well be overdetermined by a series of concerns arising from an Aristotelian context, just as a similar overdetermination in an analytic account may result from an overreliance on a computational model for naturalizing theories of action.

The terms however in which the hermeneutic account is presented, I want to suggest, keep us from seeing other aspects of actions like

Becket's than those I called attention to in discussing the analytic account. When we return to the fuller poetic description of Becket's action we find certain features which not even a comprehensive hermeneutic account is able to describe appropriately. Besides the four features of Becket's action which seem to be inappropriately described in the idiom of a naturalized analytic account, four other features of that action seem to elude the idiom of an hermeneutic account.

The first is the paradoxical character of Becket's action which is both an action and not an action but an undergoing, a willing and not a willing but a consenting. Becket's action we may say involves both the passive action and the willed consent of an enacting, neither a waiting for something nor a waiting to do something, but a waiting on what may or may not eventuate. This paradoxical feature of Becket's action is not appropriately captured in the hermeneutic reminder of passivities in action, motivational fields, and affective influences because this vocabulary, even though it can accommodate dialectic, cannot hold precisely these two aspects of Becket's action in suspension simultaneously. The elusive feature here then is the specific kinds of paradox Becket's action involves.

A second recalcitrant feature of Becket's action is its presentation as an action that arises not out of ignorance which is remediable but out of an invincible not-knowing. Becket must act in the light of ends he scarcely comprehends — to overcome temptation, to bear witness, to accomplish a spiritual metamorphosis, etc. More seriously, he must act according to a pattern and according to a design without ever being able to know either. Unlike the dancer who, in following the measured movement of his partner, accomplishes the design of the ballet without knowing its pattern, Becket must conform to a figure he neither knows nor can ever know. Thus talk of a cognitive component in action as merely complex is not an appropriate way of talking about such a feature at all.

A third obscure feature of Becket's act is its temporal specification. Although the hermeneutic account takes a step beyond the merely formal talk of temporal instant in analytic description, the hermeneutic discussion does not capture the specific peculiarities in the time of Becket's act. For this act is said to be not in time at all. It is rather situated in a 'critical moment' in the etymological sense of a moment of judgment which takes place 'always, now, and here' (61), a time described as 'too late / For action, too soon for contrition' (73), 'The moment foreseen may be unexpected / When it arrives' (63), a time seeming to lack duration where 'we wait, and the time is short / But waiting is long' (58). Becket characterizes the time of his act when he says 'out of time my decision is taken' (79). In short, the time of Becket's action is not time in some usual sense at all, but at an intersection of time and eternity, a timeless gathering of mythical, historical, and cosmic times.

Finally, Becket acts for a variety of obscure but very cogent ends. One of the goals of Becket's action is to make an end, a theme which reverberates in other descriptions to be found elsewhere in Eliot's poetry. Here to make an end is neither to die, nor to learn after Socrates how to die. It is rather to act in such a way that one will be — of all things — worthy to die. 'All my life I have waited. Death will come only when I am worthy' (75) we remember Becket saying. Being worthy here, however, is not the result of the agent's effort but the transforming effect upon the agent of the coming of death. Moreover, the particularly enigmatic element is the further suggestion that Becket is to act, that is, to make an end, in such a way that his end makes him worthy, transforms his being in transforming his beginnings — 'in my end is my beginning.' We have then another reflection of the view that Becket's act must be a response to something he must wait upon, a response which if adequate both changes his present status (he is rendered worthy to die) and mysteriously and retroactively transforms his beginnings. Even the phenomenological descriptions of action which unwind from the uses of dialectic in the hermeneutic account leave this centrally important peculiarity of acting just as unrepresented as the other three features.

In summary, however interesting in their own terms some corrected versions of a naturalized-analytic-causal account or a dialectical-hermeneutic-volitional account of human action may be, at least eight elusive features of Becket's action invite further reflection. The point in underlining these features is not so much to force further revisions in these theories but to suggest the need for reflection on whether a different idiom is required for presenting human action more perspicuously.

IV

Poetic representations of actions like Becket's deciding to wait on what may eventuate are difficult to understand. Whatever sense we do manage to make of them, these sayings could hardly be taken to apply as such to central features of intentional action. Yet I think such representations do present a challenging suggestion about at least some features of intentional action which much contemporary philosophical theory continues to overlook. Most of these features can be indicated generally, after the example of poetic representation, not so much as motivational systems or individual desires, nor as causal and volitional elements of action, nor even as cognitive and conative aspects of proximate and immediate intention, but as negativities. However, to exhibit any philosophical interest which such an overly general description might include, we need to articulate more sharply just where the analytic and hermeneutic descriptions appear unsatisfactory.

The analytic account leaves virtually no room for several important features of intentional action in general, the features I have alluded to abstractly as negativities. With Eliot's lyric poetry taking the place of the more restricted dramatic representations of action, we can now indicate four general features of many intentional actions representative analytic accounts either do not describe or simply overlook.

First, such accounts make no room for the suggestion that much intentional action involves not so much a cognitive element but a lack of knowledge. Some agents seem to act intentionally, yet without knowing what they are doing, strictly speaking. Second, some intentional actions arise not from interest but from disinterestedness. Third, some intentional action seems to be directed without regard for consequences. And finally some such action does not seem properly describable just in terms of continuous causal agency: some intentional actions are more like lettings-go, surrenderings, succumbings — uninitiated actions. Here then are four important negative features of some intentional actions which go largely unaddressed in many analytic accounts.

A hermeneutic account also leaves out more general features of many intentional actions, whether those of Becket or of someone else. When we reread Eliot's text with such a description before us, the

suggestion arises that some intentional action may involve no fulfilment of intention at all. Rather the immediate intendings of some agent
may well undergo transformation instead of fulfilment. Further, some
intentional action may not be properly describable as satisfying essential conditions, since talk of essences even in the eidetic idiom of
phenomenology involves a commitment to invariant contents which
many intentions may not involve. Third, the hermeneutic account
awards a central place to talk about the self, whether in terms of capacities of the self, self-addressed injunctions, or deliberations of a self.
But the suggestion here is that some intentional action may well be
independent of talk about the self in such a transcendental idiom, requiring in its stead another idiom for making sense out of selfless frames
of mind or selfless agents. Finally, the hermeneutic account comple-
ments the analytic view with its insistence on the role of passivity
in the nature of action. But again this point is not so much invalid
— for many actions do involve such a component — as lacking pur-
chase on what seems to be an important feature of many intentional
actions, namely this *active* consent to certain passivities which are not
merely undergone, as the hermeneutic account would have it, but in
some sense assumed. Thus four more features of much intentional action come into view — its active passivities, its non-dependence on
a transcendental self, its non-essential contents, and its frequent non-
fulfilled character.

The suggestion, in thinking twice about certain poetic representations not of what action is but what it might be, comes to a series
of negativities which neither the naturalized idiom of analytic-causal
accounts nor the transcendental idiom of reflexive-volitional accounts
seems to be able to capture adequately. This is also the case when we
reread positive features of intentional action.

The positive features of much intentional action are closely related
to the play of opposites at the opening of 'Little Gidding' — 'midwinter
spring,' 'cold that is the heart's heat,' and an epithet which echoes in
Wallace Stevens, 'the unimaginable / Zero summer' (SP 41).

> ... these co-existing opposites are not like the paradoxes of the *via negati-*
> *va* ("Our only health is the disease"), and they are very different from
> the intensifying negatives of the sestina ("the withering of withered flow-
> ers") ... Their effect is to hold in tension opposing qualities, without

resolving or reconciling them, and in such a way that the negative intensifies the positive. Thus the stress falls upon "spring"; and "Zero" carries the mind to "a summer beyond sense." This is neither negation nor transcendence, but an intensification of what is actual, or an expansion of the actual towards the ideal.[9]

In our context, the suggestion is that some intentional action may be viewed as neither inaction nor action but as the intensification of certain enacted negativities like the ones just pointed out. For example, Becket is neither agent nor patient but an actively motionless instrument of a supposed providential pattern which in him reaches out to his historical community and, through dramatic reenactment in fiction, to Eliot's community of playgoers in 1934 and his spectators and readers thereafter.

More generally, in the context of the poetic presentations of action we may say that, besides the negativities which a more adequate account of intentional action needs to address, there are as well certain positive features of such action which these negativities intensify. We can catch sight of some of these by recalling other texts from the poetry. Two passages, I think, deserve renewed attention here. In the last of the *Four Quartets*, Little Gidding III begins:

> There are three conditions which often look alike
> Yet differ completely, flourish in the same hedgerow:
> Attachment to self and to things and to persons, detachment
> From self and from things and from persons; and, growing between
> them, indifference
> Which resembles the others as death resembles life,
> Being between two lives — unflowering, between
> The live and the dead nettle. This is the use of memory:
> For liberation — not less of love but expanding
> Of love beyond desire, and so liberation
> From the future as well as the past. Thus, love of a country
> Begins as attachment to our own field of action
> And comes to find that action of little importance
> Though never indifferent. History may be servitude,
> History may be freedom. See, now they vanish
> The faces and places, with the self which, as it could, loved them,
> To become renewed, transfigured, in another pattern.

This passage raises the suggestion that a satisfactory positive description of intentional action must include some account of at least three elements. First, some intentional action is deeply implicated in a complex mental state, a state of detachment we may perhaps call evenness of mind, equanimity. Here, some intentional action requires such equanimity for its execution. Second, some intentional action also includes certain neglected central features which are closely linked with the transformation of its own accompanying awareness from a self-centered state to a selfless one, a selfless consciousness. And finally, this evenness of mind together with a movement towards selflessness in some intentional action issues preeminently in an ethical domain of values which are neither individual and private nor public and social but in both actual and symbolic senses communal and participatory, a very general if not universal solidarity.

The second passage is from very early in *Four Quartets*, a text composed not long after *Murder in the Cathedral*, Burnt Norton II.

> At the still point of the turning world. Neither flesh nor fleshless
> Neither from nor towards; at the still point, there the dance is,
> But neither arrest nor movement. And do not call it fixity,
> Where past and future are gathered. Neither movement from nor
>   towards,
> Neither ascent nor decline. Except for the point, the still point,
> There would be no dance, and there is only the dance.
> I can only say, *there* we have been: but I cannot say where.
> And I cannot say, how long, for that is to place it in time.
>
> The inner freedom from the practical desire,
> The release from action and suffering, release from the inner
> And the outer compulsion, yet surrounded
> By a grace of sense, a white light still and moving,
> *Erhebung* without motion, concentration
> Without elimination, both a new world
> And the old made explicit, understood
> In the completion of its partial ecstasy,
> The resolution of its partial horror.

This passage suggests three further positive features of many intentional actions which much current philosophical theory seems to have overlooked. One striking feature is the accent on stillness with the suggestion for us that besides a conative complex a less inappropriate description of much intentional action needs to be attentive to what I have been describing after the example here as a certain release, a letting-go, a moment of neither action nor inaction. Further, we find a strong reinforcement for the earlier suggestion that talk about the cognitive complex of intentional action needs renewed scrutiny in the light of some intentional action arising not from knowledge but from at best a quasi-cognitive background — 'I cannot say ... I cannot say' — which issues nonetheless in a kind of epistemological courage, an acting without knowing enough. Finally, the passage brings together some of the paradoxical comments we have already seen here and there about the temporal character of intentional action. Here the suggestion is that neither the formal analytic nor the informal existential analysis of time can do justice to some temporal peculiarities of intentional action, its involvement through memory and imagination with past and future but much more its apparent intersection with timeless states where history is caught up in what one is tempted to call perduring cosmological puzzles. Rather, the temporal character of some intentional action would seem to involve suspended rather than continuous moments, moments, as Eliot says, out of time whatever these could be, where time becomes a balance of infinite motions.

Eliot's dramatic representation in *Murder in the Cathedral* of Becket's action of deciding to wait, and his lyrical presentation in *Four Quartets* of what action might be, suggest the need for a wider consideration of certain negative and positive features of many intentional actions to which neither current analytic nor hermeneutic reflection does sufficient justice. The need cannot be met by merely reworking these accounts to make them more comprehensive because each is articulated in an idiom which illumines important aspects of intentional action only at the cost of occluding certain of its cardinal features. We require an idiom which is capable of articulating some of what this rich poetry suggests to us metaphorically. Such an idiom, I suspect, would require most importantly an extended critical analysis of the alternative ontologies at work here in the perplexing but challenging light of poetic fictions.

NOTES

1 Richard Rorty, 'From Logic to Language to Play,' *Proceedings and Addresses of the American Philosophical Association* **49** (1986) 747-53, 753

2 Ibid., 750

3 Ibid., 751

4 T.S. Eliot, *Murder in the Cathedral* (London: Faber 1968), 11. Further references to *Murder in the Cathedral* in my text are to this edition.

5 T.S. Eliot, *Selected Poems* (London: Faber 1961), 109. Further references to *Selected Poems* (SP) in my text are to this edition.

6 David Ward, *T.S. Eliot: Between Two Worlds* (London: Routledge and Kegan Paul 1973), 185-97

7 I rely here on Myles Brand, whose view incorporates a critical reading of work in action theory over the last twenty years. See his *Intending and Acting: Toward a Naturalized Action Theory* (Cambridge, MA: MIT Press 1984).

8 Here I rely on Paul Ricoeur, whose view incorporates a critical reading of many of Brand's references as well as a wide variety of Continental reflections. See his 'Le discours de l'action,' in *La Semantique de l'action* (Paris: Editions CNRS 1981); and *Temps et récit*, 3 vols. (Paris: Seuil 1983-85).

9 Anthony D. Moody, *Thomas Stearns Eliot: Poet* (Cambridge: Cambridge University Press 1977)

II

Social-Political Critique

Social-Political Critique

What does the contemporary rejection of foundations imply for our thinking about social and political questions? In the following set of papers we are presented with three forms of non-foundationalist political thought: Richard Rorty's 'postmodernist bourgeois liberalism,' immanent social critique, and hermeneutical dialogue.

I Bourgeois Liberalism

Rorty advocates classical bourgeois liberalism, without its historical grounding in reason or nature, as the best example of solidarity yet achieved.

Turning his debunking style against him,[1] Rebecca Comay attacks Rorty's position as a parochial canonization of the status quo. The 'we' whom Rorty invites to 'continue the conversation of the west' are not all humankind but a variously described subspecies.[2] Since Rorty ties appeals to universality to metaphysical essentialism, he prevents any critique of classical liberalism based on the contrast between its universalist pretensions and the social reality it legitimates. In assuming naively that an abstract version of democracy is enough for genuine conversation, Rorty embalms the present. He simultaneously depoliticizes philosophy, by ridiculing philosophers' delusions of grandeur, and idealizes politics, by construing social relations on the model of a conversation.

In endorsing Comay's attempt to 'interrupt' Rorty's projected conversation, Robert Burch asserts that non-foundationalists must derive their philosophical narratives from, and legitimate them by, their particular existential, practical situation. What practical purpose, he asks, informs Rorty's debunking of a philosophical tradition which Rorty claims to be impotent? Rorty's project makes most sense if he is mistaking academic constraints and confrontations for those of society, or (less charitably) if he wishes to deflect attention from social constraints and confrontations. If Rorty intends an ultimate transformation of society on the model of a republic of letters, he does not discuss such important questions as who will get to speak and be heard, or how equality and participation among different groups can be maintained without the rule of reason.

To what extent are these attacks on Rorty's position warranted? Rorty may be defended on the ground that he frees philosophers from a concern with transcendental foundations or epistemological questions in order that they may engage in social criticism.[3] But Comay doubts that social criticism will result, since Rorty's concentration on the present robs it of any tension and impetus toward anything else. As Burch puts it, ideology critique turns into pragmatic tinkering.

One can also ask to what extent the critique of Rorty's political position reflects on his strictly epistemological project. An external critique of the political programme, which presupposes values opposed to Rorty's, can be advanced along with antifoundationalist claims about the status of those values. Such an exchange seems properly described as nothing more than a conversation or a dialogue. With an immanent critique, on the other hand, one perceives oneself as belonging to a community which shares some values with Rorty and can ignore epistemological questions. Again it seems appropriate to speak about the exchange as simply a conversation. So criticizing the political programme seems not to undermine the epistemological programme.[4]

Burch's reply to this argument is that Rorty's critique of epistemology doesn't have value in and of itself, because that would be the old foundationalist project. So Rorty can't separate the epistemological critique from the resulting political ideology. Against this reply of Burch, one could hold that Rorty's anti-foundationalism is an epistemological project, which can be separated from his post-foundational political position.[5]

II Immanent Social Critique

Rebecca Comay and Robert Burch wish to hold open the possibility of a non-foundationalist immanent social critique which would contrast the universalist claims of our classical liberal tradition with the social reality which it legitimates.

Comay is less clear about the form such an immanent critique should take than she is about the need for it. Though partly inspired by Adorno, she does not defend his elitism, which in her view could lead to an impossible quietism. Adorno is politically naive and abstract, but he is in Comay's eyes preferable to Rorty in being uncomfortable about modern social reality.

III Hermeneutical Dialogue

Jeff Mitscherling introduces a distinction between conversation, the language of our cultural tradition which we are born into and learn, and dialogue, the language that lives and evolves as we speak it. According to Mitscherling, Rorty's political position results from his endorsement of conversation in this sense and his neglect of the dialogue which philosophical hermeneutics promotes. Mitscherling defends Gadamer's hermeneutics against Comay's charge that it makes critical social analysis impossible.[6] Gadamer emphasizes acculturation to one's tradition, Mitscherling asserts, because a recognition of its force is essential to a thoroughly self-conscious critique.

One may ask how far this distinction between conversation and dialogue takes us. Mitscherling thinks it helps to determine the role hermeneutic philosophy plays in social criticism, to see how social criticism is possible, and to indicate how Rorty misunderstands Gadamer. Conversation is the necessary condition for dialogue, the shared thing in common which makes it possible for two people who take different approaches to talk about a problem and compare the success which their approaches might have in solving this problem.

One may also question the accuracy of Mitscherling's comparison of Gadamer and Rorty. A recurrent theme of Gadamer's work is the need for each generation to appropriate anew the high culture of the past. Rorty is much more explicitly open to political reforms which address the conditions of the mass of humankind. It seems odd to use the perspective of a traditionalist like Gadamer to support the thesis that a liberal reformer like Rorty is too conservative.

David Hitchcock

NOTES

1 As Kai Nielsen pointed out during the discussion of Rebecca Comay's paper at the conference at McMaster University on anti-foundationalism and practical reasoning.

2 Richard Bernstein makes a similar point in an article forthcoming in *Political Theory*, along with Rorty's reply, entitled 'Thugs and Theorists: A Reply to Bernstein.'

3 Both Jean Grondin and Kai Nielsen articulated this defence during the discussion of Comay's paper at the conference.

4 Roger Shiner made this argument during the discussion of this set of papers at the conference.

5 Thus William Sullivan during the discussions referred to above.

6 Jerome Bickbenbach makes a similar charge below in his 'Legal Hermeneutics and the Possibility of Legal Critique.'

Rebecca Comay

Interrupting the Conversation:
Notes on Rorty

> ... We do not know what "success" would mean except simply "continuance"...
>
> (Rorty, *Consequences of Pragmatism*)

> ... Hence the contrast between dialectics and pragmatism, like every distinction in philosophy, is reduced to a nuance, namely, to the conception of that "next step." The pragmatist, however, defines it as adjustment, and this perpetuates the domination of what is always the same. Were dialectics to sanction this, it would renounce itself in renouncing the idea of potentiality. But how is potentiality to be conceived if it is not to be abstract and arbitrary, like the utopias dialectical philosophers proscribed? Conversely, how can the next step assume direction and aim without the subject knowing more than what is already given? If one chose to reformulate Kant's question, one could ask today, *how is anything new possible at all?* ... Pragmatism is narrow and limited because it hypostasizes th[e] situation as eternal ... .
>
> (Adorno, *Prisms*)

I

... *Liberalism without tears*: 'There seems no particular reason why, after dumping Marx, we have to keep repeating all the nasty things about bourgeois liberalism he taught us to say ... ' (CP 207).[1] Rorty's mission is clear. It is to '*continue* the conversation of the West' (PMN 394) while resisting the teleological temptation; to maintain our 'liberal habits' (SO 11) in the lapse of any philosophical convictions; to nurture the 'hopes of the North Atlantic bourgeoisie' (PBL 585) – civil society, democracy, technological progress, and so on – in the absence of the foundations which have sustained them up to now. 'Postmodernist bourgeois liberalism' (PBL 585) is the attempt to hang onto the 'ideals of the Enlightenment' (PMN 333) while dispensing with Enlightenment Reason: it is the modernist cheerfulness minus the modernist faith.

And so Rorty reproduces the terms of the bourgeois liberal tradition – cut loose from its rationalist justifications (the grounding in natural law, the appeal to the light of reason, the evocation of *homo humanus*); shorn of its universalist pretensions; cut off from its utopian 'truth.' Existing bourgeois liberalism is to be promoted, without argument, as the 'best example of ... solidarity we have yet achieved' (CP 207). 'We should be more willing than we are,' avers Rorty, 'to celebrate bourgeois capitalist society as the best polity actualized so far, while regretting that it is irrelevant to most of the problems of most of the population of this planet' (CP 210 n. 16).

Who is this 'we'? It is a 'we' which has shrugged off the authority of Hegel's magisterial *für uns*; which no longer parades as the incarnation of Spirit or the 'total horizon of humanity'; which no longer appeals to the dialectic of recognition (the encounter of natural and philosophical consciousness, i.e., the 'scene of instruction' of a Phenomenology of Spirit); which no longer insists on 'hearing itself speak.' It is a 'we' which has been stripped free of all the old essentialisms (subjectivity, objectivity, eschatology, freedom). It no longer appeals, for its legitimacy, to the light of nature (or Reason, or necessity, or *telos*). It 'asserts' itself without 'grounding' itself (Blumenberg[2]): it simply announces itself and makes no further claims.

It is a 'we' which is defiantly parochial and names itself without flinching. Rorty's 'we' contracts or expands (usually contracts) to fit any available space – 'we liberal intellectuals' (HM 173); 'we liberal democrats' (PDP 31); 'we Western liberal intellectuals' (SO 23); 'we rich North American bourgeois' (PBL 588); 'us ... educated, leisured policymakers of the West' (CP 203); 'us relatively leisured intellectuals, inhabiting a stable and prosperous part of the world' (PMN 359); 'we ... the people who have read and pondered Plato, Newton, Kant, Marx, Darwin, Freud, Dewey, etc.' (CP 173); 'we ... liberal Rawlsian searchers for consensus' (SO 12); 'us American liberals' (SH 272); constricting, eventually, to 'we philosophy professors' (CP 189) or, still further, 'we Anglo-Saxon philosophers' (SR 5), 'we pragmatists' (SO 12); or, yet again, 'we Wittgensteinian nominalists' (DC 18), 'we fuzzies' (SS 4), and so on ...

' "There is only the dialogue," only *us*' (SO 15). 'We': a 'community,' a 'solidarity,' which has been cut loose from its metaphysical moorings, from the old transcendental 'backups' (HM 173) – from Kant to Hegel to Habermas in our day: God, Reason, Nature, Freedom – cut loose from the 'theories' that had until recently propped it up. 'We' does not proselytize; 'we' is as we are. To claim more than this is sanctimoniousness; to claim less, bad manners. 'It would be better,' insists Rorty (demolishing Habermas's sweeping claims to metanarrative legitimation as just more universalist conceit) 'to be frankly ethnocentric' (HM 165). All the failures of nerve he detects in Habermas ('ideal speech situation'), Peirce ('ideal end of inquiry') (SO 5), or even in Putnam ('ideal terminus') (SO 10) simply betray a lingering idealism. It is the divine 'we' of the *sensus communis* – puffing up the partnership, pretending to be all. To posit a *telos* or end to the conversation – indeed to compare the present to the possible, so as to create a new future – is to flee time and history; it is to 'scratch where it does not itch' (HM 164); it is to reinstate all the old gods.

Philosophy, stripped of legislative function, is invited simply to 'continue the conversation' (PMN 394). 'We do not know what "success" would mean,' insists Rorty, 'except simply "continuance"' (CP 172).

II

'Progress,' shorn of its providential trappings, becomes the cheerful accumulation of the 'more and more.' History, finally freed from Reason's tyranny, becomes the incremental passage through the 'new.' Philosophy turns to 'conversation,' literally, turning over and over in its groove. It becomes a question of 'doing more interesting things and being more interesting people' (SO 10); 'we read more, talk more, write more' (PMN 375); we search for 'new, better, more interesting, more fruitful ways of speaking' (PMN 360). 'Evanescent moments in a continuing conversation' (PMN 378) – like bubbles rising to the cocktail's surface – we 'keep the conversation going' (PMN 378).

The conversation, 'floating, ungrounded' (CP 174), has the restlessness of a Faustian quest. 'New forms of life constantly killing off old forms,' remarks Rorty, 'not to accomplish a higher purpose, but blindly' (CL 6). Here the perpetually 'new' slides over easily into the already-out-of-date; history becomes a flickering succession of instants, without sequence, without end: such is 'our' modesty, our frenzy. It is the logic of sheer obsolescence, the eternal repetiton of the same. 'Since he has no extra-historical Archimedean point' the postmodernist is bound, after all, 'to become outdated. Nobody is so passé as the intellectual czar of the previous generation' (CP xl).

'Conversation' is the eighteenth-century dream of gentlemanly social intercourse adapted to the rhythms of consumer society. It is Gadamer's nostalgic evocation of classical erudition, Oakeshott's urbane 'pursuit of intimations,' the neo-classical decorum celebrated by a Pater or an Eliot. It is Old World 'high culture' done over American-style, and with the ironic awareness that 'The Tradition' is in any case no longer ours to be had. What Rorty calls 'free and leisured conversation' (PMN 389) has the frenetic pace of Adorno's 'culture industry.' Here is Rorty's own mock-facetious description of the 'post-modern bourgeois' hero, the 'all-purpose intellectual,' 'ready to offer a view on pretty well anything' (CP xxxix), scrambling to pick up the pieces of a crumbling archive.

> He passes rapidly from Hemingway to Proust to Hitler to Marx to Foucault to Mary Douglas to the present situation in Southeast Asia to Gandhi to Sophocles. He is a name-dropper, who uses names such as these to refer to sets of descriptions, symbol-systems, ways of seeing. His specialty is seeing similarities and differences between great big pictures, between attempts to see how things hang together. (CP xl)

The conversation is voracious, omnivorous; it consumes what it encounters and retains the traces of each encounter. We are close here, indeed, to the museal 'historical sense' lampooned by Nietzsche in the *Untimely Meditations*: a greed so pressing it will cram anything down — *je mehr desto besser* — books, foreign languages, 'the dust of bibliographic *Quisquilien.*'[3] It is the hungry *Neugier*, the 'lust for the new' exposed by Heidegger in *Being and Time*. It is the eclectic promiscuity of Benjamin's historicist, fingering the rosary of an already dead tradition. It is the encyclopaedic enthusiasm of the Autodidact in *Nausea* (plowing assiduously, methodically, through the local library).

It is the bizarre and monstrous humanism of Panurge; it is the versatility of Plato's sophist. – I'm dropping these names, in good 'conversational' shorthand, only to gesture towards the curious cultural dislocation which is at work here. Rorty's vaguely Dadaist blueprint marks the final crisis of historical thought. Here a debilitated humanism breathes its last gasp. Cut off from its historical moorings, devoid of utopian direction, philosophy drifts distractedly through the ruins of the Western archive. It is Gadamer's culture vision without the Gadamerian faith in History; a *Bildungsroman* without closure, a conglomeration without end.

III

The conversation continues: without interruption or impetus. Sanguine, indifferent to social criticism, it knows itself to be irrelevant and becomes an idle plaything for the sophisticates.

Rorty spares no sarcasm in puncturing the Philosophers' delusions of grandeur: they mistake 'academic politics' for 'real politics' (CP 229) and take themselves altogether too seriously. He makes short work of Derrida's 'tone of urgency' (DC 19); the 'anarchistic claptrap' (HF 9ff) of a Foucault; Lyotard's 'silly avant-gardism' (HM 169); or the absurd self-importance he detects in Heidegger. To assume a tangible political function for philosophy is to commit the old metaphysical hubris: the philosopher masquerades as legislator and forgets where he belongs.

'Who but a philosophy professor, after all, would think that the drama of twentieth-century Europe had some essential relation to the *Vollendung der Metaphysik?'* (CP 47) Or again: 'Derrida talks as if this neat textbook dilemma were a real one, as if there were a terrible oppressive force called ... "the history of metaphysics" which is making life impossible not only for playful punsters like himself but for society as a whole' (DC 14).

Rorty depoliticizes philosophy to the same degree, and by the same logic, as he aestheticizes politics. Indeed he marginalizes and aggrandizes philosophy in one and the same blow: on the one hand, refusing to grant it any 'real' efficacy and force; on the other hand, representing social relations in such idealized terms that they become indistinguishable, in the end, from a strictly cultural exchange. Thus while Rorty divests philosophy of all social relevance, he simultaneously privileges it as the model of social intercourse at large. His *exclusion* of philosophy from the political sphere is paralleled precisely by his *idealization* of politics, his onesided emphasis on discursive practices (to the neglect of, e.g., work and power), his overvaluation of the cultural sphere.

The bravura with which he insists on philosophy's political marginality — 'wildly irrelevant' to the rest of society (HM 174), an 'unimportant excursus' (HM 175), a 'mere distraction from the history of concrete social engineering which ha[s] made the contemporary North Atlantic culture what it is now, with all its glories and all its dangers' (HM 173) — this cynical bravura is matched, at every step of the way, by an unquestioning attachment to the habits and values of his own professional class. The (professional) self-importance Rorty attributes — correctly, of course — to Heidegger and company is matched only by the (professional) *comfort* Rorty takes in his self-appointed calling. 'Who but a philosophy professor,' demands Rorty, 'would take all this stuff so seriously?' 'Who but a philosophy professor,' we might in turn ask of Rorty, 'would represent society on the model of a conversational encounter?'

For Rorty's *societas* in fact looks, on closer examination, like another *universitas*; or rather, a 'better' liberal arts college with a commitment to interdisciplinary studies, nourished by a 'spirit of cooperation' (PDP 43), collegial affability, a respect for the classics combined with a healthy awareness of current events, and so on. 'Solidarity,' indeed, in Rorty's recent writings, is exemplified by the team spirit of a modern research institution (SS 8), while his 'free and open encounter' (CP 173) has the cozy respectability of sherry hour. Rorty's swipes at 'boring professional philosophy,' in this context, have the distinct ring of the disaffected 'culture critic' — appalled by the pinheadedness of his colleagues, insulted by the vulgarities of the market, avidly in pursuit of intimations, dreaming of better days. Secure in his privilege, aristocratic in his protests, Rorty only flatters philosophy as he chastizes it, and sets out to elevate its 'tone.'

IV

The conversation, continuing, leaves everything in its place. Rorty leaves philosophy dangling, as usual, between pathetic acquiescence and absurd transcendence. Observe the gentle blackmail. Either we celebrate our own society as the best of all conceivable worlds or we reveal our own essentialist stripes. Either we admit that we are 'just the historical moment we are' (SO 13) or we go chasing after the old 'metaphysical comforts' (CP 166) — grounds, essences, destinies, Human Natures — 'evading [our] contingency' (CP 166), 'clinging' to eternity (CP 165), fantasizing about the 'ultimate community' (SO 5), dreaming the 'old Platonic dream' (SH 273).

To offer a critique, to contest or refuse the present, is, for Rorty, to assume a higher standpoint and hence to play at being God (cf. SO 13). Behind the vanguardist zeal lurks the Philosopher's foolish pride. Underlying the 'Socratic alienation' is the old 'Platonic hope' (SO 5). Underlying the Habermasian suspicion is the 'too pessimistic and too exclusively German' (HM 169) sourness of the disaffected intellectual — exaggerating the difficulties, forcing his own problems on everybody else, taking himself oh, so seriously, spoiling a good time. Counterfactual thinking becomes indeed only the latest form of 'epistemology'; it is the old search for privileged touchstones (cf. PMN 210), 'universal standpoints' (SO 13) or Archimedean footholds; it is the 'neurotic Cartesian quest for certainty' (CP 161), raised to an eschatological pitch.

'Hope' — cured of its histrionic fervor — becomes, in Rorty, the happy desire that we keep on going just the way we are. 'We' — shorn of our universalist conceits — turn to patching up our tattered friendships, 'deepen[ing our] sense of community' (CP 203), 'heightening' our 'identification with our community' (CP 166), trading in the old 'metaphysical comforts' (CP 166) for the more tangible ones at hand. 'Community' — freed from global presumptions — becomes simply the place we are. 'History' — freed from the constraining *archē* and *telos* — becomes the endless continuation of the same. 'Lonely provincialism' (SO 12), faced 'frankly' (HM 165), becomes the cozy familiarity of the group. And philosophy, stripped of critical arrogance, becomes the cheerful affirmation of the 'now.' It is a collusive historicism pitted against a delusive vanguardism: the critical critic versus the well-adjusted citizen.

V

What is most striking in all this is the way in which a concrete historical undertaking has been neutralized and deflected *in the name of history itself.*

Precisely where Rorty's historicism could have been put (in pragmatic terms) to 'good use' — by exploding the 'myth of the given'; by insisting that our present conceptual modes are relative to a specific social or institutional context ('made' rather than 'found,' in Rorty's terms); by refusing to legitimate or embalm any given cultural code through an appeal to eternal or transcultural standards; by mocking the conceit of philosophy (as purveyor of essences) and thus challenging not only its intellectual hegemony but its institutional self-enclosure — precisely where Rorty's hermeneutic pragmatism, if pursued rigorously, could and should have led philosophy in the direction of a general social and political critical project, Rorty shrinks back from the potentially subversive or utopian implications of his own undertaking and retreats to safer ground.

Indeed, under the very banner of historicism, history as such is obliterated. Rorty inscribes thought and language within history, only to dissolve history itself into a timeless realm of shadows: stripped of material content, blind to its own process of formation, devoid of utopian tension or promise.

Society, in Rorty, takes the place where Nature once stood. Contemporary social practice — the final context and last court of appeal — congeals into a preformed and reified essence, frozen in its contingency, immune from philosophical criticism, invulnerable to real change. The 'community,' unproblematized, becomes the ultimate given: opaque, inert, in no need of justification, and lacking the means to interrogate itself. The 'conversation' has the homeostatic regularity of a smoothly functioning machine — without beginning, without end, without contradiction, without crisis: effortlessly reproducing itself, commanding our assent.

'History' functions here, indeed, as something 'found' and not 'made.' 'We' (bourgeois-liberal-intellectual-etc.-Americans that we are) find ourselves thrown into a world already constituted — *Geworfenheit* cut off from *Entwurf*, contingency hypostatized as fact — rowing gently down the stream in Neurath's sinking boat, mending the rotting planks with the tools the system offers, deriding the revolutionary's call to jump ship as one more piece of transcendentalist conceit (cf. SO 12).

And Philosophy functions better than ever now as the Mirror of (social) Nature, holding up its tinted glass to the order of the day. The 'correspondence' is at first glance all the tighter once you free thought from critical reflection; you simply don't *need* to talk about Glassy Essences when the fit is as exact as it appears to be here. 'Conversation,' freed of 'wholesale constraints' (CP 165), has the laissez-faire relaxation of a free-market economy (SH 262). Social existence, immunized from its material conditions and invulnerable to ideological debate, hums as quietly as a well-heeled philosophy seminar.

Had Rorty actually worried more about getting the picture to 'fit,' he would have, of course, had to deal with the discrepancies and contradictions agonizing society as a whole, rendering the whole idea of 'conversation' pretty academic, in more than one sense, and bordering on the absurd. He would have had to face the fact, for example, that the Jeffersonian 'tolerance' he cherishes in his Western liberal democracies may be more 'repressive' (Marcuse[4]) than real; that exhortations to 'civility' (CP 202) (and against what he calls 'dogmatism, defensiveness, and righteous indignation' [SS 31]) may, when applied abstractly, serve above all to legitimate the exclusion of marginal or dissident voices from the conversation; that the appearance of open pluralist debate may, as often as not, more often than not, mask the monolithic interests of the dominant power group; that the virtues of civic tolerance have in any case been rendered pretty theoretical by the ideological distortion endemic to late capitalism; and, finally, that the strictly cultural satisfactions he promotes — and here Rorty's 'we' contracts easily and spontaneously from 'we Europeans' to 'we relatively leisured intellectuals' (PMN 359) to 'we philosophy professors' (CP 189) to 'we fuzzies' (SS 4), and so on — that these esoteric aesthetic pleasures, when abstracted and isolated from their material context, not only remain necessarily restricted and elitist, but may indeed preempt and deflect the drive to fulfil more profane, noncultural satisfactions.

He would have had to acknowledge, in short, that the 'democracy' is a sham one, and that this 'let's be friends' business is disingenuous at the best of times.

What is naive is not the conversational ideal per se, nor yet the 'hope' that it might be accomplished: this should go without saying. And what is naive is not necessarily the (modernist) attachment to Enlightenment values, nor yet the (postmodernist) insistence that these values be freed from their theological props: this too, by now, should be granted. What is naive – but it is more than naive, since it actively colludes in accommodating the present – is the suggestion that the conversation is already realized, or within reach, or that it could be realized easily, or realized in the absract, or realized only by the elect few. What is naive – and here Rorty in fact does his beloved liberal tradition a disservice, since he guarantees that its promise remains opaque and formal – is the willingness to embrace an abstract version of democracy and community at the expense of more substantive and concrete requirements.

The naivety lies not in the anti-foundationalist credo as such. To strip the conversational 'we' of its divine right and power is indeed the first step we (?) must all take today. And Rorty is surely right, and demystifies things considerably, to insist on the difference between a description of a social institution and a philosophical justification for its existence. The naivety occurs rather in the suggestion that essentialism can be bypassed as easily or as immediately as Rorty implies. Here it is not Rorty's hermeneutic suspicion which is suspect, but rather the fact that *he is not suspicious enough.*

In simply jettisoning the idea of universality – instead of interrogating it and wresting it free of its essentialist trappings – Rorty tacitly accepts all the terms of classical rationalism. By dismissing the very demand for universalization as so much more transcendentalist hype, Rorty not only accedes to the verdict of the natural law tradition (universal = eidos = telos etc.); indeed he relies on this verdict so as to immunize the present from all criticism and change. Any attempt to expand or radicalize the democratic claims of bourgeois liberalism is quickly deflected on metaphilosophical grounds. Immanent critique is forestalled by an easy gesture towards the bogeyman of Reason. 'Universality' – what could have been simply a demand for a deepened or expanded democracy, what could have been simply the discomfort of a 'we' which knows itself to be all too narrow and which struggles against this narrowness – is tarred, but too easily, with the essentialist brush.

But in this way Rorty only occludes what were the real contradictions in classical liberal thought (the gap between its theoretical premises and the social practices it sanctioned, between its universalist promise and its exclusionary requirements, between the formal egalitarianism it preached and the material inequalities it legitimated). By promoting a liberalism which need no longer even pretend to loftier 'principles,' Rorty ends up shielding classical liberalism from all the embarrassments which had typically plagued it. As such he deflects all criticism of an immanent or dialectical sort and thereby seals off the liberal tradition from realizing its latent hope and promise. In handing over totality to its theological guardians, Rorty simply dissolves the tensions within liberalism as such, relieving it of the pressure to 'complete' or 'sublate' itself. His version remains purely affirmative, which is to say, conservative: a liberalism without apology, without tension, and without the means to negate or transcend itself.

But as such he embalms the present as effectively as did the natural law theorists of the eighteenth century. Whereas the latter sought to hypostatize the present by grounding it in Reason or Nature, Rorty hypostatizes it by immunizing it from philosophical critique. Philosophy formerly colluded by commission, at present by omission. If at one time philosophy sought to buttress the status quo by providing grounds or reasons, it now does so at one remove: it docs its accommodation and then quickly washes its hands of the deed. Here restraint becomes the metaphilosophical rule, and abstinence becomes the apology of the day. By relieving the present of even the pressure to legitimate itself, philosophy only ends up 'grounding' the given more securely than ever before.

VI

Meanwhile philosophy, fetishized as 'general culture,' continues as intransigently, as maniacally, as ever — indeed more so. Fleeing the social reality which it at the same time blindly reproduces, philosophy becomes simultaneously both otherworldly (i.e., apolitical) and collusive. Even as it militantly renounces its critical engagement or efficacy in the present, it becomes falsely immersed, which is to say passively reproductive of that present.

Effete, cloistered, reduced to the innocuous prettiness of *l'art pour l'art*, philosophy ends up only affirming the tyranny of the consumer society which it can in fact neither negate nor properly engage. It substitutes an illusory *transcendence* for the *critical distance* which is philosophy's real task and promise; it substitutes a blind collusion for the engagement which would otherwise open up. Simultaneously aestheticized and flatly affirmative – i.e., both excessively and insufficiently 'withdrawn' – philosophy bears all the contradictions of the 'culture industry' in general. Even as it renounces its worldliness – 'wildly irrelevant,' a 'distraction' (HM 173f.), etc. – it slides inexorably into the very facticity it would ignore or evaporate. Condemned in one blow to both superfluity and positivity, it both reproduces and mystifies the society which gave birth to it.

> To say that we become different people, that we "remake" ourselves as we read more, talk more, write more, is simply a dramatic way of saying that the sentences which become true of us by virtue of such activities are... more important than the sentences which become true of us when we drink more, earn more, and so on. (PMN 359)

Bildung, turned in on itself, becomes the disembodied quest for language. This in turn, conceived on the model of an abstract consumption, becomes in the end indistinguishable from the 'drinking more, earning more' from which it naively sets itself apart. Sinking back into the banausic everydayness which it seeks to escape without engaging, it becomes a question of sheer connoisseurship and the 'more.'

Culture is both aggrandized and debilitated here, and philosophy both idealized and belittled. The mirror, flattering philosophy's self-importance even as it condemns it to narcissistic self-enclosure, cuts off the critical distance between philosophy and its 'lifeworld,' and thus simultaneously sequesters and 'profanes' it.

To give philosophy both less and more than this would require a *genuine* historicism: it would replace an acquiescent pragmatism with a form of critical *praxis*; it would replace a yea-saying conversation with a speech which has learned to say no.

VII

The conversation, continuing, steamrollers all difference and becomes a night in which all cows are black.

Nowhere is this flattening, this collapse of tension, more evident or more revealing than in Rorty's own conversational practices. This conversation is about as 'monological' as they come. What is stunning here is the systematic way in which Rorty has managed to neutralize the potentially radical force of almost every thinker he encounters. Capacious where he sees connections, smirky where he resists them, Rorty has the assurance of someone who knows the outcome in advance and can accommodate or shrug off all positions. 'Difference' slides into uniformity, or else is laughed away as the quirkiness of fools and eggheads. This is domestication with a vengeance: nowhere has 'abnormal philosophy' (CP 106) ended up looking so reassuringly and depressingly familiar. Watch Rorty converse.

Rorty 'naturalizes' Hegelian historicism to the point of reducing what was, at its finest, a program of immanent critique into an instrument of social adjustment. He melts down the 'hermeneutic circle' into the chalk circle of the present, the quiescent reminder that we must 'start' − and no doubt end up − 'where we are' (SO 12). Heidegger, cured of his 'metaphysical' delusions (in this case: his gloomy refusal to 'mediate' the Difference), becomes the happy prophet of accommodation. Gadamer's principle of 'effective historical consciousness' (*wirkungsgeschichtliches Bewusstsein*) becomes a radical historical immanentism, a sticky inertia punctuated only by the voluntaristic frenzy of the consumer ('an attitude interested not so much in what is out there in the world, or what happened in history, as in what we can get out of nature and history for our own uses' [PMN 359]). Rorty reads Habermas as a somewhat misguided liberal reformer, the blander the better, dismissing his residual utopian tension as just so much more metaphysical conceit. He reduces deconstruction to the 'slappy *je-m'-en-foutisme*' (SR 5) of an indifferent aestheticism, and Derrida himself to a cute little jokester who should only learn how to relax.

The 'polypragmatic dilettante' (PMN 317) charms all the creatures from out of their caves and toadstools; the Pied Piper soon enough has everyone singing the same old tune. The tune, of course, is the American anthem; James and Dewey wait patiently at the end of every road. To those who step out of beat, or who refuse to learn the words, or whose accent is just too strong, or too weird for good company, Rorty turns on the macho know-nothing act and tunes out the noise – '... the word "Being" is just more trouble than it is worth. I would be happy if Heidegger had never employed it ...' (SH 267).

(Where jovial appeals to good sportsmanship don't work, there is always the threat of expulsion. 'We,' unswerving in its solidarity, becomes as stern as an Un-American Activities Committee. You don't cooperate, we see no point in continuing this conversation. This is, of course, the final privilege of the post-modern 'we': no longer pretending to be more than we are, we can now be just what we are – 'we' *simpliciter*, a tensionless monad, without discomfort or change. 'To be ethnocentric,' Rorty reminds us, 'is to divide the human race into the people to whom one must justify one's beliefs and the others. The first group – one's *ethnos* – comprises those who share enough of one's beliefs to make fruitful conversation possible' [SO 13]. As for 'the others' – the 'particularly stupid people' [PMN 349], the kooks around the corner whose 'explanation of what [they're] up to is so nutty that we brush it aside' [CP 200], the 'fanatics' [PDP 26], 'the people who have always hoped to become a New Being' [SO 12], and so on – baldly, for it comes down to this: 'there are a lot of views,' concludes Rorty, 'that we can simply not take seriously ...' [SO 12].)

By Rorty's own professed hermeneutic standards (PMN 381), the conversation is surely a failure: it is the old search for commensuration, after all, that drives the encounter on. (There is 'no difference,' as Rorty sees it, between Dewey and Tillich [SH 265]; between Dewey and Foucault [CP 11]; between Dewey and Heidegger [CP 37ff]; or for that matter between Heidegger and Carnap [SH 267]: once you get rid of all the 'transcendental German' [SH 267], you can see that it all sounds just the same.) The 'polypragmatic dilettante' becomes in the end indistinguishable from the 'cultural overseer' [PMN 317]. It is the ironic Olympian cheerfulness of the eternal go-between, obliterating all the differences, bringing it back home. What Rorty calls 'conversation with foreigners' (SO 8) looks indeed like the traditional 'conquest' (ibid.); and his tactics of 'persuasion' come close to sheer force (cf. SH 263).

A 'seamless, undifferentiated "general text,"' remarks Rorty, enthusiastically (DC 3) (speaking, incredibly enough, of the notion of *différance*). To save difference, finally, from the web of *that* 'general text' – this would take some interruption and would risk a degree of force.

*

To interrupt the conversation: this is not to '*escape* from the conversation to something atemporal' (CP 174); nor is it to close off the conversation by offering the last word. To interrupt: I mean something other than either continuation or closure. But it is difficult to interrupt this particular conversation – for I am not sure it ever began.

NOTES

1 The following abbreviations to works of Richard Rorty apply throughout this essay:

CL: 'The Contingency of Selfhood,' *London Review of Books* **8**.7 (April 17, 1986) 3-6

CP: *Consequences of Pragmatism: Essays 1972-1980* (Minneapolis: University of Minnesota Press 1982)

DC: 'Deconstruction and Circumvention,' *Critical Inquiry* **10** (1984) 1-23

HF: Commentary on Hacking's 'Michel Foucault's Immature Science,' American Philosophical Association Western Division meeting, April 1979, manuscript

HM: 'Habermas and Lyotard on Postmodernity,' in R. Bernstein, ed., *Habermas and Modernity* (Cambridge, MA: MIT Press 1985)

PBL: 'Postmodernist Bourgeois Liberalism,' *Journal of Philosophy* **80** (1983) 583-9

PDP: 'The Priority of Democracy to Philosophy,' manuscript (1986); appearing in M. Peterson and R. Vaughan, eds., *The Virginia Statute of Religious Freedom* (Cambridge: Cambridge University Press 1987)

PMN: *Philosophy and the Mirror of Nature* (Princeton, NJ: Princeton University Press 1979)

SH: 'Pragmatism without Method,' in Paul Kurtz, ed., *Sidney Hook: Philosopher of Democracy and Humanism* (Buffalo: Prometheus Books 1983)

SO: 'Solidarity or Objectivity,' in J. Rajchman and C. West, eds., *Post-Analytic Philosophy* (New York: Columbia University Press 1985)

SR: 'Signposts Along the Way that Reason Went,' *London Review of Books* **6**.3 (February 16, 1984) 5-6

SS: 'Science as Solidarity,' unpublished ms (1986).

2 Hans Blumenberg, *The Legitimacy of the Modern Age*, tr. R. Wallace (Cambridge, MA: MIT Press 1983)

3 Friedrich Nietzsche, *Werke*, Karl Schlechta, ed. (München: Hanser 1965)

4 Herbert Marcuse, 'Repressive Tolerance,' in R. P. Wolff, B. Moore, Jr., and H. Marcuse, eds., *A Critique of Pure Tolerance* (Boston: Beacon Press 1965)

Robert Burch

Conloquium Interruptum:
Stopping to Think

The bane of every hostess's life is the guest ... who refuses to be brought into the conversation, but who, on the other hand, remains in the company. When ... a hostess finds that she has erred in asking someone highly and unamusingly contentious to a party, she ... must spend the evening trying to keep the conversation away from explosive topics — explosive to the particular guest.

Amy Vanderbilt, *The New Complete Book of Etiquette*

Keinem von diesen Philosophen ist es eingefallen, nach dem Zusammenhange der ... Philosophie mit der ... Wirklichkeit, nach dem Zusammenhange ihrer Kritik mit ihrer eignen materiellen Umgebung zu fragen.

Karl Marx, *Die Deutsche Ideologie*

The conversation, continuing, leaves everything in its place.

Rebecca Comay, 'Interrupting the Conversation'

I

Conloquium interruptum! Dare it be mentioned in polite company, let alone be done publicly? Even to the 'liberally' minded, the rules of propriety and good taste would not seem that loose. The well-mannered keep the conversation going; the well-behaved never interrupt. One may kibitz but only to embellish and enliven. One may be contentious but only to entertain. To be serious about interrupting the conversation puts one beyond the bounds of civility. The obstructive are asked to leave; the ill-bred are not invited in the first place.

99

The would-be interrupter, unrefined and indecorous, also commits a logical faux pas. Short of overt violence, which breaks in abruptly to end all conversation and to coerce beyond persuasion (and thus differs essentially from 'symbolic violence' inscribed in social practices and 'exerted *through* the communication in which it is disguised'),[1] one interrupts by means of discursive strategies that commit one *eo ipso* to canons of civility. To *speak* against the conversation is still to converse, which presupposes a shared topic and at least some rules of discourse and association in common. An interruption which is not closure *sub specie aeternitatis*, nor silencing by non-communicative means, is inevitably a continuation. Yet to dwell on this sort of infelicity is itself in 'poor taste' (cf. PMN 372),[2] and is apt only to serve the interrupter's purpose.

Aside from conversational whimsy and a crude pun, the title '*Conloquium Interruptum*' has also a thematic rationale. It is meant first to signal my general sympathy with the stance that Comay has taken in our discussions and the manner in which she has secured it. That 'the conversation' has been effectively interrupted, I take as a given. In a modest way, I wish only to reinforce that stance in order to inquire futher about the 'topic' of conversation itself.

In this regard, however, the crudeness of the pun is quite deliberate. When a conversation is 'floating, ungrounded' and 'blind' (IC 85-6), when it is no longer about anything as much as itself, no longer brought forth by the nature of things or the 'matter' to be thought, then its measure is conventional, an issue chiefly of etiquette and vogue. In the event, questions of philosophic 'truth' devolve more or less into those of taste and style amid intellectual pacesetters and fashion plates; and the 'criteria' of truth devolve into the market trends which govern the production and exchange of intellectual values. To start with a *crude* pun pits one against the prevailing standards of conversational wit. To begin with a crude pun *in Latin* is to turn these standards against themselves.

In its crudeness, however, the pun is also meant to suggest two substantive points. The first concerns the way in which the 'interrupted conversation' compares with its carnal equivalent. Unlike abstinence, it does not preclude the act itself; and unlike autoerotism, it does not supplant the act with a monological parallel. Rather, for lack of better means, it refuses to lend itself to what the consummated act typically engenders. If one were to leave aside all vestige of 'puritanical seriousness,' this analogy might be pressed even further. It might be maintained (and some post-modern discourse does gesture in this direction) that, like sex, conversation is an intrinsic good that requires no external justifications; that it answers directly to a basic personal human need; that it can afford a purely 'aesthetic' satisfaction; and that it has a legitimate 'homophile' fulfilment in the sheer pleasure of talking to one's own kind. One need not be a prude, however, to see mischief in this turn. The conversation in question is public, communicative and inherently political; it is in practice inseparable from other concrete social relations; its value is interwoven with what it produces or betokens beyond the act itself; and even the well-informed can be in doubt as to how it is 'consummated' and what it 'typically engenders.' We interrupt the conversation in order to transform it, a transformation that would go beyond what is said in the talk itself.

The title '*Conloquium Interruptum*' is also intended to suggest something about the status of potential interlocutors who do not identify with Rorty's 'we' in any of its various instantiations (cf. IC 91). They do not have this ready identification, since they understand the sense, motivating rationale and disclosive import of genuine conversation differently than does Rorty, and because they speak, if at all, from a quite different place. In short, 'the conversation' is not *their* conversation. Nonetheless, under prevailing social conditions, they are neither free simply to take it or leave it, nor able on an equal footing to change its ground rules.

Yet, in our own discussions so far, there has been scarcely any talk of a plurality of voices and conversations, but only of '*the* conversation' and its sanctioned participants (as opposed to those 'we can simply not take seriously' [SO 12]). Rorty's discourse is 'frankly ethnocentric' (HM 165), yet with universal pretensions. It is the 'the conversation of the West' (PMN 394), which stands for 'the conversation of mankind [*sic*]' (PMN 398). It is here that the main intent of my title comes to the fore. The improper and unauthorized discourses of those who, for reasons of race, occupation, gender, economic circumstances, cultic practices, and so on, live on the fringes or outside the range of language games which serve to define Rorty's 'we,' can have a genuine and efficacious place in the 'conversation of mankind' only when (as a minimal condition) what is said in their discourses becomes consonant with the canonical discourse of Rorty; that is to say, they are significant participants only insofar as their discourses conform to the modish standards of polite, liberal academic talk, taken to be the discourse of humanity (or at least of that segment of humanity which is thought cultured enough really to count). The conversation, then, is not so much a 'fusion of horizons' as an expropriation or ghettoization of dissenting voices, based on a decision *in advance* about what counts as serious speech, about whose voice should be heard, and what the point of the conversation is. Thus, to have an effective voice, one must learn the canonical discourse better than the native speakers, without trace of accent or dialect, and hope that this will serve. '*Qu'est-ce c'est "la conversation"?*' a colleague from Zaire once quipped (in an imposed imperial tongue). '*C'est un mot americain que va dire "colonisation."*' To put it much less politely: Either you talk like one of 'us,' or you get screwed! Hence the allusion and the recommendation in my title.

II

By the 'metaphysical' standards which originally governed 'the conversation,' such talk of 'colonization' would have been anomalous. The real measure of 'clever speech' and 'fine words' was not (as it typically seemed) the local conventions of a particular group with position and power, but the 'whole truth,' which was beyond all *ethnoi* and special interests, and which ideally informed *all* discourse and action. The imperialism of truth was, so to speak, nonpartisan and all for the best. Moreover, this 'utopian/cosmopolitan' vision gave to the 'conversation' its unity and meaning as a homogeneous domain of discourse, whose place was 'everywhere and nowhere,' founded on a search for universal and hence transcendent truth.

'Non-foundationalism' (this itself a foundationalist label) flouts this model shamelessly. '"Supposing truth to be a woman,"' writes Derrida quoting Nietzsche. '"What then"? .... Woman (truth) will not be pinned down (*ne se laisse pas prendre*).'[3] To be sure, there has been no dearth of attempts; for the 'will to truth' is inherently 'a pinning down [*Festmachen*], a *making* true and durable' (KSA XII, 384).[4] Nor has there been a dearth of passing results; for very little seems required to found an edifice of truth—'any old popular superstition from time immemorial ... a play on words perhaps, a seduction from the side of grammar, or an audacious generalization of very narrow, very personal, very human, all too human, facts' (KSA V, 11-12). Yet, far from clearing the way for a more secure edifice, this realization casts the question of truth itself onto an entirely different plane. 'What then is truth?' Nietzsche asks: 'A moveable army of metaphors, metonymies, and anthropomorphisms, in short, a sum of human relations which have been poetically and rhetorically intensified, transferred, and embellished, and which after long usage, seem to a people to be fixed, canonical and binding' (KSA I, 880-1). It is the seducer, then, who is ultimately the one seduced, and by his own creations. His hopes of conquest are 'an essentializing fetish,'[5] his own 'projection' of an unconditioned 'metaphysical world' to which his knowledge is then supposed to correspond (cf. KSA XII, 385). Against all attempts to win 'truth in itself'—the traditional *adæquatio intellectus ad rem* — Nietzsche's tactic is to recall the 'origins' of truth, i.e., how the strategic arrays of 'worn out' and 'forgotten' metaphors have arisen and had 'currency' in human affairs, and to revalue the values which these metaphors have served to found. 'The task is wakefulness itself' (KSA V, 12). Yet this does not give rise to a 'truer picture' of things at the level of secure knowledge, but to 'a higher history than all history hitherto' (KSA III, 481) at the level of our being—a transvaluation of values that is our fundamental self-transformation.

Setting aside (for the moment) its formal dialectical difficulties, this proposed *Überwindung* of metaphysics still would not suffice to legitimate talk of a 'colonization' of discourses. Colonization presumes privilege, and privilege purely at the level of relations among discourses presumes an appeal, however disingenuous, to incontrovertible truth. To Nietzsche, however, *all* such appeals are a 'seduction' and an 'illusion.' 'The concept of "truth" is absurd nonsense. The entire domain of "true-false" applies only to relations, not to an "in itself"' (KSA XIII, 303). Thus, 'there is no "truth"' (KSA XII, 114), if one means by this a 'thing in itself' which exists *for* knowledge; yet this is not because such 'truth' is inaccessible, but because the very notion is unintelligible.[6] Still, this theoretical point is secondary to the existential demand for transvaluation. '"Truth"? Who has put this word in my mouth?

But I repudiate it; but I disdain this proud word: *no, we do not need even this*; we shall conquer and come to power even without truth' (KSA XII, 510; my emphasis).

Against all pretense to closure, this 'repudiation' of metaphysical truth would seem to favour a plurality of voices and conversations, insofar as it denies all imperial standards. Yet foundationalists would be quick to point out a twofold difficulty: Insofar as the perspectival, metaphorical character of truth is affirmed *absolutely*, the thesis is self-contradictory; and on its own terms, there seem to be no grounds for assuming that Nietzsche's thought is anything but one more passing metaphor, an ideology that merely reflects its author's self-conscious alienation from the European-Christian world. Since these issues concern the very nature and possibility of 'foundations,' nothing less than a radical confrontation of ontology with ontology would be adequate to decide them. Short of that, it may suffice here to rehearse some key points of the debate:[7]

(1) As long as 'metaphysico-logical' thinking as a form of *theoria* (i.e., a contemplation of the principles of an absolute reality in itself which, by definition, cannot be mediated or engaged in action) is held to be the model of rationality itself, the non-foundationalist critique will inevitably be judged self-defeating. (This has been so in our tradition from Plato's attack on Protagorean relativism to Husserl's critique of pyschologism.) On these terms, the negative criterion of truth is simply formal, having to do with the logical form of propositions and their relations, while our positive understanding is a matter of the correspondence of our claims as detached observers to immutable transcendent or transcendental realities.

(2) In contrast, the non-foundationalist must deny that the negative, merely formal condition is self-evidently decisive at the level of fundamental issues (assuming such 'fundamental' talk is not itself ruled out). 'It is *possible* that we have reached here the level at which logical difficulties do not bid us be silent without more ado — because it is the same level as that out of which the metaphysical root of logic is first nourished.'[8] Similarly, the non-foundationalist must challenge the primacy of 'correspondence' and its ancillary functions by inquiring about its pre-conditions. Before all 'true' and 'false' assertion, before all representation and *adæquatio*, and before all 'objective' certainty, it must ask how the 'matter' of knowledge is first given to us in truth

as something *to be* truly known? In this regard, foundationalism has two possible appeals: either to the objective self-evidence of propositions and insights as sufficient in itself to decide the true content of knowledge; or to an a priori transcendental structure that is known in *self*-consciousness. To the non-foundationalist, the first appeal would seem merely to reflect rather than confront the problem. As for the second, what is known in self-consciousness is either given reflectively as an 'object' for consciousness, which only puts the problem at one remove, or it is known as consciousness's own *product*, which qua product calls for a demonstration of its ultimate universality. Non-foundationalism would have to deny the success of any such 'demonstration.'

(3) For this critique to be both intelligible and defensible, non-foundationalists must advance their own model of cognition and their own paradigm of rationality. By affirming the primacy of practical reason, it is Kant who first decisively opens the way for such a possibility (although by no means himself a non-foundationalist). Not all cognition, nor even the most important, consists in certain judgments asserted and verified by a passive spectator. Some knowledge is obtained by a participant forced to act in the world. What is more, the 'practical' knowledge is the *ratio cognoscendi* of a philosophic truth, a truth which, as the *ratio essendi* of practical knowledge, cannot exceed but only confirm what is revealed in life.[9] For Kant, however, both the practical and the theoretical are manifestations of universal reason, and their respective truths are thus also universal.

In this regard, the non-foundationalists must hold (i) that what is disclosed practically, existentially, pragmatically is epistemologically and ontologically prior to what can be asserted philosophically; (ii) that, being beyond object-knowledge, this disclosure is also beyond 'objective' certainty; (iii) that our 'claims' to philosophical knowledge are as parochial or as universal as the contexts (practical, existential, pragmatic) out of which they arise and to which they relate; (iv) that the claims *about* truth as such and the relativity of all discourses are at root not an absolute theoretical 'position' affirmed 'objectively,' but a truth revealed in life, having first and foremost practical, existential, pragmatic significance; and (v) that outside of specialized disciplines having their pre-determined objective domains, the question of truth 'in itself' is not an ultimate concern of radical thinking.

(4) To what might be termed its 'meta'-problem, non-foundationalism has a decisive, if not convincing, answer. 'It is no refutation of the acceptance of ... fundamental conditionedness,' writes Gadamer, 'that this acceptance itself seeks to be true absolutely and unconditionally. The consciousness of conditionedness in no way dissolves [*aufhebt*] conditionedness.'[10] To be sure, the thesis of 'fundamental conditionedness' is a universal truth about the essence of truth itself in relation to human being, and not just a passing belief, destined to be superceded. Yet it is not a truth about any determinate reality at hand, but about the 'limit situation' in which we have our being, a 'limit' which is ontologically and epistemologically prior to any and all *objects*-for-cognition and objectifying judgments.[11] Furthermore, knowledge of this limit is not first furnished theoretically, nor legitimated by abstract arguments. It is disclosed rather in and through our existential attempts at radical self-transcendence, and legitimated through an appropriative interpretation whose *terminus a quo et ad quem* is 'existence' itself.[12] 'Thus the reflexive argument is out of place here. For it is not a matter of relations among judgments that must be kept free of contradiction, but of living relationships.'[13] The charge of 'logical circularity and contradictoriness is meaningless.'[14]

(5) As for the content of a particular philosophical 'narrative,' its origin and legitimation must come *ab intra* in terms of our full response to what our situation is perceived to demand. Yet the narrative directly serves practice rather than discourse about objective 'truth.' What is at stake is not an epistemically-secured correspondence between our beliefs and a presumed reality 'in itself,' but who we decide and prove ourselves to be *in medias res*, in terms of what we discern, without objective certainty or transcendent guarantees, to be appropriate to our human being.

Here, again, the case of Nietzsche is telling. In the face of the *radical* decadence of European-Christian culture, he declares the death of *all* gods: the crisis is so profound as to demand a reversal that has *final* and hence *universal* significance. In the place of all previous metaphysics, Nietzsche announces the *Übermensch* who is post-historical because capable of submitting to eternal return. The suite of past metaphysical narratives is not thereby repudiated as theoretically 'false' in favour of a 'truer' story; it is unmasked as existentially, ontologically inappropriate to the real needs of the situation. The 'thesis' of eternal return — 'the heaviest of burdens' — is above all an existential imperative, which if taken up, alters not just what we do and happen to believe, but also who we *are* as self-choosing beings and the world as our *existential* context. Yet there is no transcendent necessity to this self transformation: The spectre of nihilism and the *letzte Mensch* may indeed win the day.

Insofar as it smashes the idols of metaphysics, this non-foundationalist thinking precludes any overt 'colonization' of discourses in the form of blind submission to an unconditional truth in itself. Nonetheless, it does not offer an easy freedom from deceptions and wrong choices.

> Nietzsche does not take the death of God — the end of all horizons — as a moment to be taken lightly, as something after which we can get on with the business of making life cozy. He is not the American liberal described by Abbie Hoffman as saying: "God is dead, and we did it for the kids." For Nietzsche, the end of horizons is not cozy, for we are still left with how to live when we have admitted chaos.[15]

The result, then, is not an immunity from the seductions of a particular discourse, but the recognition that seductions are everywhere, and that we must always make our way in circumstances that are impropitious, for neither the way itself nor its signposts are given in advance or with certainty. 'We come to terms with the question of existence,' Heidegger writes, 'always only through existence itself.'[16]

III

We need not recall here the whole recent history of the affair with 'truth' to discover Rorty's place in it. He is among the once-ardent suitors who, having found himself spurned and tired of the scene, now 'would like to change the subject,' and turn his advances to more accessible goals than 'Truth' or 'Goodness' (CP xiv). At one level, this turn is simply a change of perspective; for the issue — the effort 'to be good at being human' (CP xxxix), the learning of the good life — lies within what, traditionally, was regarded as the true province of philosophy. In his effort, however, Rorty substitutes as a 'question of *practice* the on-going 'conversation' for the closure of 'reason' (CP 172). Moreover, the conversation 'has no metaphysical nor epistemological guarantee of success.' Indeed, 'we do not know what "success" would mean except simply "continuance."' The good life, then, is the continuing life of conversation, 'which is its *own* end.'

There is in this post-modern proposal a distant, though dissonant, echo of an earlier tradition which asserts that the good life is the *vita contemplativa* as an end in itself. Through contemplation, one's soul is brought into harmony with (is 'in-formed' by) the eternal order of things, and in the event, fulfils its distinctive rational *virtus*, the process of this fulfilment being the realization of true 'happiness.' This entails further a basic dualism: the active, laborious, public life, the realm of moral virtues, devoted to proximate necessity, and serving contemplation through the cultivation of discipline and leisure; and the passive, reposeful, solitary life, the realm of contemplative virtue, devoted to the consideration of truth, and enabling the wise direction of action. Although each 'way' has its appropriate role and value, the contemplative life affords human beings, severally, their highest dignity, freedom and perfection. And if there is 'conversation' essential to it, it is above all 'the soundless dialogue of the soul with itself.'

Now, to associate Rorty with this contemplative tradition will no doubt seem odd, since his pragmatism purports to overcome it decisively. The appeal to 'essential' virtues, the entrenchment of metaphysical dualisms, the contemplation of 'eternal truths' are all more or less explicitly 'deconstructed.' Beyond metaphysics, this deconstruction is also beyond the terms which originally characterized the two *vitae*. Conversation is neither simply 'action' nor 'contemplation,' neither a reversal nor a dialectical synthesis. In its pragmatic mode, conversation has its place in the public sphere as a communal activity, exigent and dialogical, guided by moral virtues and practical concerns. Yet, as an intellectual pre-occupation (cf. IC 86, 88), the form of its rationale and on-going fulfilment is that of the *vita contemplativa*, leisured, monological and theoretical, though now void of speculative content or metaphysical grounds. On the one hand, then, the legitimation in principle of this account of conversation is deemed a '*practical* question,' an issue, as it were, of exigent, pragmatic *bricolage*. On the other hand, the issues which have so far engaged this practice are insular and academic. The primacy of the pragmatic is here affirmed in such a way as to dissolve the pragmatic as such into conversational thought and yet to conceal the real relation of this thought to the pragmatic world.[17] The conversation is exemplified as a Proteus—liberal, parochial, pragmatic, hermeneutic, edifying, dilettantish, a practical concern, its own goal—changing form as is conversationally expedient, while the demand for a systematic positive account of its meaning and place is blocked by the critique of epistemic closure and transcendent truth. The whither and wherefore of the conversation thus lapse into sententious licence and utopian play.

Conversation without 'a higher purpose' (CL 6), 'floating, ungrounded' (CP 174), and thus wholly abstracted from concrete relations and even from the need for a response, is idle chatter. It is conversation purely and simply for its own sake, indiscriminately about anything and everything, impelled by the quantitative standard of 'more and more' (IC 85). It fulfils no 'essential virtue' nor presages any practical betterment, and its 'happiness' lies in the pleasure of hearing oneself talk. Without higher purpose, the critical task of conversation devolves into nihilistic decadence, the denial of all such purposes. 'They are clever and know all that has happened,' writes Nietzsche. 'So there is no end to their derision' (KSA IV, 20). At this level, one continues the conversation for fun or profit, to seduce or beguile, to sustain old habits, or finally, just because 'you've got to do something.' But, then, as this allusion suggests, one becomes just another 'rebel without a cause.'

Yet Rorty does have a 'cause.' It is to deconstruct 'the misguided pretensions of philosophical discourse,'[18] to smash the 'mirror of nature,' to undermine the false security of foundationalism. It is also 'to nurture the "hopes of the North Atlantic bourgeoisie"—civil society, democracy, technological progress—' (IC 83), to champion the American status quo. Other questions aside, it is especially puzzling here how these two agenda fit together and at what levels—whether indeed there is any intrinsic connection between the epistemological meta-critique of foundationalist discourse and the first-order political commitments and their legitimation, or merely an accidental juxtaposition. Now, on the face of it, Rorty's meta-critique is explicitly carried out in isolation as an 'intramural' concern, an abstract debate among professional philosophers and academics. Moreover, although it is punctuated thoughout by episodic hints as to the political agendum, these are not presented as integral to the argument, nor could they follow from it on theoretical 'grounds.' As an argument against all grounds, the critique can yield no pragmatic virtues except sheer, abstract openness, with the question of content being a strictly 'practical' concern. This is by no means inconsistent, however, with the further claim that it is only because Rorty has certain first-order political commitments and orientations that he comes to pose his thematic problem in the way that he does and as one that is worthy of a pragmatist's attention. Once underway, the meta-critique does take its own 'intramural' course. Yet the original decision to question along this line, its exigency, plausibility and value, along with the full range of its hermeneutic and pragmatic presuppositions, lie outside the purview of the meta-critique itself. It is a non-foundationalist tenet that our theoretical preoccupations have a natural and social matrix from which they arise and to which they relate back, deriving their sense not abstractly in themselves but from the world of everyday experience. As a pragmatist, Rorty would have to accept the coda, or otherwise appeal, surreptitiously and against his avowed aims, to a theoretical 'picture' of reality in itself to legitimate his choice of conversation and topic. In this regard, Richard Bernstein offers a telling observation: 'I think that Habermas is closer in spirit to Dewey than Rorty is. Habermas pursues what Dewey took to be the aim of the reconstruction of philosophy which enables us to cope with the concrete "problems of men" in their social-political context.'[19] Theoretically, Rorty proceeds in the direction that he does, because he has already oriented himself to these 'problems' and 'contexts' without further ado. His 'episodic hints' are thus not incidental, but a 'trace' and 'supplement.' They mark out the real topic of conversation, yet one which Rorty never openly engages. In arcadian Virginia and like climes, it seems, the 'good life' is a fait accompli.

IV

In the foundationalist/non-foundationalist debate, the central theoretical issue is this: Can there be analysis and critique of the philosophical tradition in the name of something other than the metaphysico-logical value of truth (universality, unconditionedness, omnitemporality)?[20] As ostensibly a non-foundationalist, Rorty answers in the affirmative. His avowed purpose is not to muster a new polemic in the philosophers' argument across the ages, but to call into question the unchanging ground that would support such an argument in the first place and the 'mirror' of reality that would be its result. Post-foundational hermeneutics, he writes, 'is not the name for a discipline, nor for a method of achieving the sort of results which epistemology failed to achieve, nor for a program of research' (PMN 315). It offers instead a 'therapy' to free us from illusions and self-deceptions of the foundationalist search for 'constraint.' It is (to use one of Paul de Man's best puns) a continually running *archē debunker*,'[21] without closure or finality.

Yet this is not to advance *tout bonnement* the direct opposite of foundationalism, an absolute 'discourse against truth'; for that *would* be 'impossible and absurd.'[22] It is instead to deny that the dilemmas foundationalism poses—either absolutism or self-defeating relativism, either objective certainty or mere subjectivism, either fixed canons of rationality or unintelligibility—are final and ineluctable. It is not the internal cogency of foundationalist reasoning that is in question, but its ultimate significance. And no foundationalist argument from first principles could establish that. As we have seen, the 'rational' force of the non-foundationalist critique must be legitimated in relation to practice. Between foundationalism and non-foundationalism, then, there is no mutually convincing theoretical 'refutation,' for each rejects what the other takes to be really at stake, and, on these respective terms, what counts as genuine evidence. The choice between them comes down to a 'practical interest.' 'What sort of philosophy one chooses,' Fichte once remarked in a different context, 'depends therefore on what sort of person one is.'[23]

Our question, then, is what practical interest Rorty's shift from 'epistemology to hermeneutics' serves? The answer, however, is not as straightforward as it might seem. His ostensible purpose is to acknowledge the plurality of voices and to continue the 'civil' conversation in both senses of the term 'civil.' 'Hermeneutics is the expression of the hope that the cultural space left by the demise of epistemology will not be filled—that our culture should become one in which the demand for constraint and confrontation is no longer felt' (PMN 315). One fulfils this purpose and sustains this hope by selectively 'deconstructing' the pretensions of philosophical discourse. But immediately this should strike us as odd. If one believes à la Heidegger that our history is at root the history of Being as 'metaphysics,' then deconstructing philosophical discourse might make some sense. In Rorty's view, however, only German philosophy professors with their 'pathetic' and 'fatal attachment to the tradition' (CP 52) believe that history is philosophical. But, if you do not believe that, why care about the misguided pretensions of philosophical discourse, why be concerned to deconstruct foundationalism? It cannot be because the 'mirrors' which philosophy fashions reflect 'false' images that in turn have negative social and political consequences. In Rorty's eyes, philosophy would seem too impotent to be granted such direct power. Rather it must be that philosophy is a dangerous diversion, that its 'quest for the holy' turns us away from what is really important, i.e., 'the relations between beings and beings' (CP 52). Yet, unless one is to beg the question, it is precisely the concrete meaning of these relations that is at issue.

In this regard, Rorty's 'hermeneutics' is hardly impeccable. Its purpose and hope make the most sense if one mistakes the 'constraints and confrontations' of the seminar room and the senior commons for the actual constraints and confrontations of society, if one assumes that this 'cultural space' is the limit of effective culture and of what matters. It also makes sense, to paint a more damning picture, if the intent is to deflect critical attention away from these actual constraints and confrontations. While chasing the windmills of philosophy, Rorty acts as if such constraints and confrontations did not exist in 'our society,' and could well be ignored in those of 'the others.' But surely, if interlocutors 'keep on repeating all the nasty things about bourgeois liberalism which [Marx] taught us to say' (CP 207), this is more than ill-mannered foundationalist obtuseness and a purely scholastic question. It might well be that *in practice* bourgeois liberalism still needs and deserves such things being said. Thus far, however, Rorty's ideological commitments seem to have excluded this possibility.

This exclusion is further reinforced by an odd dialectical reversal. By separating the Enlightenment ideals and liberal habits from their foundations in Enlightenment rationality, and by directing his hermeneutic attention only upon philosophical foundations, Rorty blocks a critique of the effective reality of these ideals and habits, i.e., how they have worked historically as a liberating or oppressive force in actual social conditions. In this way, Rorty's own bourgeois self-image, formed in abstraction out of these ideals and habits, is installed by sleight of hand as a foundational truth. Furthermore, it is a truth open neither to foundationalist criticism, since foundationalism has been debunked, nor to deconstruction, since that is directed to foundational claims, which Rorty demurs. It was the self-professed virtue of Enlightenment rationality to diffuse the power over us of all images that were not of reason's own making, installing one 'rational' self-image as an absolute yet freely acknowledged 'truth.' To dispense with this 'rationality,' however, does not do away with the images, only with *one* means of their production and legitimation. Yet, in bashing all mirrors, Rorty leaves one particular image, i.e., the prevailing bourgeois orthodoxy, as authoritative. Since the well-adjusted should be content with this reflection, there is now no 'slow and painful choice between alternative self-images' (CP xliv). The 'best working attitude' has already been decided, though neither on the basis of 'foundational' proof, nor from a critical assessment of how that 'attitude' does indeed 'work' in practice. Immanent ideology critique is replaced by pragmatic tinkering geared to keeping up appearances, while radical questioning dissolves into home maintenance and the preservation of domestic tranquility. In short, what is 'post-modern' in this view is that it is essentially inviolable, i.e., that it fulfils the modernist quest for foundational certitude under an assumed name.

Of course, Rorty's 'mission' could be read more charitably: that the transformation of the 'cultural space' of philosophical discourse into the conversation of bourgeois intellectuals is meant to be seen as a necessary pre-condition for the transformation of society at large into the bourgeois 'republic of letters.' Yet '"who but a philosopher professor,"' Comay asks, '"would represent society on the model of a conversational encounter?" For Rorty's *societas* in fact looks, on closer examination, like another *universitas*, or rather a "better" liberal arts college' (IC 88). This equation might have seemed plausible in the eighteenth century, for it was an age that thought of itself as about to reach the summit of rational enlightenment. As the concrete, historical objectification of the *summum bonum*, the 'republic of letters' would unite the 'rational' self-determination and fulfilment of each individual, suitably transformed by culture and education, with the 'rational' *telos* of society as a whole. In 'the pure republic,' writes Schiller, it is 'not the spiritless imitation of *foreign manners* but people's *own lovely nature* that guides conduct, where mankind passes through the most complex situations with eager simplicity and tranquil innocence, and has no need ... to encroach upon another's freedom in order to assert his own.'[24] The *universitas*, as the ideal objective union of reason and conduct, putatively the purest expression of the identification of reason and reality under the philosophically assured guardianship of universal truth, would be the model of the 'communal spirit' (*gemeinschaftlichen Geistes*). The 'liberal' in this community would be one who had been properly educated to guide his or her life by the light of reason, with equal respect for others doing the same, without 'constraint and confrontation.' In the post-modern telling, however, this story takes an odd twist.

In one sense, Rorty's view clearly reflects its place of origin.

> English societies [have] so long dominated the political world, first in the power of Great Britain and later in that of the U.S.A., that they [have been] immensely confident of their own traditions, which were those essentially of contract liberalism. Societies which are so confident of their own power in the world have little need of philosophy.[25]

Bolstered with such confidence, Rorty can happily dismiss ultimate questions as a mystification and excursus, a 'distraction' from the 'concrete social engineering which [has] made the contemporary North American culture what it is now' (HM 173). In this regard, he is the direct heir of Anglo-American philosophy, delivering not so much its *coup de grâce* as its Oedipal fulfilment. As for continental philosophy—the thought of being, *Ideologiekritik*, and so on— it is 'more trouble than it's worth' (SH 267), since our house is essentially in order and things are under control.

One need not be a fanatic or a crank, however, to find oneself unblessed with this confidence. To many of us, it is not at all assured that to succeed in the bourgeois capitalist world which Rorty celebrates, in the palpably economic and socially integrated sense he intends, is an ideal. This is not to begrudge Rorty his affirmation of 'liberal' virtues. But it is to question the relentless will-to-power under whose auspices these virtues have had their American realization. There is

more to the effective reality of the American ethos than a benign in-
vocation of liberal virtues, and more to the effective disenchantment
with that ethos, both at home and abroad, than worry over the occa-
sional pragmatic mishap or miscalculation. This is not to deny, as a
prudential reality, the dire need to have 'a sense of the feasible, the
possible, the fitting here and now,'[26] and thus to find workable ad
hoc solutions to everyday problems. But it is to deny that the demands
of our situation are well met simply through this sort of management
and calculation. The question of 'meta-narratives' aside, it is just as
essential even to our 'liberal habits' that we be acutely critical of the
values and information disseminated by the body politic, and sensitive to the dilemmas for significant differentiation and meaningful freedom that the ideology of equality and total participation poses.[27] Yet,
in Rorty's moral-practical vision, the 'all purpose intellectual' (CP
xxxix), the exemplar of our liberal habits, is no more critical and sensitive than a congenial guest at a mixed cocktail party, suitable precisely because, having read this or seen that, he is able to talk with
passing authority on all the current subjects, without being rudely
contentious or boringly serious. The stern demand of rational self-
determination and mutual respect gives way here to the socially engaging and *serviceable*.

The quality of its liberals aside, the post-modern 'republic of letters' faces a problem similar to that of its Enlightenment predecessor.
Since the 'pure republic' is realised 'only in a few select circles,'[28] the
question of its concrete, historical fulfilment, indeed its universality,
comes to the fore. The problem is further complicated in Rorty's account by the paradoxical fact that he happily 'dispenses' with the univer-
salism of Enlightenment rationality and embraces a 'lonely
provincialism' (SO 12), yet from the vantage of a secure place within
an imperial power. From there, one can afford to be broadminded,
pluralistic and tolerant. Yet, his liberalism and pragmatic bravado notwithstanding, Rorty has no account at all of the 'political economy'
which governs the dissemination of discourse in the 'republic,' the rules
and relations which in practice decide who gets to speak and be heard.
And he has no acknowledgement at all of the leveling of meaningful
diversity that in practice his liberal habits can effect. If Rorty advocates that we 'wing it' on these issues, it is because he does not grant
what is really at stake.

V

'It may be supposed,' Michael Oakeshott writes, 'that the diverse idioms of utterance which make up the current human intercourse have some *meeting place* ... As I understand it the image of this meeting place is ... a conversation.'[29] Rorty, it seems, takes this as an incontrovertible truth; it is instead the description of a question. For the 'topic' of conversation is much less evident, I venture, than post-modern deconstructionist *Schwärmerei* would have us believe. To Rorty, there is the 'seamless, undifferentiated "general text"' (DC 3), a 'text' that has *Sinn* but not *Bedeutung*. It is only the 'weak textualists' who are naive enough to ask what the text is 'about'—*die Sache des Denkens*. The shattered 'mirror of nature' is replaced with the 'mirror-play of words,'[30] while our real interest lies 'in what we can get out of nature and history for our own uses' (PMN 359). The question nonetheless remains: How does the 'ontic' *topos*, about which Rorty is expressly concerned (CP 52)—the context of things and their interrelations, physical settings, forces and relations of production, channels of power—relate to the question of the 'good life' and the 'ontological' *topos*—the lived-meanings in various worlds and the overriding sense of things as such and as a whole—in terms of which we orient ourselves critically? Rorty circumvents this question by granting a form of difference, yet denying it ontological force. The ontological *topos* is given over in theory to a neutered hermeneutics, and in practice is decided *ex cathedra*, while further discussion of the issue is ruled improper.

VI

'What is the use,' wonders the loquacious Alice, 'of a book without pictures or conversation?' If Rorty is to be believed, she need not have troubled herself overly about the former, since books with 'pictures' are of a genre well lost; and of the latter—the books without conversation—they of relatively no use at all. In one respect, Alice would no doubt concur. For when she falls through the 'ground' of commensuration and steps beyond the 'mirror' of nature there is 'nothing else to do,' she muses, but 'begin talking again.' Yet, in her adventures to continue the conversation, she discovers more perceptively than Rorty the manifold ways in which conversations can fail, the precariousness of their topics and of one's place in them. Above all, she discovers that when one moves *in practice* from the innocent discourse of polite convention to the wonderland of playful relativism, there will always be some imperial voice ready to shout, 'Off with her head!'

NOTES

1 Pierre Bourdieu, *Outline of a Theory of Practice*, tr. Richard Nice (Cambridge: Cambridge University Press 1977), 237, n. 47

2 Abbreviations for works of Richard Rorty are as given in Rebecca Comay, 'Interrupting the Conversation,' above, pp. 97-8.

3 Jacques Derrida, *Spurs: Nietzsche's Styles*, tr. B. Harlow (Chicago: University of Chicago Press 1972), 54

4 Throughout the text 'KSA' refers to Friedrich Nietzsche, *Sämtliche Werke: Kritische Studienausgabe*, Vols. I-XV (Berlin: Walter de Gruyter 1967-77).

5 Derrida, 54

6 One finds a similar argument in German idealism. Cf., e.g., J.G. Fichte, *Werke*, ed. I.H. Fichte (Berlin: Walter de Gruyter 1971), I. 435-40. Yet idealism affirms absolute knowledge of a reality 'in and for itself' on the basis of intellectual intuition, and affirms that only idealism is capable of accounting for the possibility of this intuition.

7 It is not possible here even to sketch the view of the tradition upon which the following interpretation rests. It must suffice to say that it owes a great deal to Emil Fackenheim, and in particular, to his remarkable *Metaphysics and Historicity* (Milwaukee: Marquette University Press 1961).

8 Georg Simmel, *Lebensanschauung* (Munichen u. Leipzig: Duncker u. Humbold 1922), 26

9 Cf. Immanuel Kant, *Critique of Practical Reason*, tr. L.W. Beck (New York: Bobbs-Merrill 1956).

118   Robert Burch

10 H.G. Gadamer, *Wahrheit und Methode*, 4th ed. (Tübingen: J.C.B. Mohr 1975), 424 (my translation); yet cf. Wilhelm Dilthey, *Gesammelte Schriften*, Vol. 7 (Stuttgart: B.C. Teubner 1958), 290.

11 Paraphrasing K.O. Apel, Gadamer writes: 'The discourse of human beings about themselves is on no account to be understood as objectively determining assertions about a particular being [*gegenstandlich fixierende Behauptung eines Soseins*]' (425n.).

12 The form of this argument, as well as some of the terminology, is drawn from Karl Jaspers, *Philosophie* (Berlin, Göttingen, Heidelberg: Springer Verlag 1956), esp. II. 201ff. Cf. also Heidegger, *Wegmarken* (Frankfurt: Klostermann 1967), 101ff.

13 Gadamer, 424-5

14 Ibid., 425n.

15 George Grant, *Time as History* (Toronto: Canadian Broadcasting Corporation 1969), 30

16 Martin Heidegger, *Sein und Zeit*, 12th ed. (Tübingen: Niemeyer 1972), 12

17 Cf. G.W.F. Hegel, *Phänomenologie des Geistes*, ed. J. Hoffmeister (Hamburg: Meiner 1952). 'Scepticism ... lets vanish not only objective reality as such, but also its own relation to that reality. ... What vanishes is the moment of difference' (156).

18 Richard Bernstein, *Philosophical Profiles* (Philadelphia: University of Pennsylvania Press 1986), 79

19 Ibid., 91

20 I am here paraphrasing Jacques Derrida. See *Positions*, tr. Alan Bass (Chicago: University of Chicago Press 1972), 105.

21 Paul de Man, *Allegories of Reading* (New Haven: Yale University Press 1979), 9

22 Derrida, *Positions*, 105

23 Fichte, *Werke*, I. 432

24 Friedrich Schiller, *Über die ästhetische Erziehung des Menschen* (Stuttgart: Philipp Reclam 1965), 128

25 George Grant, *Technology and Justice* (Toronto: Anansi 1986), 81

26 Gadamer, xxv

27 Charles Taylor, *Hegel* (Cambridge: Cambridge University Press 1975), 414-16

28 Schiller, 128

29 Michael Oakeshott, *The Voice of Poetry and the Conversation of Mankind* (London: Bowes and Bowes 1959), 9-10; my emphasis. Oakeshott also recognizes, as Rorty does not, the tradition for which conversation is a principal political virtue, a form of public action fulfilled in memorable speeches (ibid., 15n.).

30 John Caputo, 'The Thought of Being and the Conversation of Mankind,' *The Review of Metaphysics* **36** (1982-83), 662-3

Jeff Mitscherling

Resuming the Dialogue

A basic insight of philosophical hermeneutics is that one understands
what other people are saying not from their point of view but from
one's own. Granted, sometimes the similarity between points of view
is sufficiently extensive to enable people to share what is essentially
the same understanding, the same interpretation, of the matter at hand.
This is commonly the case in the course of our day-to-day affairs. Indeed, our everyday existence would be unthinkable without such common agreement, just as this agreement would itself be unthinkable
without the commonly-shared world of intersubjectively constituted
convictions and values upon which it rests, and from which it arises
quite naturally without any great deal of conscious effort on our part.
But such subsequent agreement upon a given matter, such 'sameness'
of understanding or interpretation, by no means follows necessarily.
Especially in the interpretation of texts — and most clearly in the cases
of literary and philosophical texts — unanimous agreement among
interpreters is rare. So it is not at all surprising that I find myself in
disagreement with the interpretation of Rorty's 'vision' of philosophy
that Comay has presented in her paper, 'Interrupting the Conversation.'

The source of our disagreement seems to me to be twofold: first,
I do not share Comay's view of the nature and purpose of philosophical inquiry in general; and second, I do not share her view of the task
of philosophical hermeneutics in particular. With regard to the former, Comay's obvious political orientation is, I think, admirable, and
perhaps it is the case that philosophical theorizing ought never to be
entirely divorced from practical application. In the concluding pages
of this paper, however, I shall question whether philosophical theory
ought primarily to be directed toward praxis. I shall be suggesting that
theory does not, strictly speaking, precede practice, but that practice
and theory develop hand in hand, with neither 'preceding' the other.
With regard to the latter source of our disagreement, I shall be arguing that the task of hermeneutics does not entail bowing down to the

121

status quo. Hermeneutics, as I shall present it, is precisely that tool which can best enable us to dismantle those hard wooden pews and pagan altars of traditional authority that Comay speaks so forcefully against. After briefly summarizing Comay's paper, I shall offer a more lengthy analysis of Rorty's *Philosophy and the Mirror of Nature*, in the course of which my view of the task of hermeneutics will become sufficiently clear to allow me to turn to my critical remarks.

I

The conversation Comay speaks of interrupting is that which Rorty describes as having begun with Plato and having continued to the present day, despite its having met with hard times of late. While she challenges Rorty on several points, the major targets of her attack are three. First, she attacks Rorty for defending the bourgeois liberal tradition. She maintains that he regards this tradition as not susceptible to philosophical critique and that he similarly views 'the present' as properly to be immunized from all critique and change, thereby supporting the bourgeois status quo. Her second attack is directed toward a (surreptitious) aggrandizement of philosophy, which, she believes, Rorty sees as 'a cheerful affirmation of the "now."' So the second target is closely related to the first, being little more than a shift in focus. While her third target is quite broad, it seems to be located somewhere in the notion of conversation itself. Rorty has called for a continuing of 'the conversation of the West,' but Comay questions both the value of this conversation and also whether it ever really began. The real issue here seems to lie in what we are to understand by 'conversation.' The notion of conversation remains vague in Rorty's book, and it might be this very lack of clarity that has led Comay to challenge his evaluation of its merits. This third target attacked by Comay strikes me as the most important of the three, so I shall proceed with an examination of the notion of conversation as employed by Rorty in *Philosophy and the Mirror of Nature*.

Rorty writes:

> Once conversation replaces confrontation, the notion of the mind as Mirror of Nature can be discarded. Then the notion of philosophy

as the discipline which looks for privileged representations among those constituting the Mirror becomes unintelligible ... If we see knowledge as a matter of conversationof social practice, rather than as an attempt to mirror nature, we will not be likely to envisage a metapractice which will be the critique of all possible forms of social practice. (PMN 170-1)

In this passage, it is clear that Rorty is rejecting the view that knowledge consists in the mirroring — i.e., the 'correct representation' — of nature. Instead, it is to be seen as 'a matter of conversation and of social practice.' It is *not* clear what it means to say that knowledge is a 'matter of conversation,' what relation conversation has with social practice, or what is meant by 'social practice.'

Further passages prompt further questions. Drawing a contrast between traditional, 'foundational' epistemology and hermeneutics, Rorty writes:

Epistemology sees the hope of agreement as a token of the existence of a common ground which, perhaps unbeknown to the speakers, unites them in a common rationality. For hermeneutics, to be rational is to be willing to refrain from epistemology ... and to be willing to pick up the jargon of the interlocutor rather than translating it into one's own. (318)

For epistemology, conversation is implicit inquiry. For hermeneutics, inquiry is routine conversation. Epistemology views the participants as united in what Oakeshott calls an *universitas* — a group united by mutual interests in achieving a common end. Hermeneutics views them as united in what he calls a *societas* — persons whose paths through life have fallen together, united by civility rather than a common goal, much less by a common ground. (318)

The notion of culture as a conversation rather than a structure erected upon foundations fits well with this hermeneutical notion of knowledge, since getting into a conversation with strangers is, like acquiring a new virtue or skill by imitating models, a matter of *phronēsis* rather than *epistēmē*. (319)

In the first of the passages just quoted, conversation appears to be viewed on the model of our day-to-day discourse with one another, the sort of conversation we might pursue in what Comay has quite

aptly referred to as 'the tranquility of sherry hour.' In the third passage, however, Rorty speaks of culture itself as 'a conversation.' He
seems here to be employing everyday conversation as a general
metaphor — indeed, as a quite sweeping metaphor. It's certainly not
clear how all of culture (whatever *that* may be) can be so neatly conceived as 'a conversation.' Who are the interlocutors? What languages
are they refusing to translate into, and what could they possibly be
talking about? Rorty's metaphorical leap may account for Comay's
accusing him of being a bit of an idealist in 'his overevaluation of the
cultural sphere.' His next mention of conversation is, however, somewhat less opaque.

Speaking of Kuhn's contribution to the 'debates about the possibility of epistemology as opposed to hermeneutics,' he writes:

> Since the Enlightenment, and in particular since Kant, the physical
> sciences had been viewed as a paradigm of knowledge, to which the
> rest of culture had to measure up. Kuhn's lessons from the history of
> science suggested that controversy within the physical sciences was
> rather more like ordinary conversation (on the blameworthiness of an
> action, the qualifications of an office-seeker, the value of a poem, the
> desirability of legislation) than the Enlightenment had suggested. (322)

The controversy in question consists in the debate among scientists
concerning which of two or more competing paradigms is to be chosen
as the received view. Kuhn's claim, as Rorty puts it, is that there exists 'no commensurability between groups of scientists who have different paradigms of a successful explanation, or who do not share the
same disciplinary matrix, or both' (323), and, moreover, that in the
absence of an algorithm that would mediate between paradigms, the
debate about the choice between them resembles a conversation much
like that which we might pursue regarding the aesthetic merit of a
work of art. Rorty has expanded on this metaphor. As we've seen,
he goes so far as to say that culture itself is a conversation. More specifically, however, he claims that philosophy ought to abandon its
view of itself as in possession — or as possibly in possession, at least
in principle — of an epistemological algorithm, and that it ought finally to confess that it too, just like the physical sciences, is incapable
of ever discovering or creating such a universal ground of agreement,

such a 'foundation.' He claims, in short, that philosophy has to abandon epistemology as its model and ideal and turn instead to hermeneutics, not as a substitute for epistemology, but rather as an optimistic attitude adopted in the hope of continuing the conversation among interlocutors who are forever talking about different things, in different languages, and with differing interests and concerns.

There is certainly something about this claim that makes it ring more than mildly utopian (despite Rorty's dislike of Habermas's 'utopian tendencies'), but we are, at this point, approaching a clearer account of the metaphor of 'conversation.' Rorty is talking about what takes place when two or more willing partners — be they individuals, groups, or whatever — come together in the shared effort to communicate in the absence of a common ground or set of shared values that would otherwise facilitate, if not already constitute, complete agreement. Such an activity is what Rorty sees 'edifying philosophers' — as opposed to 'systematic philosophers' — to be engaged in, and it is this sort of activity that he promotes as the ideal of philosophy: 'carrying on the conversation.' He writes:

> Edifying philosophy is not only abnormal but reactive, having sense only as a protest against attempts to close off conversation by proposals for universal commensuration through the hypostatization of some privileged set of descriptions. The danger which edifying discourse tries to avert is that some given vocabulary, some way in which people might come to think of themselves, will deceive them into thinking that from now on all discourse could be, or should be, normal discourse. (377)

> To see keeping a conversation going as a sufficient aim of philosophy, to see wisdom as consisting in the ability to sustain a conversation, is to see human beings as generators of new descriptions rather than beings one hopes to be able to describe accurately. To see the aim of philosophy as truth — namely, the truth about the terms which provide ultimate commensuration for all human inquiries and activities — is to see human beings as objects rather than subjects, as existing *en-soi* rather than as both *pour-soi* and *en-soi*, as both described objects and describing subjects. (378)

Philosophy ought no longer to be regarded as the search for truth, that is, as the endeavour to establish a foundation of universally agreed-on terms (values, sets of descriptions, and so on) upon which subsequent philosophical inquiry might then systematically construct an eternally enduring tower of knowledge. Rather, philosophy ought to be seen as a conversational activity through which are established transitory standards in accordance with which all our various statements and positions may or may not be deemed justifiable. In short, Rorty's claim is that knowledge is not the ground of conversation but conversation the foundation of knowledge. Just as conversation is not static but dynamic, so too is the resultant 'knowledge' not timeless and universal, but constantly evolving with the historically changing vocabulary and themes of 'the conversation.'

Rorty makes this point most clearly in the last section of his book:

> If we see knowing not as having an essence, to be described by scientists or philosophers, but rather as a right, by current standards, to believe, then we are well on the way to seeing *conversation* as the ultimate context within which knowledge is to be understood. Our focus shifts from the relation between human beings and the objects of their inquiry to the relation between alternative standards of justification, and from there to the actual changes in those standards which make up intellectual history. (390)

And in the closing sentence:

> The only point on which I would insist is that philosophers' moral concern should be with continuing the conversation of the West, rather than with insisting upon a place for the traditional problems of modern philosophy within that conversation. (394)

The passages I have quoted and my brief exegetical remarks demand no summing up. Rorty's position is clear enough, although the picture does begin to blur when we focus in on its details. By concentrating on a few of those details now, my intention is to demonstrate that the manner in which Rorty has attempted to present hermeneutics as 'conversational' might — given the vagueness of the notion of conversation discussed above — lead us not only to misconstrue the task of philosophical hermeneutics, but also to fall right back into the very conception of philosophy out of which Rorty wants to lead us.

II

I begin by calling attention to a difficulty for the claim that one can 'pick up the jargon' of another without 'translating it into one's own.' Granted, it is true that we cannot translate the technical terminology of a Husserl or a Heidegger into that of a Putnam or a Kripke. Such an attempt would be doomed from the start. Husserl's vocabulary, and perhaps still more clearly that of Heidegger, was created in the attempt to formulate adequately the new and peculiar problems that these philosophers were encountering in a new and unique way. The same holds true, although perhaps to a lesser extent, of Putnam and Kripke. The language and vocabulary with which the task of specifying and formulating a problem is undertaken is part and parcel of the task itself, and to attempt to translate that language in such a way as to be able to apply it in the formulation of problems encountered in a different manner, or to attempt to translate these problems themselves into a context foreign to them, simply makes no sense. Such an attempt could meet with no more success than the effort to produce a convincing forgery of the *Night Watch* in watercolour. Nevertheless, if the artist specializes in watercolour, he or she might well first come to appreciate the power of Rembrandt's oil, and thus first approach a deeper understanding of his work, by comparing it with the power of watercolour — that is, by trying to *translate* it, and to some extent accomplishing this translation. My point, to state it quite briefly, is that it is impossible simply to 'pick up the jargon' of another without at the same time 'translating it into one's own,' at least to some extent. This, I believe, is also Gadamer's point when he speaks of the event of understanding as a 'fusion of horizons': You cannot simply leave your own language behind and start speaking that of another (be that 'other' a person, community, or historical epoch). We always understand from our own point of view — that is, from what we bring with us in our encounter with another — and to deny this, as I think Rorty does in the passage in question, is to ignore precisely that 'basic insight' of philosophical hermeneutics which I discussed in the opening paragraph of this paper.

A second difficulty is this: Rorty, rephrasing Oakeshott, states that hermeneutics views persons as 'united by civility rather than by a common goal, much less by a common ground.' If I have understood Rorty correctly, he is mistaken about both the goal and the ground. There clearly is a common goal — namely, coming to under stand the other, and thereby coming better to understand oneself. Without such a shared goal, no conversation can ever take place. (Or perhaps I should say no *dialogue* can take place. I shall discuss this distinction between 'conversation' and 'dialogue' in what follows.) As for Rorty's claim that hermeneutic philosophical conversation proceeds in the absence of a common ground, nothing could be further from the truth. He appears to have overlooked two basic phenomenological observations that lie at the heart of philosophical hermeneutics: the notions of 'intersubjectivity' and the 'life-world.' The crucial point was already noted by the later Husserl. In his early work Husserl, still so much the Cartesian, concentrated on the importance of 'subjectivity,' identifying the agent of the constitutive activity of consciousness solely as the individual subject. Heidegger criticized this view of subjectivity, and one of the results of this criticism is a new emphasis, in the later Husserl of the *Crisis*, on the role played in constitution by the *community* of subjects, a community that is established largely upon a set of shared, culturally inherited values. Such shared cultural values are intersubjectively constituted while at the same time providing the ground of the activity of intersubjective constitution. They comprise the value-laden world we live in, our *Lebenswelt*. Such shared values seem almost to have a life of their own, separate from that of the subjects among whom they are shared. One of the best examples of this is to be found in the language we speak: It lives only as long as it is spoken by us, and it evolves in the course of its life — but we first learn to speak it by listening to it and learning its rules, rules that naturally change, over time, in the course of our speaking the language. The rules of our language-games evolve, just as do the meanings of the words we employ. Moreover, to our language belongs a set of a particular sort of 'values' that we, as subjects among subjects, inherit and later pass on in a slightly altered condition. It is such shared, intersubjectively constituted values as those we find in language — in the meanings and connotations of words and the import of syntax — which establish that 'deeper agreement' among subjects which I described above as necessary if any dialogue is ever to get underway.

I am now speaking of *dialogue*, not conversation. The distinction marks a difference between the sort of conversation Rorty appears to envision and that which philosophical hermeneutics deals with. Dialogue, for hermeneutics, exists as the language that lives and evolves as we speak it, while conversation — as Rorty has presented it — is nothing more than the language that each of us is born into and must learn in order subsequently to engage in dialogue. In Aristotelian terms, we might say that language qua conversation is potentially language qua dialogue, and that dialogue is actualized conversation. Moreover, such actualization always alters the potentiality remaining yet to be actualized. We are born into a conversation — namely, that of our 'tradition,' the shared, intersubjectively constituted values of our *Lebenswelt* — and as soon as we enter into dialogue, we proceed to alter the nature of the conversation into which those who follow us will be born. Dialogue is, in short, always a creative and dynamic process, whereas 'conversation' is static. Yet such conversation remains, nevertheless, the only starting point to be found for any and all dialogue. This leads me to a third difficulty for Rorty's book.

Recall Rorty's closing sentence: 'The only point on which I would insist is that philosophers' moral concern should be with continuing the conversation of the West, rather than with insisting upon a place for the traditional problems of modern philosophy within that conversation.' It strikes me that, contra Rorty, the problems of modern philosophy are in fact *partners* in the dialogue — or at least they *ought* to be. To the dialogue that philosophical hermeneutics regards as essential to the event of understanding necessarily belong different points of view, different perspectives and approaches. In this sense, the 'traditional problems of modern philosophy' possess a thoroughly legitimate claim to membership in the 'conversation of the West.' Indeed, without acknowledging these problems as our interlocutors we would not be able to engage in that critical dialogue which challenges their privileged status. That is, in attempting to refute their claim, Rorty has already recognized them as essential to that very conversation he sees them as breaking off. But, like Rorty, the hermeneutic philosopher does not acknowledge the unquestioned *authority*, the 'privileged status,' of these problems. The hermeneutic philosopher will grant the legitimate claim of traditional problems and differing philosophical positions, but only while at the same time limiting the historical and conceptual field in which these problems and positions enjoy their legitimacy. This is part of the *critical* task of hermeneutics.

Inquiry — be it in the field of natural science, ethics, epistemology, or politics — is always *human* inquiry, and as such, it too is characterized by that 'historicity' which Heidegger identified as essential to the being not only of *Dasein* but of all human pursuits and creations. Dialogue, in the form of critical inquiry, is pursued by persons who are born into a conversation, into a tradition of values and convictions, which it is their human task to alter as their lives demand. And to alter the values that constitute tradition is to change that tradition itself. To engage in dialogue is to alter the course of the historical conversation in which one found oneself prior to such engagement. Tradition makes us what we are, but it is we who make the tradition that we shall leave to others. In short, while hermeneutics recognizes the *power* of the status quo, it does not attempt to promote the status quo merely because of its power. There is no question here of 'defending' the status quo — it's merely a question of recognizing the power of the powers that be.

III

This leads me, finally, to my critical remarks on Comay's paper. She has claimed that Rorty defends the status quo, having 'surreptitiously aggrandized' philosophy, viewing it as 'a cheerful affirmation of the "now."' These two sides of a single criticism follow also from my own argument that Rorty's notion of conversation (and thus also his presentation of hermeneutics) is misleading. To this extent, Comay and I are in agreement. Rorty's view of conversation, along with his vision of philosophy as properly concerned with 'carrying on' that sort of conversation, might indeed reduce philosophy to little more than an ethereal game played by the sort of irresponsible sophists Aristophanes so deftly lampooned — an ongoing game whose theoretical results have little if any practical application. But ought philosophical inquiry always to have as its goal the practical, social-political application of its theoretical results? In other words, is philosophy to be defined in terms of a telos of political praxis? And is hermeneutic philosophy — which Comay reads Rorty as representing — denied critical content? That is to say, is hermeneutics incapable of legitimately engaging in the critical analysis of those problems and positions that constitute such a great portion of our tradition?

Comay suggests affirmative answers to both questions. With regard to the former, my own political convictions persuade me to lean in Comay's direction, yet what I have said above precludes my complete agreement. This should be clear: I have come to adopt certain political values, and these have influenced not only my view of philosophy, but also my choice of the other interests and activities I currently pursue. In turn, these interests and activities — which include political activities — exercise a continuing influence on both my view of philosophy and the sort of philosophy I engage in; that is, the sort of 'philosophical theorizing' I pursue. My point in saying this is to indicate that there exists no clearly drawn line between theory and practice in this case, and it is unreasonable to stress one over the other by restricting the scope of philosophical inquiry to within the field of possible political action. Perhaps Comay and I shall, after all, wind up in agreement on this. In any event, this is precisely the sort of 'conversational' stuff of which hermeneutical dialogue is made.

This observation leads me to the second question raised above. In order to show that hermeneutics is capable of critical analysis, I shall address two seemingly casual remarks about Gadamer. Comay writes:

> "Conversation" is the eighteenth-century dream of gentlemanly social intercourse adapted to the rhythms of consumer society. It is Gadamer's nostalgic evocation of classical erudition, Oakeshott's urbane "pursuit of intimations," the neo-classical decorum celebrated by a Pater or an Eliot. (86)

And:

> It [Rorty's view] is Gadamer's cultural vision without the Gadamerian faith in History; a *Bildungsroman* without closure, a conglomeration without end. (87)

The expression 'nostalgic evocation' is entirely inappropriate when speaking of Gadamer's treatment of 'erudition.' Indeed, 'erudition' is itself an unfortunate and desperately misleading translation of the

German, for *Bildung* — as a technical term in the philosophical vocabulary — enjoys a far richer meaning than that. The sense which it has
in Gadamer's work can be appreciated only if we take into account
the roles played by intersubjectivity and historicity in the spiritual
development of both the individual and the society as a whole. This
sense is already to be found in Hegel. S-J. Hoffmann has described
it as follows:

> The concept of *Bildung* refers to the development of an individual's
> potential in the context of the cultural tendencies of a given time and
> place. Johannes Hoffmeister, in his *Wörterbuch der philosophischen
> Begriffe* (Hamburg 1955, p. 124), defines *Bildung* as
>
>> Vor allem die Entwicklung und Förderung der Anlagen des her-
>> anwachsenden Menschen nach einem Vorbild (Ideal, Typus), das
>> durch die jeweiligen Kulturtendenzen wesentlich mitbestimmt
>> ist ... [above all the development and nurturing of the abilities
>> of the maturing person in accordance with a model (ideal, type)
>> which is essentially codetermined by the cultural tendencies of
>> a given time ...]
>
> The educated or cultured man neither merely absorbs factual knowledge
> by means of schooling nor merely shows himself to be apt in social
> graces. Rather, his education teaches him to think for himself, and en-
> dows him with the ability to make judgments and to grasp the possi-
> bilities and limits of knowledge.[1]

Gadamer's intention is not, as Comay seems to believe, to glorify the
view of bygone days regarding the value of a well-rounded education.
Rather, when Gadamer speaks of *Bildung*, he is speaking of the manner in which an individual grows to become an active, responsible
member of a society, this society being characterized by
intersubjectively-constituted values that evolve over the course of time
through the contribution made by the individual members. It was along
these lines that I earlier distinguished between 'conversation' and 'dialogue.' The conversation is the tradition into which the individual is
born, and the dialogue, engaged in by present members of society,
gives rise to the tradition, the conversation, into which future members of that society will be born. There is no 'nostalgic evocation' here.

There is only a description of the manner in which the individual and society are dialogically related to one another.

Comay's second remark is also misleading. To refer to 'the Gadamerian faith in History' would seem to imply that Gadamer enjoys some sort of unfounded, optimistic confidence in the benevolence of 'History.' This is not the case at all. His extensive discussions of history are not intended as arguments in favour of throwing in the political towel and endorsing the status quo. Quite the contrary. His faith is not in the worth of any particular set of historical, traditional values, but in the very power of tradition itself. His concern, in short, is not to demonstrate that ours is the best of all possible traditions, but that all traditions, all 'histories,' are possessed of a force that cannot simply be denied. And his further concern is to demonstrate that we must first recognize the power that our tradition is exercising upon us if we are ever to be able sufficiently to extricate ourselves from its grip in order to discern and rectify its shortcomings. In sum, he has attempted to lay the groundwork for a philosophical critique of society — not a mere critique of ideology, which itself remains bound to values that are inherited from a particular tradition, but a critique of such critiques itself, a thoroughly self-conscious critique, pursued through dialogue, of those intersubjectively-constituted values in which the conversation of our tradition so greatly consists. This is clearly no 'faith in History,' nor is it the return to the 'optimistic attitude' of pre-modern, 'pre-epistemological,' philosophy that Rorty seems to be advocating. It is a call to recognize our responsibility, as individuals, to enter into that creative dialogue by means of which alone can the 'conversation,' the tradition, of the present be preserved, altered, and passed on. This conversation did, obviously, begin at some point, and most certainly far before the days of Plato. And it has *not* been interrupted. What *has* been interrupted, however, is the dialogue, the self-conscious and self-critical participation in the intersubjective constitution of those values that will create a vital tradition for the future.

In his praise of the 'conversation of the West' and his rejection of 'modern epistemology,' Rorty has, I feel, lost sight of the task of hermeneutics. In doing so, he has interrupted the hermeneutic dialogue. Comay, by challenging Rorty and by questioning the very existence of our 'western conversation,' has not interrupted that conversation at all. She has resumed the dialogue.

NOTE

1 S.-J. Hoffmann, 'The World of Culture in the Phenomenology of Spirit' (unpublished MS).

III

Moral
Reflection

Moral Reflection

The prospects of finding an axiomatic method for resolving moral questions in a public context are currently very slim. Even if an individual philosopher somehow managed to uncover self-evident starting-points and became convinced of their worth as such, the community probably would not follow suit. The spirit of the age is very much one of subjecting everything to further considerations, without conceding anything as a possible moral axiom.

Contemporary epistemology offers at least two moderately attractive ways to construct a methodology without advocating a search for axioms. One is normally labelled 'modest foundationalism,' the other 'coherentism.'[1] A modest foundationalist asks us to look for 'initially acceptable' starting-points and then explains how something initially acceptable can be transformed into something acceptable. The explanation usually urges us to find some kind of 'fit' with other initially acceptable things. A coherentist, on the other hand, dispenses with a concern for the initially acceptable and operates solely with the notion of fit, advising us to find a set of beliefs the members of which hang together more effectively than the members of competing sets.

In 'Searching for an Emancipatory Perspective,' Kai Nielsen outlines a methodology which falls on the coherentist side of this divide. Although he acknowledges a need to start somewhere, he attaches no importance to assigning the starting-points an initial epistemic value. They are simply points of current general agreement which can be used provisionally to work toward a coherent whole. If some of them cannot be accommodated in the set which exhibits maximum harmony, they should simply be dropped along the way, with no epistemic regrets.

For Nielsen, the best way to develop a coherentist methodology is to hold out for a wide reflective equilibrium. The demand for reflective equilibrium ensures that common intuitions and general principles are both accommodated. And the demand for width ensures that judgments and principles are harmonized with broader social theories, not just with each other. The width requirement is important for two reasons. First, if moral conclusions are to serve the end of rational justification, they must have a certain stability, and that stability seems best achieved by casting the harmonizing net as widely as possible. Second, if moral theory is to make a difference in practice, it has to reach as broad an audience as possible, including individuals who are professionally charged with the task of guiding and shaping public policy.

Of course, one of the central questions Nielsen faces is whether there is sufficient consensus among interested individuals to make this methodology work. He maintains — albeit with reservations — that there is. True, he acknowledges the existence of moral sceptics like J.L. Mackie who refuse to accept ordinary moral judgments. But he thinks that their wholesale rejection of ordinary judgments means that they are simply quarrelling with a philosophical characterization of ordinary moral responses, not rejecting the responses themselves. Hence he thinks that the necessary consensus remains intact.

Things may not be quite this straightforward, however. Nielsen's eventual goal is not merely to justify a set of moral beliefs but to justify morality as a way of life. Some sceptics may link the characterization of moral beliefs which they as sceptics reject with the kind of practical justification which Nielsen seeks. In that case, the fact that they share the primitive moral responses of ordinary people does not commit them to a consensus about the ends of conduct. For example, sceptics may initially respond by saying that dishonesty is wrong and yet be dishonest whenever it pays, precisely *because* of the way they characterize the response; they may regard the response as too subjective to serve as a guide to their conduct. Nielsen's methodology needs some fine-tuning if it is to sidestep a sceptical challenge of this kind.

Nielsen also acknowledges another possible obstacle to getting the necessary consensus when he concedes that even non-sceptical philosophers disagree in very fundamental ways, where their disagreements reflect lay differences. But he finds it unlikely that such disagreements will survive wide reflection. Although he cannot find a basis for this prediction in the history of traditional philosophical reflection, he feels that pushing the range of considerations beyond narrow traditional boundaries will make a crucial difference. Dieter Misgeld, in 'The Limits of a Theory of Practice,' rightly expresses serious misgivings on this point in the light of actual developments in social theory. Misgeld makes a good case for thinking that social critics who are sensitive to the demands of a wide-ranging coherence often have as much trouble reaching agreement as traditional moral philosophers.

The incidence of stubborn disagreement also raises the more basic question of the significance of coherence. A coherentist methodology has little to say about cases in which the prescribed method is unable to secure theoretical agreement. It can merely exhort us to try harder. Consequently, if alternative coherent schemes emerge, a coherentist methodology is under some pressure to find another ground for deciding between them, in which case it falls back into the same foundationalist's trap from which it seeks to escape. Similarly, as Barry Allen points out in 'Groundless Goodness,' if coherentists find themselves at odds with theorists who deny the need for coherence, they are forced to treat coherence as a ground of the very sort they want to avoid enlisting. The status of coherentism as a genuine form of antifoundationalism thus turns heavily on its establishing agreement of a sort the contemporary human mind has not even approximated.

Misgeld also points to a tactical difficulty in Nielsen's methodology. Nielsen's ultimate motivation is practical. He wants a method for constructing a theory which will disclose worthwhile ends of human actions and worthwhile ways of achieving them. The theory must therefore be able to cope with practical concerns and there must be a suitable fit between theoretical conclusions and practical judgments. Misgeld describes several problems which social theorists have had in reconciling the two levels of inquiry, making one seriously wonder whether the goal can in fact be achieved. The search for a wide-ranging and useful coherence may turn out to be just as futile in practice as a Cartesian search for incorrigible foundations.

Moreover, recommending a search for 'wide' coherence may be a case of investigative overkill. There is a question of how wide the range of considerations has to be before a member of a set of beliefs can be said to be justified. The range must be finite and restricted to considerations which are in some sense available at the time. Yet the coherence requirement must also be satisfied for any *extension* of the range, since the methodology has to generate a guide for future conduct. Hence the question is: What things must actually be considered if we are to be entitled to say that the set will remain coherent as new things are considered? Nielsen's answer is: A 'wide' range of things. He thinks that by taking into account the widest possible range of considerations which is currently available, we are in a better position to predict what will happen as the range is extended. That seems wise methodological advice, given that the considerations which are taken into account are relevant to the question at hand. Furthermore, if the question is as fundamental as something like 'What should the structure of society be?', the relevant considerations are highly diverse and encompass the findings of social theory broadly conceived. But is this true for more restricted moral questions, including questions about the conduct of a private individual? In order to determine whether you should read a graduate student's thesis draft before working on an article for publication, do you really have to employ such a comprehensive methodology or draw on the conclusions of theorists who have employed it? We need a better understanding of how the scope of the considerations which have actually been taken into account bears on the acceptability of a resulting belief before we can give an affirmative answer to this question. Wide reflective equilibrium may be a methodology which has to be practised only by certain kinds of investigators, not by everyone engaged in moral reflection.

Yet even if the proposed method is only suitable for theorists who share Nielsen's broad social concerns, it still contains a potentially important message. Although it may not contribute much in cases of radical disagreement, it does have useful advice to give to theorists who share an appropriate framework. It also sets the standards for judging their inquiries at a commendably high level, higher than the level often set at present. And, within the same general framework, it offers a benchmark which outsiders — especially individuals in public office — can use to appraise competing theories. The methodological inquiry started by Nielsen in these pages therefore should be studied carefully, and continued. Although using his method probably will not eliminate the vertigo which he himself feels when he looks at the full spectrum of moral positions to date, it can help to keep the feeling within the bounds of philosophical sanity.

Douglas Odegard

NOTE

1 For representatives, see, respectively, James Cornman, *Skepticism, Justification, and Explanation* (Dordrecht: Reidel 1980), and Laurence Bonjour, 'The Coherence Theory of Empirical Knowledge,' *Philosophical Studies* 30 (1976) 281-312. The theories are not primarily intended to provide a method for securing public agreement, but they might be enlisted for this purpose. For a nonaxiomatic foundationalism which gives intuition a central role, see Paul K. Moser's *Empirical Justification* (Dordrecht: Reidel 1985).

Kai Nielsen

Searching for an Emancipatory Perspective: Wide Reflective Equilibrium and the Hermeneutical Circle

I

How to start in reflectively thinking about ethics, and more generally in thinking about what sort of people we would like to be, and about what sort of society and world-order we would like to see obtain or come to obtain? If we look about us at what has been said on such grand themes by people who are knowledgeable and reflective it is enough to give one a kind of vertigo. We have varieties of utilitarianism, contractarianism, duty-based theories, rights-based theories, perfectionist theories (some harking back to Aristotle), relativism or conventionalism, projectivist error theories, new forms of subjectivism, and new forms of noncognitivism. These are all theories, in themselves in many ways and at a number of different levels very different, which get articulated within the dominant Anglo-American analytic tradition.[1] When we step out of that ambience to traditions that tend to look at ethics rather more broadly, and not so much as a distinct philosophical subject matter to be pursued as a distinct branch of philosophy, the motley of voices is even more of a motley. Jürgen Habermas's communicative ethics integrally linked with his systematic critical theory of society is one thing, Michel Foucault's ethics of 'practices of the self' on the other side of a firm turning of his back on the project of constructing systematic moral foundations is quite another thing again, as is Hans-Georg Gadamer's still very different hermeneutical placement of such matters, as is — to point to still further radically different ways of doing things — the pragmatist approach of John Dewey, Wittgenstein's approach to such matters, or Rorty's very contextualist, neo-pragmatist, neo-Wittgensteinian approach in the service of a conservative form of liberalism.

The differences here, both substantive and methodological, are not infrequently very deep. It isn't that these theorists more or less agree about what is at issue and give different answers to roughly the same questions as, say, Richard Brandt, Robert Nozick, David Gauthier and John Harsanyi do. Rather, the differences sometimes go so deep that it is not at all clear that there is a common subject-matter. The differences in conception are such that it may well be the case that no comparisons can be usefully made, not to mention the scouting out of anything like a unified project. What is there in common between R.M. Hare, Gadamer, Dewey, and Foucault that would make such scouting and comparisons fruitful? Do we not just have a tower of Babel here?

With a certain amount of trepidation and some ambivalence, I want to suggest that perhaps we do not. If we look carefully at what is involved in what I shall call (following Norman Daniels) an appeal to considered judgments in *wide* reflective equilibrium (a conception central to the work of John Rawls, but a conception which others, myself included, have adopted, adapted, modified, and have, as well, argued is a central underlying methodology in setting out an account of morality or of ethics), we shall come to see a way in which very diverse strands in thinking about ethics can be brought together into a unified whole.[2] When the method of wide reflective equilibrium (WRE) is integrated with a substantive critical theory of society developed with an emancipatory intent, we *may* have a project that can articulate a legitimate conception of a normatively acceptable order to set against the reality of what is now disorder and illegitimacy. Such a project, I shall suggest, would, in a fruitful articulation, use insights (insights valuable in themselves) drawn from Rawls, Williams, Foucault, Gadamer and Habermas, in a unified account which both makes sense of the moral terrain and gives us a coherently-integrated set of normative criteria to appeal to in social assessment and criticism and for making sense of our lives: lives that often, particularly under contemporary conditions, have the look of being senseless.

This, if it has any chance at all of success, cannot be an eclectic hodge-podge of diverse and incommensurable items. The items are indeed diverse and they are stressed by their authors for very different purposes and often under very different frameworks; but, collected together and unified by WRE, the diverse elements can be seen to fit together into a coherent whole.

II

What we need to see is what WRE comes to and how it fits in with a critical theory of society. In responding morally and in reasoning morally we cannot escape starting from tradition and from some consensus. In this fundamental sense we unavoidably start from morality as *Sittlichkeit* and refer back, however far we go in a reformist or even in a revolutionary or iconoclastic direction, to that *Sittlichkeit*. We go back, that is, to a cluster of institutions and institutionalized norms, sanctioned by custom, through which the members of an actual social order fulfil the social demands of the social whole to which they belong. This must not be mistaken for an implicit defense of conservativism, for the reflective moral agent, starting with a distinctive *Sittlichkeit*, can and will reject certain, indeed perhaps whole blocks, of such institutional norms, refashion some of them, or perhaps forge some new ones. What we cannot do is to coherently reject, or stand aside from, the whole cluster of institutional norms of the life-world in which we come to consciousness and, so to say, start afresh. We cannot avoid starting from the deeply-embedded cultural norms that go with our interlocked set of institutions.

The norms that we, starting from our own culturally derived *Sittlichkeit*, would most resist abandoning, the ones that humanly speaking are bedrock for us, are the norms that Rawls takes to be our firmest considered judgments (convictions). They are norms that for him have a very strategic but still non-foundationalist place in our moral reasoning and in our conceptions of how we would justify our moral beliefs.[3] Here, in spite of what otherwise are enormous differences, Rawls and a hermeneuticist such as Gadamer have a common point of departure.

Starting with our firmest considered judgments and then turning a Rawlsian trick by utilizing a coherentist model of justification and rationalization, we will seek to get these judgments into *wide* reflective equilibrium. This would involve, in our reasoning from such a *Sittlichkeit*, a winnowing out of these culturally received norms. Rawls, like Habermas, and in the tradition of the Enlightenment, will not just stick with tradition, with what Hare called 'received opinion.'[4]

Let us see a little more exactly what wide reflective equilibrium comes to. Narrow or partial reflective equilibrium, the method in effect used by contemporary intuitionists, consists in getting a match between our considered particular moral convictions (judgments) and a moral principle or set of moral principles (which may themselves be more general considered convictions) which will systematize the more particular considered convictions so that we can see how they all could be derived from that principle or those principles, or at least recognize that they are best explained and rationalized by that principle or these principles, so that together the more particular moral convictions and more generalized moral principles form a consistent whole perspicuously displayed. This gives us a coherence theory of justification but not an adequately wide one.

Wide reflective equilibrium is also a coherence theory of justification and moral reasoning but it casts a wider net. It seeks to produce and perspicuously display coherence between 1) our considered moral convictions, 2) a set, or at least a cluster, of moral principles, and 3) a set or cluster of background theories, including most centrally moral theories and social theories, including in turn, social theories which are quite definitely empirical theories about our social world and about how we humans function in it.

We cannot take the point of view from nowhere or see ourselves as purely rational noumenal beings with no local attachments or enculturations.[5] If we self-consciously seek to place ourselves, vis-à-vis our considered moral convictions and overall moral and intellectual perspectives, in the perspective of some radically different time and place we will in considerable measure fail. Whether we like it or not we are children of modernity, and we are deeply affected by its conditioning and by its dominant consensus. (Even Islamic fundamentalists extensively educated in the West are not free of it. In certain key respects their reaction is more like the Counter-Enlightenment reaction of the German romantics to the Enlightenment.) It is perfectly true that this is a matter of degree. Some strata and some subcultures of industrial society are more influenced than others by modernity, but my point is that all are deeply influenced. And, as the demystification of the world runs apace, we are becoming increasingly and more pervasively so influenced.

Within the culture of modernity there is disagreement as well as consensus, but what is important for WRE is that there is consensus. As in any justificatory venture, it is unavoidable that we start from there.[6] Questions of justification arise when we disagree among ourselves or when we, as individuals, are of two minds. To resolve these questions we must proceed from things that everyone involved in the dispute holds in common.[7] For justification to be possible we must find some common ground. Even when any of us are of two minds about some issue, we need, in thinking it through, to retreat as individuals to some relevant set of beliefs that, for the time at least, holds fast for us.

So we start in WRE from what we have a firm consensus about. In the broad cluster of the cultures of modernity there is, fortunately, a considerable overlap of considered convictions, including agreement in what I have called moral truisms, such as: it is wrong to torture the innocent, to break faith with people, to fail to keep one's promises, and the like. It isn't that these things can never be done, no matter what the circumstances. What is the case is that to do any of these things is ceteris paribus wrong. There is always a presumption against doing them and, particularly in the case of torturing the innocent, that presumption is very stringent indeed. These are deontic considerations but the moral consensus includes, as well, truisms such as: pleasure is good, pain is bad, it is a good thing to develop one's powers and to have meaningful work and meaningful human relationships. There is, in fine, a vast consensus about both deontological and teleological moral truisms. All ethical theories, ethical scepticism and its country cousins aside, accept these judgments and compete to show which best reveals their underlying rationale and coherence. Moreover, ethical scepticism only rejects them in the course of rejecting *all* moral judgments as somehow unjustified, perhaps because there is and can be, as J.L. Mackie put it, no objective prescriptivity.[8] Ethical sceptics do not single out these particular moral conceptions for rejection as having some distinctive defect; they reject them because they do not think any moral beliefs at all can be objectively warranted. (In its very generality perhaps such moral scepticism is suspect.) We should add to the list of items over which there is now a firm consensus what Charles Taylor says we have developed a particular concern for since the eighteenth century, namely, 'a concern for the preservation of life, for the fulfilling of human need, and above all for the relief of suffering ... .'[9] There are, of course, deep disagreements over the right and the good, but there is plainly much agreement as well and we can and should *start* from the consensus in trying to rationalize morality, in trying to show, against nihilism, how the very institution of morality has a purpose and a point.

We start with our firmly-fixed considered convictions filtered for convictions that we would only have under conditions in which we would make errors in judgment, the errors we typically make when out of control, enraged, depressed, drunk, fatigued, under stress, in the grip of an ideology, and the like. But we do not rest content, as an intuitionist would, with simply making a fit between our particular moral convictions so pruned and our more general moral principles. WRE, unlike partial or narrow equilibrium, is not just the attaining of a fit between the considered judgments and the moral principles we remain committed to on reflection or the principles which are the simplest set of principles from which we could derive most of those considered convictions. Beyond that, WRE remains committed to a fit which also includes the matching of principles which not only satisfy the conditions just mentioned but as well match best with ethical theories, theories which are the most carefully elaborated and rationalized and in turn fit best with what we know about the world and the full range of our considered convictions, including convictions brought to bear in defense of these theories or in defense of background social theories relevant to them and which involve moral convictions, some of which are distinct from and logically independent of the considered convictions with which and from which we started. We shuttle back and forth between considered convictions, moral principles, ethical theories, social theories, and other background empirical theories and those considered judgments (at least some of which must be distinct from the initial cluster of considered judgments) that are associated with or are constitutive of or partially constitutive of the moral principles, social theoreies or other background theories. (The association will be such that they are standardly appealed to in justifying those principles or theories.) In such shuttling we sometimes modify or even abandon a particular considered conviction; at other times we abandon or modify a moral principle or come to adopt some new principles; and sometimes (though of course very rarely) we modify or even abandon a social theory or other background theory or even come to construct a new one. We move back and forth — rebuilding the ship at sea — modifying and adjusting here and there until we get a coherent and consistent set of beliefs. When we have done that, then we have for a time attained WRE. (It is important in such coherence accounts that we have a large circle involving many considerations rather than a small one.) This does not rule out the possibility that at a later time this equilibrium will be upset and that we will then have to seek a new equilibrium.

Put another way, the account of morality is the most adequate which most perspicuously displays the conceptions we should accept and act in accordance with. That is the account which a) fits together into a coherent whole the at least provisional fixed points in our considered convictions better than alternative accounts, b) squares best with our best knowledge and most plausible hypotheses about the world (including, of course, our social world), and c) most adequately (of the alternative accounts) provides guidance where we are, without recourse to a reflective application of the theory, not confident of what particular moral judgments to make or indeed, in the more extreme case, are at a loss to know what to do. Where we are unsure about a considered moral judgment, WRE will provide guidance concerning whether to continue to accept it or whether and how to revise it. In new situations (say in arguments about nuclear matters) it will better guide us in what extrapolations to make from the stock of judgments at hand than alternative accounts of morality. Such an account, to expand the last part a bit, will best show us what extrapolations to make in such situations from our stock of considered judgments in the light of what we know or reasonably believe about the world. Accounts which do these things better are the better accounts, and the ones that best do these things are the best accounts, i.e., the accounts which are for the nonce in reflective equilibrium.

Of course, a given account of morality might be better in one of these dimensions and worse in another. Where this obtains, and we cannot devise an account which unites these virtues for a time, then we will not have achieved WRE. We should also note, with Rawls, that a Socratic element remains in all such reasonings. We unavoidably make reflective contextual judgments, all along the line, in any effective thinking about particular considered moral judgments, moral principles, ethical theories, rationalizing particular judgments and principles, making assessment of the facts, and in considering critical social theories with an emancipatory intent. In all those contexts we make reflective judgments about what to do or be. Moreover, in choosing ethical and social theories there will be an appeal to considered judgments and a reliance on our particular reflective judgments. We do not, anywhere along the coherentist path, get anything that is utterly value-free; there is no avoiding the necessity of making reflective judgments. If we say, for a given population at a given time and place, that they have put their judgments into WRE, and have shown that they are justified, that reflective equilibrium will not be one which thus could have been attained without their making such reflective judgments. We can have no algorithms here.

Our justificatory account of morality will be a holistic, antifoundationalist coherentism, in which to gain an adequate conception of morality and to represent the best moral point of view we can at a given time garner is not a matter of per impossibile getting a conception derived from, or in some other way based on, unchallengeable general principles. Neither is it a matter of deriving such principles from a set of self-evident propositions or squaring this moral point of view with a set of particular considered judgments which are not even in principle revisable or challengeable. No such quest for certainty, no such tacit appeal to foundationalism, is in order. Instead the justification of a claim that we have such a moral point of view is 'a matter of the mutual support of many considerations, of everything fitting together into a coherent view.'[10] Here, unlike in intuitionism or in another view which would stick with narrow reflective equilibrium, our sense of what is right and wrong, good and bad, while starting from tradition, may undergo extensive change at the behest of critical reasoning and investigation. On this thoroughly fallibilistic coherence account, where all claims, including any considered judgments at any level, are, at least in theory, revisable, there is no foundationalist appeal to some moral beliefs (say some of our concrete considered convictions) as basic or self-warranting. Our grounds for accepting moral principles are not that they systematize pretheoretical considered judgments which carry epistemological privilege. None of the moral judgments, moral principles, moral theories, or background social theories carry any privilege. The point is to get these diverse elements into a coherent whole which does justice to the importance and relevance of our firmest convictions, to our best rationalized social and moral theories, and to what we know or reasonably believe about the world. No elements are uncriticizable: none form a justificatory base which we simply must accept, though indeed some of them may never in fact be doubted or actually be subjected to criticism, and it is, as the pragmatists stressed, impossible to doubt them all at once. Something must for the nonce stand fast while we doubt other beliefs, but, this, as Peirce showed against Descartes, does not mean that any belief is permanently indubitable. Indeed for some of them it is astronomically unlikely that there will be any point at all in doubting them, but this does not mean they are indubitable.

So at no place along the line is there a foundationalist claim, not even with our firmest considered convictions. The point is not to try to find such an Archimedean point but to gain instead, for a time, and always subject to future revision, the most coherent package of beliefs relevant to how our life in society is to be ordered and how we are to care for our own lives as individuals. Justification in ethics comes to getting these beliefs in WRE.

III

A persistent worry about WRE is that, starting from a particular agreement in considered judgments at a particular time and place, it will in one way or another be ethnocentric: it will be skewed from the beginning along class or cultural lines and the like. Such unavoidable starting points in local attachments cannot, the claim goes, but skew the outcome.

This worry does not take seriously enough what WRE is or attend carefully enough to how it works. We *may* possibly get such cultural skewing in the end, that is after we have for a time achieved WRE, just as we have it at the beginning, but there is no necessity about this, and it is unlikely if we resolutely reason in accordance with WRE. We can have no guarantees here — we should avoid taking the

a priori or transcendental road — and we would not know whether
this non-skewing was so until we had carried through such reasoning
thoroughly and in turn had reflectively reconsidered it. Nevertheless,
we can have good hunches about the critical potential of WRE.

Suppose we started not from a consensus we could actually at
tain in a Western society such as ours, but from a *Sittlichkeit* which
was that of an Anscombeish-Donaganish Hebrew-Christian morality
(by now a rather out-of-date Hebrew-Christian morality) that actual
ly might have been our *Sittlichkeit* in an earlier period in our history.
Among the core considered convictions that would be a part of our
consensus in the initial situation in such a life-world would be that
voluntary sterilization is impermissible because it is a form of self-
mutilation, that casual sex must be evil because it cannot but be ex-
ploitative, that abortion, suicide, euthanasia, and sex outside of mar-
riage are all *categorically* impermissible. But that we would start with
such a consensus does not mean that we would end with it after pro-
tracted cultural debate *where the contestants would be committed to us
ing WRE*. To have such a commitment means not only appealing to
a partial reflective equilibrium which might take it as sufficient to get
our considered judgments to fit with the first principles of the natural moral law, but, more radically and extensively, to get them into
equilibrium with the best rationalized moral theories, social and other
relevant empirical-cum-theoretical theories, and with the best factual
knowledge we have about the world. It is, to put it minimally, very
doubtful indeed whether such an initial consensus in considered judgments could survive the justificatory demand that we get such judgments into the most coherent package of this whole range of beliefs.
We unavoidably start with local attachments, firm bits of our culture,
and we can never break out of the hermeneutical circle or the web
of belief and just see things as they are *sub specie aeternitatis*. But, to
refer again to Otto Neurath's metaphor, we can rebuild the ship at
sea. We have with WRE the conceptual and empirical equipment to
criticize the considered convictions from which we start. Nothing in
that starting point justifies metaphors of conceptual or cultural imprisonment. WRE is not a disguised form of subjectivist and ethnocentric intuitionism which views itself self-deceptively as a form of
objectivism. We will not get certainty, but knowledge with certainty

is not pleonastic and fallibilism is not scepticism or subjectivism. It is rather late in the day to have nostalgia for the absolute.

IV

Norman Daniels, to whom my account of WRE is indebted, gives, as does Rawls, too traditionalist an account of the relevant background theories. Traditional moral (normative ethical) theories, I agree, do have a considerable role in displaying such background theories, as does a conception of a well-ordered society.[11] Moreover, I also agree with Rawls and Daniels that at the next level of WRE a theory of the role of morality in society, a theory of persons, and a theory of procedural justice should be appealed to. And finally, I agree that, furthest in the background as vital feasibility tests for the other claims, there should be a general social theory and a theory of moral development. In assessing proposed moral principles, such as a self-realizationist (perfectionist) principle, the principle of utility, or Rawls's two principles of justice, it is vital to examine closely the claims and rationales of various moral theories and to see what they can say for the principles they propose and against the principles they criticize. In turn, in assessing these theories we need a theory of the role of morality in society. So far so good. In Daniels's account, however, too much stress in these assessments is placed on working out a theory of persons and a theory of procedural justice. More attention than necessary or desirable is placed on typical philosophical and legal concerns, and not enough on characterizing and exploring the role of general social theory in such contexts and on specifying what kind of social theory we need. Too much attention is directed to philosophy as traditionally conceived, not enough to sociology and critical theory.

In showing that this is so, I shall proceed indirectly. Michel Foucault, in responding to the question why he should be interested as well in politics, a question he took to be self-answering, responded as follows:

> ... what blindness, what deafness, what density of ideology would have to weigh me down to prevent me from being interested in what is probably the most crucial subject to our existence, that is to say the society

in which we live, the economic relations within which it functions, and the system of power which defines the regular forms and regular permissions and prohibitions of our conduct. The essence of our life consists, after all, of the political functioning of the society in which we find ourselves.[12]

To be seriously interested in ethics, at least in societies such as ours, is to be deeply interested as well in politics. In ethics we care about the quality of our lives and our relations to others. Thinking in a theoretical way about ethics, we know that these matters are central objects of concern in the moral life. That they are so much a part of the moral life means, if we care about morality (as given our conditioning most of us will), that we must also care about our society. Plainly, the care of ourselves, care for the quality of our lives and the kinds of relations we can have with others, is deeply and pervasively affected by the kind of society in which we live. Moreover, our hopes for human enhancement, for the extensive and equitable satisfaction of our needs, and for self-development are importantly tied to what it is reasonable to hope concerning the possibilities for social change and concerning the kind of society we can reasonably expect and, with or without optimism of the will, sensibly struggle for. To have any reasonable understanding here, we must, if such knowledge can be had, understand at least how our society works and hopefully how societies generally work. We need to understand our society's social and economic structure, its structures of legitimation, what holds it together, what could change it, the direction and limits of change, and how permanent those changes are likely to be.

We need, if anything like this is to be had, as much knowledge of these things as we can get to help us in coming to know what we should strive for, how we are to live, and what is right and wrong. Ethics and politics (pace Henry Sidgwick) are inextricably intertwined, but traditional ethical theories are of little help here.[13] Indeed it is very likely that ethical theory, at least as traditionally understood, is more of an impediment than an aid to both understanding and reasonable advocacy and that metaethical theories are no help at all, except to explode the myths of ethical rationalism. In developing an adequate WRE we need more sociology and less philosophy (at least as traditionally understood). While in the past figures such as Aristotle, Augustine, Montesquieu, and Hobbes were of central importance over such matters, it is now thinkers in the mold of Marx, Weber, and Durkheim that should be our models for the kind of social theory we need, not philosophers. (Dewey is a partial exception, but he did not march lockstep with the tradition. It is not uncommon for philosophers to think that he was hardly a philosopher at all.)

V

Given such a conception of WRE, it is vital to see if we can develop anything intellectually respectable that counts as a holistic critical theory of society with an emancipatory intent. (My interest here is to schematize such a theory. I am not concerned with how it matches or fails to match Habermas's account.) I am also largely indifferent to whether this critical theory is to be called philosophy or a part of a successor subject to philosophy. If 'philosophy' is construed broadly as an attempt to see things in a comprehensive way in an attempt to make sense of our lives, then a critical theory of society is also a part of philosophy, but many would want to construe 'philosophy' more narrowly as part of a distinct disciplinary matrix. What is important is not whether a critical theory of society is or is not philosophy but whether it makes a disciplined set of claims that can be warrantedly asserted and will provide us with an adequate account of what society is like and how it can change.[14] Critical theory wants to help us to come to understand how things hang together and how some ways in which things could hang together could answer more adequately to human needs and be more liberating of human powers than others. In seeking WRE, having a social theory which really did such things is of considerable importance. If such a theory is not to be had, that would considerably diminish the force of WRE. What it could achieve without such a theory would be far less than what could be achieved with a viable critical theory.

The critical theory we are seeking, on the perhaps illusory hope that it is attainable, is a holistic theory which will display and explain in a comprehensive way how things hang together. It is a descriptive-explanatory theory, an interpretive theory, and a normative critique. In such a theory elements of philosophy as more traditionally conceived will be amalgamated with the human and social sciences with none of the elements claiming hegemony and with philosophy giving up all pretensions to being an autonomous 'guardian of reason.' (To claim this is not to defend irrationalism or to rage against reason, though it is to reject philosophical rationalism. Friedrich Waismann's dictum that the heart of rationalism is irrational is salutary.)

Critical theory, while remaining descriptive-explanatory, will also provide a comprehensive critique of culture, society, and ideology. It is here, of course, where it will have its critical-emancipatory thrust, though it will have this to a very considerable extent indirectly by way of its descriptive-explanatory and interpretive power. It will help us not only to see better who we were, are, and might become; it will, where there are alternatives, help us see who we might better become and what kind of society would be a more just society, and not only a more just society but also a more humane society that more adequately meets human needs and aspirations. Here WRE and a critical theory of society mutually require each other, at least if we are to have anything more than an impoverished WRE. It is important to recognize that critical theory is not a fancy word-picture – a grand philosophical-social vision – but an empirical-cum-theoretical theory that must meet empirical constraints.[15] It is a descriptive-explanatory theory, showing us the structure of society, the range of its feasible transformations, and the mechanics of its transformation.

Critical theory is a project of modernity, growing out of the Enlightenment. To give post-modernism its due, it is reasonable to be sceptical about whether social theories on such a grand scale can meet anything like reasonable empirical constraints. They may, after all, their authors' intentions to the contrary notwithstanding, be just grand theories or meta-narratives providing us with accounts which are nothing more than dressed up word pictures. Whether critical theory can be something more (can, that is, be a genuine critical theory) will depend on whether it proves able to solve some determinate human problems, e.g., whether it gives us guidance for what to say and do about abortion or terrorism, whether it develops a theoretical practice that has a clear emancipatory pay-off, whether it is a theory whose descriptive-explanatory structure actually can be utilized so as to yield explanations which are true or approximately true, and finally whether these explanations, together with the evaluative and normative claims contained in the theoretical practice, are set together into a well-matching, interlocking, comprehensive, and persipicuously articulated framework. This is, of course, a portion of WRE, for it requires a theory of society; and, unsettlingly, it is also the case that the prospects of carrying such grand theory to successful completion, or even to a promising temporary closure, are daunting. (Perhaps talk of 'completion' for such a program is a mistake.) But it is one thing to find the prospects daunting and quite another thing again to say there is something incoherent about the very idea of such a project. That latter conceptual stopper has not been made out. It has not, that is, been shown that there is something incoherent about the very idea of a comprehensive critical theory of society. The difficulties concerning scope, the problems posed by the knowledge-explosion, the complexity of the social world, and the like appear at least to be empirical difficulties and not difficulties in the very idea of a holistic social theory. The proof of the viability of critical theory will be in the self-critical carrying out of something like this program of a critical theory — a program, if achievable, which would provide the appropriate social theory for WRE and, more generally, have an emancipatory potential.

Post-modernists will resist such claims to theory. Not a few will claim that the incommensurability of competing theories and forms of life runs too deep for grand theories to be possible. What we get instead with the attempt is ideology disguised as theory. Great unmaskers like Marx and Freud are, the claim goes, unwittingly wearing a few masks themselves. Habermas, defending the ideals of the Enlightenment, responds by arguing, correctly I believe, that critical theory requires and permits the firm distinction between theory and ideology without which the very possibility of social critique is undermined.[16]

Critical theory argues that in our life-world there is embedded a whole array of distorted legitimating beliefs which, taken together, provide us with legitimating myths. (Talk of 'legitimation' here is, of course, in a sociological sense only.) These false beliefs and the associated mistaken attitudes go into the make up of our world-picture and our social consciousness, and they prompt us to commend, or at least accept as necessary, a network of highly repressive institutions and practices, including the acceptance of certain conservative political attitudes and an authoritarian work discipline. These are very central, ideologically distorted beliefs — a system of legitimating myths — that underwrite our repressive social system.

Given this, a critique of ideology is a vital element in a critical theory, but this very claim also dramatically underscores the need to be able clearly to distinguish critical theory from ideology and more generally ideology from non-ideology, distorted discourse from un-distorted discourse. What, in fine, would a cluster of non-ideological legitimating beliefs look like? What would it be to have a true account of society where, against post-modernist irony and a pervasive scepti-cism, we would come to have a correct picture of our needs, their proper scheduling, and an ideologically cleared-up self-understanding, enabling us in this important way to see the world rightly? (Post-modernists will, of course, challenge the very idea of seeing the world rightly.)

Let us see, roughly following Habermas, whether we can charac-terize a set of circumstances in which, if they were to obtain, legitimat-ing beliefs could plausibly be said to be nonideological. This is, of course, a model. We are talking about counterfactual circumstances and not about our class-divided and pervasively sexist societies, but it is important for the coherence of this model that the circumstances are not so 'otherworldly' that we could not conceive what it would be like for them to obtain. That they have this empirical significance does not mean, for the model to do its work, that we have to be able to spell out the causal mechanisms that would bring them into exis-tence. It must be a situation in which our legitimating beliefs (includ-ing, of course, central moral beliefs) are formed and argument for them is sustained in conditions of absolutely free and unlimited discussion and deliberation. All parties to the institutions and practices being set up must be in a position such that they could recognize that they are freely consenting to their establishment under conditions in which the only constraints on their acceptance derive from the force of the better argument or the more careful deliberation. Where we so dis-course we have undistorted, non-ideological discourse. Moreover, where we so reason and actually succeed in achieving a consensus we do not merely have a consensus, we have a rational consensus. In our class-divided, ethnically-divided and religiously-oriented cultures (with the religious divisions that standardly brings) we do not get such a consensus; but if we were to get a consensus under the conditions of undistorted discourse I have just described, a consensus which would plainly be an unforced consensus and a consensus which is conceivable no matter how unlikely it may be, then in such a circumstance we would have conditions in place for undistorted, nonideological discourses. A critical theory of society articulates a model of discourse which, if followed, would take us beyond the distortions of ideology and give us a certain kind of objectivity.[17] WRE, in appealing to a theory of society, should appeal to a critical theory, for critical theory would adumbrate a conception of a theory of society which could help provide the corrections needed for the not infrequent ethnocentrism of partial reflective equilibria.

There is also the problem of incommensurability. There are those who say that the history of ethics, like the history of philosophy and the history of culture more generally, is a series of contingencies or accidents of the rise and fall of various, often incommensurable, language-games and forms of life. Philosophers stubbornly retain a nostalgia for the Absolute; but, after all, like a return to pure laissez faire, that is just nostalgia, for no such Archimedean point is available to us. There are no ahistorical standards of rationality or objectivity providing us with ahistorical reasons for acting, reasons that can be seen to be good reasons independently of time, place, and circumstance.

What should be challenged (Peter Winch, Thomas Kuhn, Jacques Derrida and Richard Rorty to the contrary notwithstanding) is whether there really are such incommensurable abysses, whether we really suffer from a conceptual imprisonment, caught up, as it is claimed we are, in various incommensurable hermeneutical circles.[18] There is much in both our intellectual and political culture which sees us as being ineluctably creatures of incommensurable perspectives. There just are rival points of view concerning the truth or falsity, the warrantability or unwarrantability, of scientific theories or moral conceptions, the propriety of political arrangements or the aesthetic qualities of works of art. On examination, the claim goes, we find we have incommensurabilities here incapable of being brought under a set of rules which will tell us how rational agreement can be achieved or how we could reasonably settle matters where we differ.

However, we are – or so I would claim – not stuck with rival points of view. WRE, rather than sanctifying or rationalizing our alleged stuckedness, can be generalized in such a way that we can free ourselves from 'conceptual imprisonment.' When faced with an in-

commensurability claim, the claimants on either side of the putative
abyss should, for a time, bracket the contested claim and, as in the
initial stages of WRE, try to isolate whatever assumptions and procedures they both take to be noncontroversial in the context of that
controversy.[19] Where some common ground is found, as is virtually
certain if the search is more than perfunctory, then further deliberations between them should start from a point of view where only these
shared assumptions and procedures are taken for granted. The strategy is again to work outward toward the contested areas from a consensus and indeed from what predictably will be, if we continue in
this way, a widening consensus; and then, with that consensus firmly
in mind and perspicuously arranged, to again make an onslaught on
the disputed area, working carefully with lines of inference from the
area of consensus. There can, of course, be no a priori guarantees that
we will find such a background consensus or be able, reasoning carefully from that consensus, to resolve the issues or even narrow them.
But that there are no a priori guarantees should not be worrisome
if we have good empirical reasons to believe such a consensus is achievable. And we do have this. And, even if we only have the initial consensus, we then can know that strong incommensurability theses are
mistaken. We are not caught in radically different conceptual universes,
points of view or forms of life between which there are, and can be,
no bridges to a rational and objective resolution of what sets us apart.
We do not have to be rationalists not to believe in a post-modernist
alienation of reason.

NOTES

1 There are a variety of criss-crosses here. There can be contractarian
theories which are utilitarian and projectivist or non-cognitivist theories which can be construed as ontological theses about values, as theses
about the logical status of moral utterances, or as epistemological theses
about whether, and if so in what way, some moral reactions can be
knowledge claims. But a non-cognitivist or projectivist might also be
a utilitarian, a perfectionist or a deontologist. We have, in fine, a considerable range of combinations and permutations here.

2 John Rawls, *A Theory of Justice* (Cambridge, MA: Harvard University Press 1971), 19-21, 48-51, 577-87; 'The Independence of Moral Theory,' *Proceedings and Addresses of the American Philosophical Association* **48** (1974-75) 5-22, 7-10. Norman Daniels, 'Wide Reflective Equilibrium and Theory Acceptance in Ethics,' *The Journal of Philosophy* **76** (1979) 256-82; 'Moral Theory and Plasticity of Persons,' *The Monist* **62** (1979) 265-87; 'On Some Methods of Ethics and Linguistics,' *Philosophical Studies* **37** (1980) 21-36; 'Reflective Equilibrium and Archimedean Points,' *Canadian Journal of Philosophy* **10** (1980) 83-103; 'Two Approaches to Theory Acceptance in Ethics,' in David Copp and David Zimmerman, eds., *Morality, Reason and Truth* (Totowa, NJ: Rowman and Allanheld 1985); and 'An Argument About the Relativity of Justice,' *Revue Internationale de Philosophie* (1987). Jane English, 'Ethics and Science,' *Proceedings of the XVI World Congress of Philosophy*. Marsha Hanen, 'Justification as Coherence,' in M.A. Stewart, ed., *Law, Morality and Rights* (Boston: D. Reidel 1983) 67-92. Kai Nielsen, 'On Needing a Moral Theory: Rationality, Considered Judgements and the Grounding of Morality,' *Metaphilosophy* **13** (1982) 97-116; 'Considered Judgments Again,' *Human Studies* **5** (1982) 109-18; and *Equality and Liberty* (Totowa, NJ: Rowman and Allanheld 1985), Chapter 2.

3 John Rawls, 'Justice as Fairness: Political not Metaphysical,' *Philosophy and Public Affairs* **14** (1985) 223-51; 'The Independence of Moral Theory'; 'The Idea of an Overlapping Consensus,' *Oxford Journal of Legal Studies* **7**.1 (1987) 1-25

4 John Rawls, 'The Independence of Moral Theory'; 'A Well-Ordered Society,' in Peter Laslett and James Fishkin, eds., *Philosophy, Politics and Society*, Fifth Series (New Haven, CT: Yale University Press 1979) 6-20

5 G.A. Cohen, 'Reconsidering Historical Materialism,' in J.R. Pennock and John W. Chapman, eds., *Nomos XXVI, Marxism* (New York: New York University Press 1983); Isaiah Berlin, *Vico and Herder* (London: Hogarth Press 1976), 145-216

6 Rawls, *A Theory of Justice*, 580-1

7 Ibid.

8 J.L. Mackie, *Contemporary Linguistic Philosophy – Its Strength and Its Weakness* (Dunedin, New Zealand: University of Otago Press 1956); *Ethics: Inventing Right and Wrong* (Harmondsworth: Penguin Books 1977); *Hume's Moral Theory* (London: Routledge and Kegan Paul 1980).

For a discussion of Mackie's views and, more generally, of projectivism and the rejection of objective prescriptivity, see the essays in Ted Honderich, ed., *Morality and Objectivity* (London: Routledge and Kegan Paul 1985).

9 Charles Taylor, *Philosophy and the Human Sciences* (Cambridge: Cambridge University Press 1985), 155. Given the slaughter and degradation of humans by humans so characteristic of the twentieth century, from Hitlerism and Stalinism, to South Africa, to the actions of the United States Government in sustaining what it regards as its own sphere of influence either on its own or through its proxies, it is hard to believe that there really are out there the beliefs of which Taylor speaks. What can be said is that while the people portrayed in Icelandic sagas could hack away at each other with a clear conscience, we need complicated rationalizations to butcher and torture each other, and without these rationalizations there is a widespread horror and revulsion at the killing and the infliction of suffering. So there is a tortured way in which we really do believe that needless suffering is to be avoided. However, even with us there may be subcultures without such a belief.

10 Rawls, *A Theory of Justice*, 21, 579

11 See the references in Note 2 and most particularly Daniels's 'Reflective Equilibrium and Archimedean Points.'

12 Michel Foucault, 'Human Nature: Justice versus Power,' in Fons Elders, ed., *Reflexive Water* (London: Souvenir Press 1974), 168. This is a debate with Noam Chomsky.

13 Bernard Williams, *Ethics and the Limits of Philosophy* (Cambridge, MA: Harvard University Press 1985), 74, 120, 151-3, 171-3, and 198

14 It would have to be what has been called 'grand theory.' See Quentin Skinner, ed., *The Return of Grand Theory in the Human Sciences* (London: Cambridge University Press 1985). To be valuable it would have to have the constraints Frederick Crews notes in 'The House of Grand Theory,' *The New York Review of Books* **33**.9 (May 29, 1986) 36-43.

15 Frederick Crews, 'The House of Grand Theory,' rightly stresses the need for such constraints but wrongly claims that Marxist or Freudian theories must be retrograde in this respect, functioning more like religious *Weltanschauungen* than scientific theories. Richard Miller shows how Marxist accounts can be genuine social science, meeting

the constraints Crews requires without the positivist fetters that Crews takes to be hobbling. See Richard Miller, *Analyzing Marx* (Princeton, NJ: Princeton University Press 1984). See also Rodger Beehler's critical notice of Miller's book in the *Canadian Journal of Philosophy* **17**.1 (1987) 199-226.

16 Perhaps the most crucial thing to see here is his exchange with Rorty. See Richard Rorty, 'Habermas and Lyotard on Postmodernity' and Jürgen Habermas, 'Questions and Counterquestions,' both in Richard J. Bernstein, ed., *Habermas and Modernity* (Cambridge, MA: The MIT Press 1985). But see, as well, Habermas's 'The Genealogical Writing of History: On Some Aporias in Foucault's Theory of Power,' *Canadian Journal of Political and Social Theory* **10** (1986) 1-9, and his 'Modernity versus Postmodernity,' *New German Critique*, **22** (Winter, 1981) 3-14.

17 For a sense of the complexity of the concept of objectivity see Thomas Nagel, 'The Limits of Objectivity,' in Sterling McMurrin, ed., *The Tanner Lectures on Human Values*, Vol. 1 (Salt Lake City: University of Utah Press 1980) 77-139. See also Bernard Williams's *Ethics and the Limits of Philosophy* and discussions of his book by H.L.A. Hart, *The New York Review of Books*, **33**.12 (July 17, 1986) 49-52, and by Thomas Nagel, *The Journal of Philosophy* **83** (1986) 351-9.

18 Isaac Levi, 'Escape From Boredom: Edification According to Rorty,' *Canadian Journal of Philosophy* **11** (1981) 589-602; and my 'Scientism, Pragmatism and the Fate of Philosophy,' *Inquiry* **29** (1986) 277-304, and 'Can There Be Progress in Philosophy?', *Metaphilosophy* **18**.1 (1987) 1-30.

19 Levi, 'Escape From Boredom'

Dieter Misgeld

The Limits of a Theory of Practice: How Pragmatic Can a Critical Theory Be?

What is ethical theory to look like in the face of the present attack on foundationalist modes of inquiry in philosophy? Kai Nielsen turns to classical pragmatism and the critical theory of society in his several answers to the conundrum produced for ethical theorists by antifoundationalism:

1. Philosophy can become a form of social critique, addressing real and large scale social problems. Here it pays off, he thinks, to reexamine classical pragmatism as a social theory as well as critical theory.

2. Philosophers can adopt the neo-pragmatist stance of reflective critics of culture and contemporary ideologies. They can practice ad hoc and piecemeal criticism in determinate contexts.[1]

3. Philosophers can practice the method of wide reflective equilibrium and appeal to our most considered judgments, in order to organize them into a coherent package of beliefs, always open to revision.[2]

For Nielsen this third answer is the strongest answer to acquiescent relativism and a 'retreat from liberalism' frequently entailed by antifoundationalist positions.[3]

My argument is that Nielsen's first and second answers to antifoundationalism are better than his third, because they aim at less. They also pose the relation between a critical theory of society and pragmatism as a problem. I attend to this problem in the first two sections of the paper, with heavy emphasis on Rorty's neopragmatism in the second. I argue in the third section that we need a different reconciliation of critical theory with the neopragmatist critique of foundationalism from the one Nielsen intends. This last step leads back to a Deweyan conception of the relation between philosophy and the social disciplines.

I The Rejection of Pragmatism by Critical Theory

Critical theory has never merely been a normative theory of society or neo-Hegelian social philosophy. It has seen itself as continuous as well as discontinuous with the classical and non-empiricist traditions of philosophy. It aimed, in its beginning phase, at an alternative to the transformation of philosophy into either a methodology of scientific discovery or an articulation of experiences untouched by the process of scientific rationalization and Weberian disenchantment.[4]

At least since Horkheimer's seminal essay on 'Traditional and Critical Theory,'[5] critical theorists have looked for a theoretical position, not available in most forms of academic philosophy, which would permit them to say in what way twentieth-century societies were deficient. They did so in a manner quite opposite to pragmatism. Theirs is a different sense of what 'large scale social problems' are from, for example, Dewey's. First-generation critical theorists such as Benjamin, Horkheimer, Adorno, and Marcuse vehemently rejected the spirit of problem-solving with which Dewey's philosophy is imbued, and they did not believe in elaborating a procedure for identifying social problems which would be geared toward potential solutions of these problems. In short, they rejected successful action as a criterion for the truth of their diagnoses of twentieth-century societies.

Some earlier critical theorists developed a method of social and cultural criticism which consisted in a mixture of apparently ad hoc observations and general reflection. It was meant to provoke startled awareness of the absence of any non-repressive reconciliation between individual autonomy and social solidarity in modern societies. Reflection on the absence of reconciliation was to help people experience the extent of coercion and collective violence present in history. The existence of suppressed violence was traced in the mute fragments of modern everyday life as well as in the dominant philosophies. This method teaches by example, letting 'determinate negation' illuminate a particular event, practice, or institution, as if rearranging it into a new constellation of elements. Things, persons, societies in their concrete detail are confronted with what they are not, thus making us see them in their incompleteness.[6]

Critical theory, when practised in this form, is more critique than theory. It displays everyday life in modern societies as fragmented and senseless without calling upon a well-worked-out theoretical apparatus. It is as fragmentary in its own theorizing as the life which it reflects. Thus, while not piecemeal critique in the form Nielsen alludes to, i.e., a critique which presents concrete alternatives, it is critique in the form of determinate negation. This approach is clearly opposite to that of classical pragmatism and the search for creative solutions to concrete problems which Nielsen wishes to continue in his own domain.

Horkheimer linked Dewey's pragmatism to the practical-mindedness of American business culture, thus expressing aversion to the accommodation of reflective thought to existing society.[7] In their 'Dialectic of Enlightenment,' Horkheimer and Adorno lumped pragmatism, Leninist Marxism, and any 'Baconian' philosophy of science or theory of knowledge together, branding all of this 'blindly pragmatized thought.'[8]

For Adorno theorizing had no method other than the systematic negation of all modes of reflection which accommodate thought to reality. The method of 'Negative Dialectics' is philosophy as anti-methodology. This is the essence of the critical-theoretical critique of positivism, indebted as it may be to Hegel's or Marx's conceptions of societal totality as the 'object' of dialectical assertions. 'Negative-dialectical' assertions do not offer positive statements about reality which add up to a comprehensive view. Critical theory can only educate our sense of anticipation about possible solutions to social problems by making any particular solution appear partial to particular interests. The perspective is eschatological and non-naturalist, but also secular. It is an argument for utopian hope versus pragmatic expectations. Critical theory is concerned with imagining new possibilities of life for societies.

There is a further reason for the rejection of pragmatism by critical theorists before Habermas. Critical theorists believed (and mostly still believe) that technological and scientific methods of social regulation are a more serious problem for modern societies than philosophy. They think that we need to examine the consequences of social engineering, its 'glories and its dangers.'[9]

While earlier critical theorists saw no glory in social engineering at all, Habermas, for one, recognizes that it has some merits. Regardless of their differences, however, critical theorists cannot approach social engineering with much optimism. They do not share Dewey's belief that the problem-solving capacities accumulated in science, technology, and industry can serve as a measure, directly or indirectly, of social institutions (such as law and morality). For them pragmatist conceptions of social reconstruction can lead to the imposition of engineering criteria upon social institutions which are much better understood by a method of internal and normative critique.

While Horkheimer and Adorno certainly recognized that the soft rule and mass-indoctrination of American business culture differ from direct coercion and the genocidal policies adopted elsewhere, they attempted to draw attention to the long-term implications of the practical utilitarianism of this culture. They allude to the need to reconnect the ideas and ideals of Enlightenment emancipation with the social experiences of the population. Speculative thought is to reclaim itself from philosophies which direct it towards practical tasks, such as the elaboration of methodologies, logics of inquiry, or practical ethics. Speculative thought and esoteric modernist art have to take the place which religious conceptions once held. They have to be cast in such a form that they cannot be incorporated into the organization of social progress by way of the implementation of scientifically aided programs of social regulation.

If there is to be an integration of critical social theory into moral philosophy, as Nielsen wants, it ought to take note of critical theory as a critique of instrumental rationality. This critique needs to influence our sense of what a social problem is, how it is distinct from a moral problem, and how we need to look for solutions in a domain different from social policy and practical deliberation about current problems. Critical theory is incompatible with both the straightforwardly moralistic claim that present society is illegitimate and the claim that we know how to secure an ever widening consensus in moral and political judgments via the method of wide reflective equilibrium. Neither of these claims does justice to the fact that society is geared toward the suppression or the rhetorical manipulation of ethical questions.[10]

In sum, critical theory is capable of social and cultural critique in determinate contexts, but its sense of large-scale social problems, such as that of technical or instrumental rationality, contradicts pragmatism's, and possibly Nielsen's. It is a large scale narrative of modernity (as Nielsen perhaps wants), having as its theme the growth of scientific and technical knowledge and the concomitant domestication of reflective and aesthetic capacities. As such it is compatible with German romanticism and idealism, the Weberian diagnosis of capitalism, and some forms of cultural criticism and pessimism practised in Weimar Germany. Its picture of modernity is thus thoroughly anti-pragmatist.

II The Neopragmatist Reply

In order to see how pragmatism and critical theory can be joined, as welcomed by Nielsen and made possible by Habermas's transformation of critical theory into a theory of problems of societal reproduction in the late-capitalist welfare-state democracies,[11] it is important to learn whether neopragmatism is a serious alternative to both.

Rorty may be willing to let us indulge in talk of universal and non-repressive reconciliation as the earlier critical theorists did, but for him this talk can only express private desires and hopes. It is not acceptable as a social and public ideal. For Rorty, having these notions and making the negative dialectical claim that reality is deficient in failing to meet the expectations expressed in them is not an advance over pragmatism. For once again philosophy would be put ahead of democracy, of the working out in practice of different conceptions of public life and its quality. Rorty thus views the critical theory of Horkheimer and Adorno as unduly pessimistic. They underestimate the beneficial role of social engineering in the formation of liberal democracies and welfare-state social policies, turning social engineering into the villain, and hoping for ways to overcome it with philosophy, rather than distinguishing good from bad social engineering and leaving philosophy to explore new possibilities of life in the imagination.[12] Moreover, they treat universal emancipation as a necessary concept rather than as an expression of contingent possibilities available from the actual histories of modern societies.

Critical theorists such as Adorno may also be taken to look for a foundational discipline, such as the critique of political economy, which is to give a rock-bottom kind of knowledge of why things go wrong, whereas this critique should be taken to be merely one conception of the fate of modernity against which a variety of other accounts have to be kept in the running.

Most of all, critical theorists, whether they follow Horkheimer and Adorno or Habermas, seem to expect more of theory than it can give. Instead of talking of theories, they talk of a theory of society in the singular, and the theory is to have social practice as its object rather than its starting point.

Nielsen also looks for an 'adequate account of what society is like'[13] and this account is to be delivered in the form of a warrantably-asserted set of claims which emphasize sociological over purely moral considerations. In his 'Theory of Communicative Action' Habermas has produced just such a theory, giving prominence to sociology over ethical and political theory. This procedure has the effect that, in Nielsen's terms, the 'best moral point of view which we can garner' at a given time already is a view of the limits and possibilities of practical and moral reasoning and of the interpretive freedom available to us within the parameters of societal reproduction in late capitalist societies. This social theory of morality has a scope which may make neopragmatists recoil in disbelief, but it is attractive for a moral theorist cum critical theorist such as Nielsen.

However, this theory requires us to distinguish large-scale social problems from more common types of moral dilemmas. The theory is to assure us of the meaning of modernity as a whole and of the possible completion of this meaning in the future. It is for this reason, and not in order to clarify more ordinary forms of moral disagreement, that Habermas pursues a counterfactual model of normative deliberation. Pragmatic and local elements have to be removed from our model-conceptions of practical deliberation because our vision of the possible completion of modernity otherwise succumbs too quickly to present and unexamined exigencies. It is the removal of *all* obstacles to probing convictions in arguments and freeing deliberative capacities which, for Habermas, makes up the Enlightenment project and a conceivable future meaning of modernity and its idea of universality.

Neopragmatists can understand a search for procedures to resolve present moral disputes but find it odd that critical theorists believe theory capable of knowing wherein the completion of the future might consist. They might agree that Habermas has found a very cogent new formulation for interpreting processes of unblocking inquiry, democratic deliberation, and public will-formation, one that repeats Deweyan insights in a manner adequate to our times. However, Habermas would make more sense, neopragmatists might say, if he just dropped allusions to some underlying historical compulsion or to the idea that we can extrapolate from the processes in question toward the future of modernity. There is no need to look below the surface for such profound dimensions: the drama is exciting and challenging enough. Thus Habermas, and Nielsen, aim in the wrong direction when they look for perspicuous general models of normative deliberation to be put into place as part of the reconstruction of modernity.

Sometimes Habermas seems to recognize that his theory can merely help the social sciences come to terms with the universalist assumptions of modern democratic thought, thus releasing the potential of the social sciences to aid us in strengthening our commitments to universal value-beliefs and to the inclusion of everyone in processes of normative deliberation. But, given his preference for the theoretical components of the social sciences and concomitant indifference to the applied social disciplines,[14] neopragmatists will suspect that there is still too much of the legacy of the critique of instrumental reason operative here — of Horkheimer's and Adorno's attempt to salvage Enlightenment reason by placing it beyond any practical implementation. I wonder whether Nielsen has accounted for this legacy in his own optimistic embrace of critical theory as a remedy to the shortcomings of ethical theory?

And what about the central question of Habermas's recent work: whether developed industrial societies are capable of reconciling their enormous economic and administrative knowledge with the communicative and moral knowledge we intuitively possess of ourselves and our social traditions?[15] It is not merely our moral intuitions and political beliefs which clash but also different institutional and organizational logics. This is not a process out of which we can work ourselves by analyzing our moral beliefs one after the other as Nielsen would have us do, for here we come across politics. Habermas's question is whether we can identify an historical logic of the development of institutions and social movements pointing toward a politics capable of responding to the exhaustion of forms of intuitive moral and social knowledge acquired in everyday communication. As the exhaustion is due to economic, administrative, and (as one might add) military rationalization, the politics in question must protest the primacy of economic and administrative conceptions of the social good. The notion of communicative rationality central to Habermas's work functions as a symbol for a variety of attempts to make the imperatives of run-away instrumental system-rationalization in advanced capitalism responsive to people's needs and concrete experiences.

The Rortyan picture of society, the social disciplines and morals basically denies that it makes sense to carve up society into domains of instrumental knowledge on the one hand and of moral and communicative knowledge on the other. It does not share either the Horkheimer-Adorno premise that the growth of instrumental reason is potentially totalitarian or Habermas's fears that social reproduction is endangered unless the cultural resources of communicative reason can be mobilized against rationalization pressures emanating from concentrated corporate and state power. Rorty believes that welfare-state democracies are not nearly as endangered by their internal dynamics as Habermas thinks; and, if they are, theoreticians are not in a position to do much about it.[16] Habermas's ideal of communicative rationality appears to him to be no more than an expression of the need to continue to develop and maintain the relevant liberal democratic and social democratic convictions.[17]

It is misguided to expect that the social disciplines can set us straight about these matters (as Nielsen thinks) by helping us distinguish useful social knowledge from ideological claims or (as Habermas thinks) by finding a truly critical social science. These disciplines are insufficiently responsive to the employment of various forms of engineering knowledge, problem-solving, or other kinds of knowledge and interpretation addressed to specific problems arising in particular contexts. Habermas and Nielsen proceed as if having some general idea of solutions to specific social problems is the same as having a general normative theory of such solutions or a systematic theory of the direction which modern societies must take. All such conceptions distract from the need to come to terms with present circumstances in the best possible way, given whatever there is in terms of useful methods, theories, or rules of thumb, which are in rough conformity with democratic ideals available in the relevant traditions.

III The Integration of Critical Theory into Pragmatism

My summary of potential neopragmatist arguments against critical theory (and against an undertaking such as Nielsen's) does not seek to endorse the partial retreat from progressive liberalism, which seems to be a side-effect of Rorty's anti-foundationalist arguments regarding the relation between philosophy and democratic societies. Rather it raises the questions (1) whether there indeed is a role for critical theory in the examination of large scale social problems and (2) how this role is to be pursued if social inquiry can only be what Rorty says it is, namely, a contribution to work on particular circumstances and problems.

(1) In response to Rorty (and his use of Lyotard's arguments)[18] Habermas reaffirms that one can still speak of 'rationality' in the singular. It is the task of philosophy, albeit a modest task, to preserve the difference between 'valid and socially accepted views, between good arguments and those which are merely successful for a certain audience at a certain time.'[19] Because we have learned to live with dissenting convictions, we need to preserve these distinctions, although Rorty denies that they can be sustained within Habermas's view. Dissent and 'faith' in its possible resolution are incentives for learning processes which, as Habermas says, can only be nurtured by the expectation of future resolutions. This expectation is an unconditional element in our momentary and ad hoc deliberations. A similar expectation underlies Nielsen's belief that by adopting the procedure of wide reflective equilibrium we can work toward rational consensus and overcome the inhibiting effect of believing that all we can achieve is passing agreement. But is there not still an important difference between hoping that disagreements can be overcome in argument and pursuing solutions to large scale social problems (which Nielsen recommends as a task for the future)?

Habermas is convinced that in order to look for the right solutions in the right way we need to be committed to the idea of a rational society. A society is rational which has instituted procedures for open deliberation and argument as the mechanism of conflict resolution in all domains of social life where conflicts may arise. Habermas grants to pragmatists that they have the proper sense of how problems arise. Problems arise because they 'objectively happen to us,'[20] not because philosophers instigate them. A fortiori this holds for large scale social problems. What then, do philosophers such as Nielsen and Habermas want when they argue for rational consensus as a goal to be pursued? They mean to incite doubt about the validity of the institutions and practices we have. Many present institutions and practices are illegitimate, or may yet become illegitimate, and we can notice this illegitimacy by developing a comprehensive social theory. Their strong emphasis on normative considerations as the core of this theory thus suggests that making existing institutions and practices appear as in need of improvement is among its central tasks. Since this is far from addressing specific social ills in their concrete manifestation, Habermas and Nielsen share the antipragmatist stance of the earlier critical theorists. They differ from the earlier critical theorists in arguing that a holistic critical theory is a research program to be confirmed or infirmed in the future.

In Habermas's case, this research program is to be tested in the development of the social sciences themselves as well as in the actions of emancipatory social movements. In Nielsen's case the research program is to be tested in the achievement of consensus, by way of building up a coherent set of moral/practical beliefs beginning with our most evident moral certainties. In either case the holistic theory is not testable in the same sense as are specific hypotheses about institutional practices. It is not a program for institutional reform, addressing one social practice after another in order to see whether it can indeed be reformed. Thus the theory is not directly at stake in institutional reform. The question is whether critical theory can be a research program of any kind under these conditions. Indeed, it cannot be.

(2) I propose as an alternative, that critical theory be fused with pragmatist elements, with something like Dewey's trust in problem-solving and social research as a form of practical experimentation as well as his belief that both are compatible with the common practical sense of people living in democratic communities. The critical-theoretical doubts about 'scientific' problem-solving can be inscribed into the design of practical social experiments testing the limits of present-day societies. One need not work out a new and more theoretical social science (as Habermas wants), but merely employ available *or* future research imaginatively and cautiously at the same time. Thus critical-theoretical reservations over the power of instrumental

rationality could be combined with pragmatist faith in the legitimacy of and need for social experimentation. The issue would always be the compatibility of problem-solving capacities with democratic will-formation. A pragmatically reconceived critical theory can understand itself to be in question in the very process of testing the limits of present day societies and practices.

Deweyan pragmatism argued for the acceptability and desirability of such tests, but it optimistically believed in their success before their outcome could be known. With critical theory we may accept that this optimism is less warranted after technological and scientific criteria of social development have lost their plausibility as the dominant criteria of social progress. Thus critical theory can make pragmatism more critical of itself, but one can still maintain with pragmatism that our sense of social problems depends on practical experimentation. This sense of problems can certainly be deepened by appealing either to a comprehensive conception of democratic will-formation or to our 'most considered judgments.'

Nielsen's and Habermas's views are ambiguous. On the one hand they privilege an idealized conception of rational consensus in order to say that an existent consensus may be less than rational, supportive of illegitimate interests, or not fully attuned to the need to bring forth argumentation to treat dissent and conflict. On the other hand they appeal to existing practices of deliberation, or their presumptive conditions (such as universal pramatic ones in Habermas's case), and want to move from these practices to normative ideas without considering the intermediate domain of specific problems in which creative social intelligence is called upon to invent solutions. So far, they only offer a set of metatheoretical considerations, possibly applicable to a great variety of heterogenous problems (from the environment and nuclear war to the political effects of social movements and new forms of dependency and paternalism resulting from welfare-state practices). A theory of discursive and uncoerced will-formation gives the illusion that all these problems can be seen to be a problem of 'reason' and its embodiment in present institutions. This view of the role of theory is neither practically helpful nor does it help to clarify our more diffuse sense of what is desirable.

Rorty is closer to Deweyan views of these matters, including Dewey's conviction that the relation of individual freedom to organizations is a question of social experimentation addressing specific details of the relation.[21] It is not a question of wholesale theory. Solutions to social problems, even where they require justificatory theory, must appeal to practical results; the better argument at a given time addresses the conceivable and available results of attempts to achieve solutions. However, while Habermas's and Nielsen's views are clouded in ambiguity, Rorty is too 'cheerily indifferent' to most of the social issues mentioned above. He ignores the detailed accounts given of them in a great deal of critical theory.

Critical theory is important as an articulation of these large-scale problems because it is something like a theoretical narrative of how they are linked, rather than a rigorous explanation of their emergence or a construction of normative conceptions equally applicable to all of them. It states a set of difficulties and survival-problems for modern societies which can inform our practical sense of any immediate problem. Critical theory, therefore, ought to be taken simply as a narrative which can inspire us to look beyond piecemeal solutions to social problems by deepening our sense of how they are all linked in the history of societies. It is a mistake to think (and here Rorty is right) that having notions of undistorted discourse and communication can really be regarded as a solution or, as Nielsen wants, turned into a method for solving specific problems.

A critical theory is a background to concrete steps in social learning in particular contexts belonging to the history of modernity. From the Deweyan point of view this history primarily consists in the acceptance of democracy, the taming of capitalism in social democracy and the welfare state, and the use of science and social research for the sake of improving public policy and individual self-understanding. From the standpoint of critical theory, however, it consists in the suppression of democracy, the possibly fatal conflict between military/economic blocs, the use of science and social research in maintaining the conflict, and public and private corporate policies leading to the exhaustion of human capacities and the natural environment. Critical theory has developed a picture of modernity in all its facets, much more thoroughly and eloquently than Dewey or any other philosophy. It is a narrative indispensable for any interpretation of our overall contemporary sense of social problems, and it does what philosophers like Nielsen want when they seek a place for theory in our articulation of social issues. It is a vision of a rational society, combined with the depiction of the irrationalities of the present.

Because such a theory does not give answers to the questions of the day, it cannot take a position on the advisability of social change or reform. It cannot show how society can change except in the most general sense. In the face of any concrete problem it will not help to know that social engineering can be used as a shibboleth, confounding distinctions between practical-moral problems (such as abortion) and technical ones (such as methods of birth-control and contraception), between questions of democratic will-formation and expert competence. When real reforms are at issue merely drawing clear conceptual boundaries around engineering knowledge versus moral knowledge will not do, nor will it suffice to articulate a final goal for these reforms, known in advance of real experimentation. Critical theorists need to recognize their dependence on those engaging in practical social experimentation. They should not, as do Habermas and Nielsen, expect theory far removed from the 'daily detail' to achieve clarification about the fundamental values underlying experiments with social conditions; nor should they claim, as Habermas sometimes does, that theory is not part of social experimentation. Critical theorists have something to contribute nevertheless.

As theorists concerned with general principles, policies and forms of social organization, they can single out cases of social experimentation and reform where increases in social efficiency can be achieved exactly by way of democratic participation. From here they can move to other cases, where the relation between participation and effectiveness is less clear. They can engage in a detailed appraisal of social engineering with reference to ideas of democracy and the possible institutionalization of forms of association which require a decreased reliance on instrumental relations between people. They can also point out to social movements engaging in a high-minded form of moralizing and critique that to neglect pragmatic, prudential, and other considerations regarding the possible effectiveness of actions will not help them achieve their goals: it can also lead to fanaticism and dogmatism.

From time to time, then, one may venture beyond the realm of pragmatic decision-making and entertain Habermasean conjectures about a future society: that post-conventional identities can be formed, that post-material values can be institutionalized, that there can be a systematic exchange between expert knowledge and every-day reasoning, that socialism may still have a future. These are speculations which theory cannot articulate further until the relevant new social movements have brought about the institutional changes required or until more basic problems have been solved. Social experiments in this domain have to operate at their own risk for the time being, as Habermas always has argued.

By working through a number of cases of social reform and policy deliberation which have the relation between effectiveness and democratic participation as a theme,[22] philosophers may find that they can indeed identify the points at which the critical-theoretical vision of modernity makes a practical difference. Together with social researchers, planners, and others, they can work on methods which overcome the traditional division between technical and practical knowledge. The perception of contemporary realities which critical theory has begun to assemble into one picture can inform a philosopher's involvement with the tasks of real communities.

What can theory contribute to improving practice? What are the implications for theory of the application of this criterion? A pragmatic awareness of the limits of theory needs to be built into our design of theory. Otherwise theorizing becomes a comforting substitute for practice rather than a guide operative in it — 'reflection-in-action,' as Dewey envisaged it. Dewey distinguished the pragmatist social-democratic vision from both the traditional liberalism which is indifferent to theory and social critique and from the revolutionary Marxism which is obsessed with theory and oblivious to the need for caution in the translation of theory into practice. A holistic critical theory, despite its obvious advances over traditional liberalism and Marx's theory of history and critique of political economy, has, as yet, not sufficiently accepted the exigencies of practice as limits to its own theorizing.

NOTES

1 Kai Nielsen, 'Scientism, Pragmatism and the Fate of Philosophy,' *Inquiry* **29** (1987) 277-304; and 'Searching For an Emancipatory Perspective: Wide Reflective Equilibrium and the Hermeneutical Circle,' above.

2 Nielsen, 'Searching for an Emancipatory Perspective,' 144 ff.

3 Kai Nielsen, 'Can There Be Progress in Philosophy?', *Metaphilosophy* **18**.1 (1987) 1-30

4 I am alluding to Horkheimer's critiques of logical positivism and of 'Lebensphilosophie' in Max Horkheimer, *Critical Theory* (New York: Herder and Herder 1973), 10-47 and 136-87. I also have Theodor Adorno's critique of Husserl and Heidegger in mind. See his *Against Epistemology. A Metacritique* (Cambridge, MA: MIT Press 1983) and *Negative Dialectics* (New York: Seabury Press 1973). Herbert Marcuse's attack on linguistic philosophy also belongs here. See his *One-Dimensional Man* (Boston: Beacon Press 1984), 123-202. All of these are critiques of foundationalist tendencies in philosophy, arguing against renewals of 'first' philosophy or against the independence of philosophy from social practice. But they are not reductionist critiques, as is evident from Horkheimer, *Critical Theory*.

5 Max Horkheimer, 'Traditional and Critical Theory,' in his *Critical Theory*.

6 Cf. Martin Jay, *Permanent Exiles: Essays on the Intellectual Migration From Germany to America* (New York: Columbia University Press 1985), 115. See also Walter Benjamin, *Das Passagenwerk* (Frankfurt: Suhrkamp 1983); and Walter Benjamin, 'Theses on the Philosophy of History,' in his *Illuminations*, ed. H. Arendt (New York: Schocken Books 1973), 253-65. Adorno developed his negative dialectics out of Benjamin's micrological studies of historical change and cultural transformation. Susan Buck-Morss has traced the relation of Adorno to Benjamin in *The Origin of Negative Dialectics* (New York: The Free Press 1977).

7 Max Horkheimer, *Eclipse of Reason* (New York: Seabury Press 1974), 42-91

8 Max Horkheimer and Theodor Adorno, *The Dialectic of Enlightenment* (New York: Herder and Herder 1972), xiii. For the two critical

theorists Bacon's slogan that 'knowledge is power' represents the degeneration of reason to instrumental reason. Their view is opposite to Dewey's, who regarded Bacon as the earliest hero of modernity. See John Dewey, *Reconstruction in Philosophy* (Boston: Beacon Press 1972), 28-38.

9 Richard Rorty, *Consequences of Pragmatism* (Minneapolis: University of Minnesota Press 1982), 203

10 Jürgen Habermas, *Toward a Rational Society* (Boston: Beacon Press 1970), 106-8

11 Jürgen Habermas, *Legitimation Crisis* (Boston: Beacon Press 1973) and *Theorie des kommunikativen Handelns*, vol. 2: *Kritik der funktionalistischen Vernunft* (Frankfurt: Suhrkamp 1981), 489-549

12 Rorty, *Consequences*, 203

13 Nielsen, 'Searching For An Emancipatory Perspective,' 155

14 I am referring to Habermas's belief that philosophy, by defending universalist claims, can hold the place for those sciences or social sciences willing to examine strong theoretical claims. This is why he believes that his is not a foundationalist theory. It only anticipates possibilities of inquiry for the social sciences and is not self-sufficient. See Jürgen Habermas, *Moralbewusstsein und Kommunikatives Handeln* (Frankfurt: Suhrkamp 1982), 9-27. See J. Forester, ed., *Critical Theory and Public Life* (Cambridge, MA: MIT Press 1986) for attempts (including my own) to develop an understanding of the applied social disciplines commensurate with critical theory.

15 I am alluding to the widely discussed theme of the 'colonization of the social life-world' in Habermas, *Theorie des kommunikativen Handelns*, Vol. 2, 489-547. This theme stands for a reinterpretation of Marx's theories of 'Verdinglichung' and alienation.

16 Richard Rorty, 'The Priority of Democracy to Philosophy,' in M. Peterson and R. Vaughan, eds., *The Virginia Statute of Religious Freedom* (Cambridge: Cambridge University Press 1987)

17 Richard Rorty, 'Habermas and Lyotard on Postmodernity,' in R.J. Bernstein, ed., *Habermas and Modernity* (Cambridge: MIT Press 1985)

18 See ibid.

19 Jürgen Habermas, 'Questions and Counterquestions,' in Bernstein, *Habermas and Modernity*, 194

20 Ibid., 198

21 John Dewey, *The Public and Its Problems* (New York: Henry Holt 1927, 1957), 282

22 Carole Pateman, *Participation and Democratic Theory* (Cambridge: Cambridge University Press 1970), chs. 3 and 4, has examined the compatibility of efficiency in the workplace with its democratization.

Barry G. Allen

Groundless Goodness

Kai Nielsen's paper, 'Searching for an Emancipatory Perspective,' draws from two currents of philosophical thought: the Frankfurt School and especially Habermas, and the Social Contract and especially Rawls. Dieter Misgeld's comments on the paper concern the former component; mine concern the latter. I disagree with the use to which Nielsen puts Rawls's idea of reflective equilibrium, and to explain why I will draw from other sources in contemporary philosophy, in particular from Davidson and Derrida.

I

Inquiry owes its success to its own previous fortune. It knows no absolute beginning nor uniquely proper method, no finally valid answer nor teleological end. It has always already begun with questions already posed by answers already given. Impressed with this, Heidegger wrote: 'any interpretation which is to contribute to understanding must already have understood what is to be interpreted.'

> But if we see this circle as a vicious one and look out for ways of avoiding it, even if we just sense it as an inevitable imperfection, then the act of understanding has been misunderstood from the ground up ...
> What is decisive is not to get out of the circle but to come into it in the right way.[1]

The right way will, of course, differ according to different concerns and contexts of inquiry. When we are thinking reflectively about moral subjects Nielsen thinks we come into the circle in the right way by ranging broadly in all that we once called the moral sciences, aiming for equilibrium in the well-considered moral judgments that make us a body politic.

This is not moral philosophy as usual. At least since the Enlightenment moral theory has inclined toward what Nielsen, Norman Daniels, and others call a narrow or partial equilibrium.[2] This we get when, with one or a few general moral principles, we can articulate the prevailing intuitive moral consensus. In contrast to this familiar conception of moral theory Nielsen urges that reflection on our considered judgments should range beyond moral intuitions to draw upon what we know of the biological, social, and historical forces responsible for these intuitions. From this more reflective perspective some judgments may appear conditioned by class or culture in a way that undermines their apparent legitimacy.

This theoretical reorientation seems motivated by difficulties inherent in the traditional conception of a moral theory. Whether it claims self-evidence for its principles or guidance from an intuitive faculty for its selection of considered judgments, ethical reflection in partial equilibrium is committed to a foundationalist moral epistemology. But the epistemology of intuition and self-evidence merely serves an historically particular consensus, presenting it as the very substance of rationality. This may make us suspicious of any distinctively *moral* epistemology, and one way to circumvent such theories is the way of wide reflective equilibrium. A moral theory in wide reflective equilibrium would make explicit the principles underlying that consensus which animates ethical life, and yet it would not merely be an intellectual stamp of approval for prevailing prejudices. Intuitions are but provisionally fixed starting points, and under pressure to realize a truly wide equilibrium no considered judgment is immune to revision. The resulting picture would permit those committed to ethical life better to understand just what they are committed to and how that commitment bears on issues whose complexity baffles the unreflective moral consciousness.

I agree with the motives for much of this. I agree that reflective thinking on moral subjects can only be a not-intrinsically-different part of inquiry as such. I also agree that such reflection must be wide-ranging, for the web of belief resists Kant's partition of it into spheres of Science, Morals and Art. But I do not think that merely modifying the form of moral theory in the way Nielsen recommends adequately reflects the reason for dissatisfaction with foundationalism in moral theory.

II

What assumption makes it even seem possible to partition off properly moral judgments from other kinds, like the properly scientific? To understand this we need to see how our moral philosophy is at once modern and ancient. An ancient idea is that the rationality of what we say and do depends on there being something whose presence makes those sayings true, when they are, and those actions good. On this view the possibility of theory demands something for theories to be *true to*: some *thing* whose presence makes one sentence true, another false. Yet even in matters not of theory but of practice this metaphysics still demands something (it may be God or Reason or Nature) capable of determining which commitments are really valuable and rationally compelling. Unless we are irrationally attached to a fabric of illusions, there must be something such that its presence makes life, character, action, or intention really valuable. Anything less would be groundless, mere appearance.

This antique underlies Kant's split between morals and science. As for Aristotle before him, rational judgment for Kant meant grounded judgment. But unlike Aristotle, Kant also had to grant that the Nature Newton's science was true to could not also be the thing whose presence made actions right and character good. He invented the idea of a 'transcendental' kind of reflective thinking, capable of taking not just this or that particular commitment or theory but whole 'spheres' like Science or Morals into view and passing judgment on the adequacy of their grounds. Reflecting in this way on morality, Kant found that no transcendent deity or natural purpose but only practical reason in its pure (disinterested) state must be there to make an intention properly moral. And even though Kant was thus convinced that reflection would return a reassuring verdict on the grounds of moral judgment, after Hegel the consensus held that Kant's moral law was just local *Sittlichkeit* dressed up with groundless universal pretensions. Counterexertions in neo-Kantian moral theory were directed toward an ever more narrowly academic audience, and Hegel's relativism generally prevailed. Yet the emergence of a profoundly non-Aristotelian conception of nature did nothing to dislodge the ancient identification of the rational and the grounded. Not only does this motivate Kant's stubborn differentiation of science and morals; it is responsible for the contemporary illusion that one might bracket all specifically moral commitments while retaining those proper to science. This has made it seem as if moral commitments might just be arbitrary.

Few still believe in something whose presence determines the rightness of action or the goodness of character and life. Rather more common is belief in something whose presence determines which beliefs and theories are true. This peculiar historical situation has made ethical life the target for all those who would transcend the 'moral sphere' and tell us what such commitments are really nothing but: really nothing but ideology; really nothing but a sublimated paternal No; really nothing but the bourgeois sensibility it is Art's higher calling to shock. After more than a century of this, even those who have never read Marx, Nietzsche, or Freud routinely suppose that moral commitments must be really nothing but *something*. Something not properly compelling. Something irrational. Groundless.

This is the situation Philip Rieff describes when he says: 'A reorganization of those dialectical expressions *Yes* and *No* the interplay of which constitutes culture, transforming motive into conduct, is occurring throughout the West ... .' He finds it predictable that 'some instruments appropriate to our organization of permissions and restraints upon action will not survive the tension of fundamental reorganization. But' – and here he poses a question I want to consider:

> suppose the tension is driven deeper – so deep that all communication of ideals comes under permanent and easy suspicion? The question is no longer as Dostoevski put it: "Can civilized men believe?" Rather: Can unbelieving men be civilized?[3]

It is true that there can be no return to a time when common sense confirmed a power not ourselves that makes for righteousness. Yet there is nothing inevitable about that species of Unbelief that believes it knows what ideals are really nothing but. Before we can become Unbelievers we must first believe that ideals, if they are proper objects of commitment, must be made ideal by a correspondingly ideal reality. Only then can conversion to one or another school of the Really-Nothing-But render us suspicious of ideals as such. We are indeed long disabused of belief in an ideal reality making one fabric of ethical reactions and social organization uniquely rational. Mental equilibrium lies not in the direction of rehabilitated ideas of moral truth and objectivity but in a firmer recognition of what for a long time we have done very well without, namely a presence which does for theory what metaphysicians of morals asked God, Reason, or Human Nature to do for practice. Unless we already believed that there must be something whose presence determines the virtue of one disposition, or the truth of one theory, to the exclusion of all competitors, there would be no point to somebody's telling us that there is no such thing and that our ethical life (or our science) is really nothing but ... . If we see not separate 'spheres' but only many lines of inquiry and fields of endeavour, everyone inextricably woven in a fabric of belief and commitment shared just because we share a language (that is, a culture, a history), then it will not even seem possible for somebody to step outside of any specifically ethical relationships, look at them whole, and claim that they, unlike the rest, are groundless. The only 'outside' is outside inquiry, outside history, outside language. As this is scarcely a position to occupy, and no place from which to speak, we would do better without the spatial metaphor. When we judge and act we are not peculiarly and comprehensively inside of anything at all.

III

I agree with Nielsen in 'Searching for an Emancipatory Perspective' when he says that reflective thinking on moral subjects 'cannot avoid starting from the deeply-embedded cultural norms' (145). I also agree that 'our sense of what is right or wrong, good or bad, while starting from tradition, may undergo extensive change at the behest of critical reasoning and investigation' (150). This applies to reflection on moral subjects what Quine and pragmatism say of inquiry generally: 'We are limited in how we can start if not in where we may end up.'[4]

According to this conception of inquiry, in justifying ourselves (and I speak indifferently of opinion, theory, action, or choice) we appeal to other opinions, theories, actions and choices. At no point do we break out of the circle, neither with the self-evident principle nor the intuited good. Now there is a certain picture that may naturally attach itself to this understanding of justification but which I think we would better resist. The picture locates our beliefs, ideals, and behaviour within a comprehensive whole which, however, does not rest on sure foundations but somehow holds itself up merely by its internal coherence. There are two reasons to be dissatisfied with this picture. First, it encourages us to think of language (or culture) as having an inside (where we are) and an outside (where equally coherent and self-supporting spheres might sustain persons and projects we find flatly incomprehensible). Davidson has argued, I think very cogently, that radically incommensurable conceptual schemes are not a real possibility.[5] Second, to take a stand against foundationalist epistemology ought to mean more than simply doing without unassailable certainties. A comprehensive structure (whether Science or Science plus Morals, or maybe just 'everything' we believe) is something about which it seems to make perfect sense to ask on what principles it is constructed and whether these principles leave it well-grounded. *Structures* are just the sort of thing to which such questions apply. So why affirm this comprehensive whole but deny it any foundation? I can't blame unreconstructed metaphysicians for rejecting the suggestion that it manages somehow to hold itself up. That is as if something we would like to have (namely, foundations) just can't be found; as if the question of grounds were quite in order, and as if we had to make do with mere equilibrium where some want rock-solid certainty. To step away from foundations is to step away from the picture of culture as containing spheres (or its being itself one comprehensive sphere) to which a supposedly 'transcendental' reflection may attach predicates like 'justified' or 'rational.' This is a step away from the ancient metaphysics that recognizes as real only what is grounded.

Nielsen says that where wide reflective equilibrium is achieved (by means of undistorted discourse) 'we do not merely have a consensus, we have a rational consensus' (158). In the light of my last remarks, this seems to me covert foundationalism. It expects reflective equilibrium to do what Kant asked of the moral law or St. Thomas of his God, namely, to be the thing whose presence determines the justice and rationality not of this or that, but of some proper whole. In the same spirit Nielsen says that if 'a given population at a given place and time ... have put their judgments into WRE' then they will 'have shown that they are justified' (150). Writing of those 'beliefs relevant to how our life in society is to be ordered and how we are to care for our

lives as individuals' he says: 'Justification ... comes to getting these beliefs in WRE.' Why advocate equilibrium in 'all' these beliefs, unless
one assumes that anything less would leave them groundless? Nielsen
sounds like a foundationalist who says that to be properly worthy
of commitment and respect there must be something whose presence
determines that propriety. But there needn't be any such thing, and
there is not. Beliefs and commitments ground other beliefs and commitments, but there is no determinate whole that is everything a person or a people believes and respects and which is, or might fail to
be, well-grounded.

Here I think important differences between Nielsen and Rawls
come to light. Rawls wants reflective equilibrium to settle out 'the
kernel of an overlapping consensus ... sufficient to underwrite a just
constitutional regime.'[6] He describes the envisaged consensus as overlapping precisely because

> liberalism assumes that in a constitutional democratic state under
> modern conditions there are bound to exist conflicting *and incommen-
> surable* conceptions of the good. This feature characterizes modern cul-
> ture since the Reformation. Any viable political conception of justice
> that is not to rely on the autocratic use of state power must recognize
> this fundamental social fact.[7]

This makes justification solely a matter of particular and specifically
political arguments for and against particular and specifically political arrangements. This is rather different from the thought that reflection may look down upon a whole (whether discretely political or
more comprehensive) and pronounce it justified *in virtue of* its
equilibrium.

Also, when Nielsen urges movement toward equilibrium in beliefs about 'how we are to care for our lives as individuals' he seems
to expect consensus on matters rather far beyond Rawls's strictly political conception of justice. Thus it is not clear whether Nielsen would
accept the priority Rawls assigns to justice over the good. Rawls seems
not to believe that justice as fairness could itself overcome the 'deep
divisions between opposing and incommensurable conceptions of the
good' which are characteristic of Western democracies. Instead, it would
provide a way in which those differences could be set aside for the

practical purpose of agreeing on political arrangements under which various and even incommensurable pursuits of happiness might coexist in stable political society.

IV

Wilfrid Sellars is a metaphysician of genius, and he voiced the vision of metaphysics when he said that philosophy is the attempt to understand how things (in the broadest sense) hang together (in the broadest sense).[8] What is metaphysical is precisely the idea of a broad sense of 'things' and a broad sense of their 'hanging together.' Since ancient times a 'way' things hang together is a way things are, and since ancient times that has meant a way things might be said to be — a significant assertion objectively true or false. In the broad sense, things and the ways they hang together are presences called up to make true sentences true. Of course something whose presence makes a given sentence true can scarcely be described with any sentence other than that very one.[9] That is the problem with the broad and metaphysical sense of things hanging together: Things are things under descriptions if they are anything to us at all; but their possible descriptions are many, and nothing is such that it absolutely cannot be variously described. Whatever there may be, there are no things such that their presence is just what it takes to make a belief or theory true.[10]

This should undermine the pessimism of those, such as Bernard Williams, who see a 'genuine and profound difference' between science and ethics; 'enough,' Williams says, 'to motivate some version of the feeling (itself recurrent, if not exactly traditional) that science has some chance of being more or less what it seems, a systematic theoretical account of how the world really is, while ethical thought has no chance of being everything it seems.'[11] What does science seem to be, except what is best in the way of belief, as ethical thought grapples with what is best in the way of choice? There is no good reason to insist there is something for the scientist, but not the teacher, politician, or parent, to be true to.

Movement away from foundations begins with this step away from true-making presences. From there it develops into a general reaction to that originary metaphysics which disdains as mere appearance all that is not demonstrably grounded in something 'really there' whenever sentences are true, dispositions virtuous, or distributions just. Really to be an antifoundationalist is to oppose the appearance that rationality (whether in belief or choice) depends on the presence or absence of something. Call it God or call it wide reflective equilibrium, a ground is a ground, and what faces us is the need to be good without grounds.

And not just to be good but to be cheerful. There is nothing — not reason's law or real interests, not God or Nature or Reflective Equilibrium — such that its presence rationalizes practice. To advance the claims of one of these in favour of the others is to engage in the moral version of what, aiming more broadly, Derrida calls 'the metaphysical ... quest for the proper word and the unique name.'

> There will be no unique name ... And we must think this without *nostalgia*, that is, outside of the myth of ... a lost native country of thought. On the contrary, we must *affirm* this, in the sense in which Nietzsche puts affirmation into play, in a certain laughter and a certain step of the dance.[12,13]

NOTES

1 Martin Heidegger, *Being and Time*, tr. J. Macquarrie and E. Robinson (New York: Harper and Row 1962), 194-5

2 See Norman Daniels, 'Wide Reflective Equilibrium and Theory Acceptance in Ethics,' *Journal of Philosophy* **76** (1979) 256-82.

3 Philip Rieff, *The Triumph of the Therapeutic* (New York: Harper and Row 1966), 4

4 W.V.O. Quine, *Word and Object* (Cambridge, MA: MIT Press 1960), 4

5 See Donald Davidson, 'On the Very Idea of a Conceptual Scheme' and 'The Method of Truth in Metaphysics,' in his *Inquiries into Truth and Interpretation* (Oxford: Oxford University Press 1984). Also see his essay, 'A Coherence Theory of Truth and Knowledge,' in E. LePore, ed.,

Truth and Interpretation: Perspectives on the Philosophy of Donald David-son (Oxford: Blackwell 1986); and Richard Rorty, 'Pragmatism, David-son and Truth,' also in the LePore volume.

6 John Rawls, 'Justice as Fairness: Political not Metaphysical,' *Philosophy and Public Affairs* **14** (1985) 223-51, 246-7

7 Ibid., 245; my emphasis.

8 Wilfrid Sellars, 'Philosophy and the Scientific Image of Man,' in his *Science, Perception and Reality* (London: Routledge and Kegan Paul 1963)

9 See Davidson, 'True to the Facts,' in *Inquiries*, esp. p. 49.

10 See Davidson, 'On the Very Idea of a Conceptual Scheme,' in *Inquiries*, esp. pp. 193-4.

11 Bernard Williams, *Ethics and the Limits of Philosophy* (Cambridge: Har-vard University Press 1985), 135; cf. p. 199. Freed of the ontology of presence our understanding of scientific practice is enhanced. John McDowell draws attention to Williams's caricature of science 'as a mode of inquiry in which the facts can directly imprint themselves on our minds, without need of mediation by anything as historically condi-tioned and open to dispute as canons of good and bad scientific argu-ment': Critical Notice of Williams, *Mind* **95** (1986) 377-86, 380.

12 Jacques Derrida, 'Différance,' in his collection, *Margins of Philosophy*, tr. A. Bass (Chicago: University of Chicago Press 1982), 27

13 My thanks to Arnold Davidson for helpful discussion of an earlier ver-sion of this essay.

IV

Legal
Deliberation

Legal Deliberation

For over two decades now, Anglo-American legal philosophy has enjoyed a renaissance spearheaded by the influential work of H.L.A. Hart. Hart's success in rekindling interest in this discipline was largely due to his powerful and elegant restatement of legal positivism, a view which many theorists and practitioners of law find intuitively appealing. John Austin's classical version of positivism, with its central claim that all laws can ultimately be traced back to the commands of a single sovereign, was replaced with a new species which preserved the strengths of the old while overcoming many of its shortcomings. A master rule of recognition, displayed principally in the practice of judges and other legal officials, replaced the Austinian sovereign as the ultimate source from which the validity of all laws and decisions within the legal system could be derived. Primary (obligation-imposing) and secondary (power-conferring) rules replaced the sovereign's general commands.

The same basic model of law remained. Laws were conceived as a special set of norms (primary and secondary rules) distinguishable now by their satisfying validity criteria contained within the rule of recognition. In virtue of this master rule, valid laws could be clearly distinguished from moral and other non-legal standards — objects of great controversy, uncertainty, disagreement, and ultimately conflict. On the positivist's picture, one of the salient features of law is its capacity to extricate us from this quasi-Hobbesian pre-legal world of moral uncertainty. As Neil MacCormick, himself an inheritor of the positivist tradition, argues in 'Smashing the Two-Way Mirror,' practical reason suggests the necessity of legal authority as a means of rendering determinate what would otherwise be indeterminate, uncertain, and ultimately dangerous.

Positivism might reasonably be referred to as a brand of 'legal foundationalism.' For the positivist, valid laws are ultimately traceable to a source from which their validity and the validity of decisions based on them follow. Legal judgments typically involve applying valid laws to particular cases, and as Jerry Bickenbach suggests in 'Legal Hermeneutics and the Possibility of Legal Critique,' the model here is deductive reasoning, in particular the application of the universal (the valid law) to the particular (the case before the judge). Judgments are objectively correct or mistaken depending on whether they 'follow' from legally-sanctioned norms whose validity and authority is a function of their foundational source. This is so whether that source lies in the will of an Austinian sovereign or a Hartian rule of recognition.

Positivists are aware that even legal rules are incurably incomplete or 'open-textured,' and that fact-situations, as Hart put it, do not await us clearly labelled as instances of our valid legal norms. In many cases it is indeterminate whether a particular fact-situation is covered by a valid legal rule. In other situations more than one valid legal rule applies, with no agreed method for determining which takes precedence. Judges will sometimes be able to draw upon 'canons of interpretation' and other procedural rules designed to deal with conflicts and indeterminacies, but often these rules will themselves prove indeterminate. In such 'hard cases,' the positivist argues, the person who must ultimately decide the case – i.e., the judge, the authority – must resort to a kind of quasi-legislative judicial discretion. Because the law, to use a well-worn metaphor, has simply run out, the judge is left to his or her own devices in determining how the law shall respond. The judge can no longer deduce the legally correct decision from pre-existing valid law. He or she must decide in some other way.

But in what way? Here positivists have characteristically been silent. As Ronald Dworkin has suggested, positivist theories of legal reasoning tend to let us down just at the point where we are in most need of a theory. Simply to say that in hard cases judges must do their best, must exercise their discretion wisely or in a reasonable manner, is of little use. It is for this reason, among others, that Neil MacCormick's attempt to fashion a 'moderately foundational' account of practical reason is of such interest to both positivists and their critics. If MacCormick's attempt to formulate the rules and forms of practical, and hence legal, reasoning and discourse should prove successful, then a very large gap in the positivists' account of legal adjudication will be filled. They will have an interesting and possibly instructive account of judicial reasoning in hard cases. To what extent MacCor-

mick's theory is only 'moderately' foundational, and whether, in being foundational at all, it is simply wrongheaded from the start, are
questions for which answers might be found in the preceding sections
of this volume.

The foremost modern rival to positivism is Ronald Dworkin's
hermeneutically-flavoured views. Dworkin rejects entirely the
positivist's vision of law as a set of special norms validated and distinguished from all others by a foundational criterion like a rule of recognition. He also rejects the related view of legal reasoning as requiring
either the application of valid norms to particular cases or the exercise of discretion. In Dworkin's view such an account is not true to
the facts of adjudication as it is practiced in modern legal systems. It
fails to reflect accurately what Bickenbach calls 'the participant's point
of view.' Judicial reasoning is not, Dworkin argues, divided into two
spheres: deductive application, where the law binds, and discretion,
where the judge is left to his own devices. Rather the (legal) constraints
judges feel persist to the decision itself. They never experience step-
ping beyond the law's reach into a quasi-legislative realm where the
law is silent and the judge must act as a legislator, creating new law
ab initio.

Although judges feel legal constraint at each step of their reasoning, these constraints are not the forces of special legal rules validated
by a rule of recognition. Rather they are constraints in some way embodied in the legal/political/social/cultural tradition in which judges
find themselves 'hermeneutically situated.' These constraints are experienced as legal, and yet they have no foundational source. Legal
reasoning, viewed from the participant's point of view, simply does
not fit the positivist model of law and legal reasoning. Law cannot
be a closed system of validated rules which must be applied in all cases
where this is possible and which can be ignored when not. Rather,
legal adjudication is an interpretive enterprise in which a variety of
rules, principles, maxims, conceptions, and theories from all facets of
our culture play vital roles. There is no foundation for laws and hence
no foundation from which legal judgments can be derived. Judgments
in law are more like interpretive judgments in literature. As Dworkin argues in *Law's Empire*, the attempt to discover the law bearing
on the case before them requires that judges 'interpret' legal history
and tradition. In so doing, they must attempt to make legal practice

(e.g., a body of statutory law, a string of precedents, or perhaps even the entire legal system) 'the best it can be,' much as the literary critic's interpretive judgment of a novel or play must attempt to make it the best it can be. In each case, Dworkin argues, the interpreter's task is to find meaning, significance, and value in what is interpreted. This bears little resemblance to either of the positivist's two forms of judicial reasoning: deduction from valid law or discretion.

Critics of Dworkin have been quick to note certain problematic consequences of his conception of law and legal reasoning. It has been suggested, for example, that Dworkin's swelling of the law to include much more than the positivist's valid norms simply pushes back the inevitability of judicial discretion. Just as interpreters of literature disagree dramatically over their interpretations, indeed over how properly to go about fashioning an interpretation, judges too will disagree radically. In the absence of consensus about interpretations or about how to go about constructing and evaluating them, judges are inevitably left to their own devices, to the exercise of judicial discretion. This potential difficulty is alluded to by Bickenbach, who sees in our modern societies a significant lack of consensus of the sort which is essential to any hermeneutic/interpretive enterprise, whether it be law or literary interpretation. In the absence of a consensus, or something like Neil MacCormick's foundational canons of practical reasonableness, we may yet be left in the discretionary void. If so, what does this say about the rationality and justifiability of judicial decisions?

Bickenbach also raises a problem for legal critique. Here the positivist may have the upper hand. With his clear separation of valid law from other moral and social norms, the positivist can easily provide for legal critique. His theory leaves room for an 'external' vantage point from which legal practices can be evaluated and criticized. But if 'the law's resources' in some way or other include everything within our social/moral/political culture, then how may we sensibly subject the law to moral criticism? Are we left searching for foundational canons of the sort advocated by MacCormick?

Dworkin's analogy between legal and literary judgment is instructive if only because it provides a viable alternative to the positivist's model and challenges us to think hard about its presuppositions and limitations. But instructive analogies can sometimes be taken too far, as Roger Shiner points out in 'The Hermeneutics of Adjudication.'

Shiner's paper attempts to chart four important differences between legal adjudication and literary criticism. These differences, he thinks, are of sufficient weight and importance to preclude any straightforward inference from the fact that literature has certain properties to the conclusion that law has those very same properties. If Shiner is right, then legal adjudication may be no more like literary criticism than simple deduction from valid laws — and we may have yet another reason to follow MacCormick in his search for a 'moderately foundational' basis for legal judgments.

Wilfrid Waluchow

Neil MacCormick

Smashing the Two-Way Mirror

I The Question of Foundationalism

It is a fine thing to take part in philosophical conversations whose aim is to dispel anglophonic ignorance of Continental philosophy and to test out how far English-speaking and (mainland) European philosophers may have lately been converging in the ideas they propound without realising it. Anti-foundationalism is presented to us, for example, as a possible candidate for the point of hitherto unnoticed convergence among us all. There is here an implicit — almost an explicit — suggestion that antifoundationalist is not only that which we all have become, but also the very thing to be. Enlightened persons who wish to embrace all that is best in Euro-American thought seem exhorted by the very terms of debate to incinerate their mental girdles and consign their foundationalist garments to the flames.

This paper goes but half-way with such burning enthusiasms. It is all too true, and shamefully so, that those who philosophize in English as their native language tend to be bred up in contented ignorance of what is said in other tongues. It is a remarkable fact that reputations for scholarship can be established and retained among us by persons who are obstinately and perhaps even incurably monoglot. Our language is a mirror, if not our philosophy a mirror of nature, and the mirror shines our own thought back at us. But this is not a universal condition; it is no more than *le vice anglophonique*. The English language is not one of your honest-to-God one-way mirrors but rather a two-way mirror like those which feature in the lurider accounts of vice and folly spiced with voyeurism, wherein one set of actions can be remunerable as two performances. English is a two-way mirror on one side of which the actors see only their own reflection but on the other side of which everyone else keeps pretty well up-to-date about what is going on.

In short, there is little evidence that Continental philosophy lacks awareness of British, Canadian or American work, though differences of fashion and style sometimes inhibit useful contact. Here, I find striking and startlingly revealing Jean Grondin's remark that Francophone philosophy has been moving from reflections on reason towards investigations of language while the Anglophones have been moving in the opposite direction, from linguistic studies to a new concern with practical reason, the moment being with us now for a meeting en route.[1] Still, it is on our side that the more formidable barriers to comprehension lie. In terms of the earlier metaphor, the task of today is to smash the two-way mirror. I am all for that and, as to this half, I swim cheerfully with the tide.

It is as to antifoundationalism that I allow myself less commitment to the swelling theme. In a recently published paper,[2] I have put forward a case for legal philosophy (or 'jurisprudence') as foundational in legal education. There seems but little virtue in any educational programme which does not confront students with the demand that they take up a position on such questions as: What is there? How do we know, by what title can we make knowledge-claims? How are things structured, how do they hang together? By what methods can we pursue understanding of things and their structured interrelations? How do humans stand in relation to whatever else there is? How ought humans to behave in the light of their relations to one another and to whatever else there is? The task of philosophical disciplines in liberal education and in civilized thought is none other than to pose such questions and to keep alive debate about them. In law, that task is performed, or anyway should be attempted, by those who teach or study jurisprudence.

That philosophy has this central role in education would not be a very startling proposition for most strands of European thought. In Scotland, with its historical links to Europe, especially France and the Low Countries, but Germany increasingly in the nineteenth century, it is not so either. George Davie's classical book, *The Democratic Intellect*,[3] shows how the philosophical tradition in Scots education survived, albeit precariously, into this century. It was part of the European inheritance which survived the greater insularity consequent on the union with England. The historical point is worth taking here, since it insists on a connection with Europe rather than a disconnection therefrom in the tradition of the democratic intellect, and also, I think, in a tradition of the democratic intellect in the law. Within the European tradition, philosophy was taken to be central to humane education because there were ontological and epistemological questions which people had to face as questions whatever else they were doing, and whatever answers they might give to these questions.

Alan Hunt has recently mounted a brisk attack on my advocacy of this tradition.[4] It is a case of the foundationalist fallacy, says he, to give special, privileged status to such questions as those I listed above. It is, he suggests, above all a mistake to shut them off into separate philosophical or jurisprudential ghettoes away from the rough trade of real life or real law. Theory is not confined to such questions, nor have they any special priority in it. We must take our questions as we find them, not line them up cap and categories in hand (to quote from a tradition not favoured by Hunt). The question, then, is whether I ought to be, or am, now repentant and sensible of error in my ways. Or do I remain obstinate in upholding an old-fashioned Scoto-Continental view of philosophy's place in the great chain of thinking? Need I ask? Need I answer?

Certainly, things change, and doubtless they change everywhere. I claim no better than an imperfect grasp upon Richard Rorty's thought,[5] but take it to be his point that both there and here an awakening, not to say renaissance, is upon us, sweeping away the old primacy of ontology and epistemology, freeing us from the illusion that philosophy can clear the ground for the subordinate sciences to do their work on a sure foundation of sound metaphysics, unerring theory of knowledge, and reliable methodology. Dogmatic slumbers may keep us still heavy-lidded, Kant's Humeanism may have been incomplete, and enlightenment was surely claimed ahead of time. But awakening is with us now; and alike so in continental Europe and Oceania.

There are two ways to read this: one can take it as advocating that very attractive moderate scepticism commonly and properly associated with the name and work of David Hume. Probabilities, not certainties, are all that humans can find in matters of fact and of existence. Programmes, systems or mere projects which set their or our ambitions higher and aim to rest knowledge on some footing of indubit-

able certainty are both delusory and, worse, delusive. They flatter our
desire for intellectual repose, but flatter only to deceive. Moderate scepticism of this sort is a sound view, at least it is my view. But I observe
it to be grounded in an epistemological thesis. In Hume, moreover,
it is tied up with the ontology of impressions and ideas and of the
unknown but undeniable external world. It is likely to turn out that
any version of it presupposes some ontological commitments.

The alternative reading of Rorty's antifoundationalism, perhaps
the one more in harmony with the picture of philosophy as continuing conversation, goes beyond mild scepticism about the chance of
certainty in answers and denies any special structure, rhyme or reason in the questions. Whether Rortyan or not, this view seems implicit in Alan Hunt's critique of my argument in 'The Democratic
Intellect and the Law.' Let me therefore say that I do adhere to and
hereby commend a version of foundationalism (if that is what it is)
which insists that:

(a) There are some questions which are specifically philosophical
in the sense that they are crucial to a systematic understanding
of our world and that anyone who purports to be a philosopher
or to have a philosophy needs to have some considered and discursively stable view about them;

(b) One of the philosophical questions is which other questions belong in the list (my list of such other questions having been stated above);

(c) These questions are of concern to all thoughtful humans, not
only those who hold paid jobs as Lecturers in or Professors of
Philosophy or cognate disciplines; but

(d) A large part of the most worthwhile prior discourse upon these
and related questions has been carried on by recognised
'philosophers,' and so a study of their ideas is of particular utility
to anyone who wants to carry forward his or her own thought
or discourse upon them;

(e) Answers can be put forward persuasively (rhetorically) and may
be more or less plausible, never demonstrable with certainty;
nevertheless

(f) Some ordered and structured taking up of position, with a discursively stable and defensible internal logic, is necessary to
every serious engagement with the questions.

One who believes in that creed can certainly acknowledge the
attractiveness of Rorty's image of philosophy as a continuing conversation or dialogue between the living and the glorious dead. (This may
not be disconnected with the hope that someone will go on talking
to *us* after *we* are dead.) The idea that there is a certainly true and
absolutely demonstrable set of answers awaiting us like a holy grail
at the end of a purifying quest is as probably false as anything can
be. So there is a debate, a multipartite discourse, on the go. And there
is nothing for it but that anyone philosophically minded has to join
in. But the debate or discourse is about the foundations of our thought.
So the position to opt for looks to me to be better described as moderate
or sceptical foundationalism than as antifoundationalism. If the conception of philosophy as conversation goes farther than that, it de-
grades the subject into nothing better than a high-falutin chat show
of no value greater than entertainment value. I have nothing against
entertainment but do not hold out high hopes for the box-office appeal of philosophy as pretentious chat-show.

II Some Continental Thought: Alexy

In his recent book on legal theory, Mario Jori rightly upbraids British and North American scholars for their ignorance of European
work, observing that no converse ignorance exists among, for example, Italian legal and political philosophers.[6] To mention this is merely to repeat my zeal for kicking through the two-way mirror. The
first work I wish to discuss to this end is Robert Alexy's study of legal reasoning as a special case of practical discourse.[7] To speak per-
sonally, I can certainly put it in the class of work in one tradition
which converges unknownly and unknowingly with work in another.
I first learned of Alexy's work in 1979, shortly after the publication
of a book of my own on a similar theme, the main thrust of whose
ideas and conclusions ran along lines similar to Alexy's.[8]

Alexy, however, makes far more thorough use of British and American writing than I of work in German or French (not much beyond Josef Esser and Chaim Perelman). His argument reviews in its first part a general theory of practical discourse, working from analytical philosophers such as Hare, Toulmin, J.L. Austin, Singer and Baier, from the 'new rhetoric' of Perelman as followed also in works of Viehweg and Larenz and taken farther in Esser's *Vorverständnis und Methodenwahl in der Rechtsfindung*,[9] German analytical philosophy as represented by Günther Patzig, the Erlangen School of Lorenzen and Schwemmer and finally, most influentially and significantly of all, Jürgen Habermas's theory of rational discourse and of truth in discourse.[10]

Any work across this range starts with the Oxford style of linguistic analysis of the post-war period. Understanding in moral philosophy was, if not equated with, certainly pursued through analysis of the use of moral words and expressions in ordinary language. A classic case is Hare's attempt to establish the theses of prescriptivity and universalizability by these means.[11] Toulmin used similar techniques in his analysis of the uses of, and rules governing, argument.[12] Meanwhile, however, the new rhetoric was focussed on issues like those of what amounts to rational persuasion, what are the grounds of persuasiveness in non-demonstrative arguments, and what intersubjective criteria can be set up for correctness in practical arguments. With Habermas, a similar search leads back to language and to something like Austinian speech-act theory; for the theory of theoretical and practical rationality is located in the distinction between doing and discoursing (*Handlung* as against *Diskurs*). An analysis of the ideal conditions governing correctness in discourse gives a conception of rationality in human affairs; also, through the notion of consensus in an ideal speech-situation, a conception of truth or at least correctness. The key to rationality lies in universal pragmatics.[13] This rather noticeably echoes Grondin's idea, mentioned earlier, that Anglophones started with language and moved on towards reason whereas Continentals, having started with reason, moved into language. Recent work by Paul Amselek in Paris confirms the trend.[14]

However that may be, Alexy's aim is to construct a general theory of practical discourse, indeed a theory of 'General Practical Discourse,' and then to build out of that a theory of legal reasoning as a special case of general practical discourse. His strategy is to work out by critical reflection on the writings mentioned above what are the rules and forms of argument implicit in our practical discourses, leaving aside those which have arisen from discursively indefensible conditions or circumstances. Let me give some examples:

First come the 'Basic Rules,' common to all forms of discourse, theoretical as well as practical. These include a rule against self-contradiction, a rule against insincerity (saying what you don't believe), a rule that one must univeralize one's application of predicates of any sort (but especially practical predicates) to subjects, and a rule against equivocation in terms. Next he offers 'Rationality Rules' – conditions of the possibility of discourse, or indeed conversation, among rational beings – such as: Anybody who asserts something has to be willing to give a reason for it if challenged; All persons are entitled to enter into discourse on equal terms with everyone else – no exclusions on arbitrary grounds; Everybody's wishes, desires, needs, or world-views are equally relevant and admissible in discourse with those of every other person; But if they are introduced into discourse, they are subject upon challenge to scrutiny for their genuine relevance to the topic in hand.

In practical discourse as such, these basic rules and rationality rules come under further controls, such as an insistence upon Harean universalizability as improved in the light of work by Singer and Habermas. Where competing practical arguments from competing practical premises are in play, one properly has recourse to consideration of the consequences of either set of premises. And so on. Elsewhere, I have given a fuller account of Alexy's rules and forms of argument as criteria for sound practical discourse, and a complete translation of his work is now under way;[15] so I shall not repeat them *in extenso* here. Enough has been said to convey the flavour of the project. He is trying to establish what would be the conditions of and limits on practical discourse among humans on any practical subject at all if humans lived up to their capacity for rationality.

Alexy (with whom I fully agree on this) holds that these rules and forms have a very particular significance. For they allow us to identify 'discursively possible,' 'discursively necessary,' and 'discursively impossible' opinions or statements. Whatever is unsayable without breaking the rules is impossible. The possible defines itself *e converso*, and where only one saying is possible in context, it is discursively necessary. So proposals for action, when sieved through the practical-discourse rules, may reveal themselves as possible, impossible, or necessary (permissible, impermissible, or obligatory). Again, we get at the point of practical reason by reflecting on the conditions of possible speech. It follows that reason alone, rationality of itself, rules out quite a lot of the things we might be tempted to do. But alas not everything. Or, rather, it may fall short of eliminating all but a single necessary course of action. Many possible courses of action are excluded discursively as irrational (discursively impossible), some are rendered obligatory (discursively necessary) by reason alone applied in the circumstances of a given case. But quite often more than one course will prove discursively possible (permissible), none being discursively necessary (obligatory).

Thus the necessary and the impossible fall far short of covering every case. A plurality of courses almost always lies open, sometimes because of conflicting courses arising out of competing projects. Even if everyone behaved solely as rational practical discourse reveals to be permissible, that is, even if everybody always behaved rationally (in the relevant sense), we should not always know what to do. There would be inevitable conflicts, not necessarily resoluble through rational practical discourse. So it becomes a datum of practical discourse that we need in such matters to have recourse to authorities. No doubt there ought to be restrictive conditions upon authority as such, but within these restrictions we ought to have it. We need institutions of legal governance and practices of legal reasoning (both legislative and adjudicative) which apply practical reasonableness to resolve the conflicts and antinomies surviving at the level of general practical discourse and to supply enforcement of the requirements of reasonable conduct in general.

This general line, according to which the indeterminacies of rational practical discourse operating at large themselves reveal the rational practical necessity of acknowledging the necessity of limited government under law, is of course not radically new. One can pursue its roots through thinkers like Kant, Rousseau and Locke. Its special originality in Alexy's statement lies in the way in which he beds it into discourse theory. From it one can derive not unimportant implications for topics germane to interpretation and foundationalism.

III Implications

The argument which says that general practical discourse needs to be supplemented in special cases and special spheres by legal discourse as a special case of general practical discourse implies that intrinsic to the legal discourse there has to be a concept, not necessarily of 'law' but certainly of 'the law.' For this purpose that concept denotes the very set of norms which are established by authorities having it as their particular point that they render determinate our basis of reasoning where general practical discourse leaves too much at the level of the discursively possible. Thus for a certain purpose we give to the term 'law' a certain semantic significance, not extraneous to the reasoning enterprise but as a specific part of it. We shall have settled upon using this term to denote inter alia the particular rules and other norms or normative generalizations which we settle upon as the very ones which the organs of political authority must in their various ways administer and apply in their specialist discourse. To propose or accept such an understanding of the term is not to appeal to some wholly independent semantics, but to the semantics intrinsic to the legal enterprise as an enterprise of reasoning and discourse. And to say this is to offer an interpretation of practical discourse and of legal discourse as encapsulated therein.

    This approach is clearly enough interpretive or 'hermeneutic' in that it seeks to see the point of a certain discourse ab intra and to interpret a concept used in it and crucial to its special point. But it is then quite obvious that an interpretive approach is not of itself one which necessarily excludes deductivism. In fact, both Alexy and I hold that one of the reasoning forms properly used within legal discourse is a deductive form, wherein subsumption of a set of factual findings under a rule which is a 'law' generates a conclusion properly deemed legal.[16] This puts in dispute the view, stated below by Jerry Bickenbach, that an interpretivist or hermeneutic approach in the sense advanced by Ronald Dworkin automatically excludes recourse to deductive argument in law.[17]

    In any event, and here I am firmly in agreement with Roger Shiner,[18] there is a risk of our depriving 'interpretation' of usefulness in our discourse by giving it itself an excessively broad interpretation. When I said that deduction has a place in law, I should have added that its place is in turn embedded in an interpretive process. It is always possible to raise doubt as to the proper interpretation of the rule from which somebody proposes to deduce some conclusion. On a rival interpretation of the rule the conclusion may not follow. So too for factual findings. On one interpretation or classification, they may supply the very minor premiss which generates the desired conclusion given the preferred interpretation of the rule; but not otherwise. Only if no issue of interpretation arises, or after any that arises has been settled, does the deductive phase of argument proceed. In turn, the interpretive conclusion which forms the basis for the deductive phase has to have its justification. Sometimes rules of interpretation suffice, but rarely so. In some, though not all, cases of interpretive difficulty, one is driven back to evaluating consequences of rival readings of the rules. In doing so, one needs to have regard to the guiding principles and values of the law. In the last resort (and always as a side constraint on arbitrariness) one has to go beyond the specifically legal, even at its most general and abstract level, and have recourse to the general practical reasoning from whose indeterminacies we in the first place fled unto the sanctuary of the law.

In all this, there is a proper place for reflection upon and (if you will) interpretation of the legal and political tradition in which one locates oneself. There is a proper place for reflection upon and (if you will) interpretation of the practice of legal argumentation and discourse, bearing in mind that it is not independent of, but a special case of, general practical discourse. But these interpretations or modes of interpretation are at several removes from the first level of interpretation in legal discourse, where we try to settle among disputed possible meanings of a legal text. On that account, I join Shiner in protesting that, although all that we do in law may involve interpretation in some sense, the senses need differentiation, and interpretation *sensu stricto* should not be dissolved into interpretation *sensu largissimo*.[19] The fact that in any legal dispute somebody might if they chose press the argument right back through strict-sense interpretation into general debate on legal principles and values, and beyond that to debate about unrestricted practical reasonableness, does not mean that all these remoter reaches of argumentation are somehow shadowily present in the simple run-of-the-mill case where the parties are agreed about relevant rules and their meanings and settle for a simple proof or trial of the issues of fact, these issues being also assumed to be unambiguous in their classification. Run-of-the-mill law may be boring, but it is at least as expressive of the point of law as the grand-scale argumentation of the highest instances of appeal.

These views about the practical point and working of legal argumentation are, I believe, substantially common to Alexy and myself. Where conclusions match, examination of premises is tempting. Alexy's self-location in Habermasian discourse-analysis sets him in a different tradition of thought from that in which I start and, perhaps, finish. Yet the power and systematic vigour of his theses make it tempting for one who goes along with the conclusions to think of adapting to the tradition which generates them through so powerful and systematic a presentation. To wrestle with that dilemma is a private problem for myself, and not vital to the present issue.

As to that, what is needed is some attention to the matter of foundationalism in the light of the reading of Alexy offered here. For someone to embark on the highly ambitious project of stating and formulating the whole set (or set of sets) of rules and forms presupposed in and authoritative for practical reasoning and discourse and likewise those of legal discourse, even to embark on that project by way of summarizing in orderly terms the best current thought on issues of practical reasoning, is to tackle an undertaking with a foundationalist ring to it, albeit in a new form. To bring it off with substantial success is to lay bare, it may be thought, the foundations of practical thought. The like might in principle be done for 'empirical discourse' and 'discourse-theoretical discourse.' When accomplished, such a project would map out the limits and boundaries of the rationally sayable and the rationally thinkable, and therewith the limits of whatever, for us, is 'real.' En route, and not by accident, answers would emerge to the kinds of questions I sketched above.

To say that is not to impute to Alexy or anyone else the crazy claim that the job is already done, or that anyone will ever do it with final and conclusive certainty. His work does not claim to be more than a progress report on results achieved so far through work done according to a certain job-specification. The point, however, is about the specification, not the job. That seems to me to fit better with what I am disposed to call moderate foundationalism than with out-and-out antifoundationalism. And so much the better for that. Working in the spirit of Habermas may not guarantee one's antifoundationalist credentials after all.

IV Further Thoughts and Further Implications: Weinberger

My other exemplar of current European thought seems even less promising for the thesis that antifoundationalism is the sole and sufficient meeting point of European and British thought. Ota Weinberger of Graz and I recently brought out a book called *Grundlagen des institutionalistischen Rechtspositivismus*[20] and yet more recently an English version entitled *An Institutional Theory of Law*.[21] This project arose out of the discovery that each of us had, unknown to the other, written an essay on 'Law as Institutional Fact'[22] and had developed that line of thought in subsequent papers, but had done so from starting points in different legal, jurisprudential, and general philosophical traditions. What we both thought we had discovered was the utility of the concept 'institutional fact' outlined by Anscombe and then by Searle for the solution of the problem of how to talk about the existence of thought-objects like law and laws and instances of institutions internal to law like contracts, corporations, trusts, *Stiftungen*, etc. We also both thought we could refine the concept and make its legal and philosophical applications yet more perspicuous.

In doing so, however, we seem to have come dangerously close to having committed out-and-out foundationalism. The following quotation from the Introduction to our English version makes the point:

> Our Institutional Theory of Law aims first to provide a sound ontological and epistemological foundation for two equally valid and mutually complementary disciplines, legal dogmatics and the sociology of law, aims secondly to make a contribution to the understanding of legal structures and of the methods proper to legal study, and aims finally to show the place and limits of practical reason in law and human social life. These are matters with which any comprehensive theory of law must deal. We hope this book makes a contribution to dealing with them.

There indeed one has the claim and the ambition which some find so objectionable in philosophy, viz., that it should concern itself with 'foundations' for other disciplines. For myself, who am after all also an academic lawyer, that is, a practitioner of legal dogmatics, I cannot see anything in the least disreputable about this activity of investigating and testing the existence-assumptions and knowledge-claims implicit in that other activity of mine. If disciplinary specialization should result in two quite separate persons doing the two jobs, neither becomes eo ipso disreputable, though we may all regret the narrowing of perspectives brought on by the advanced division of labour.

What Weinberger and I are arguing, after all, is no more than that truth-claims can be quite legitimately made by those who set out to give a representation of the law of a given jurisdiction at a given time. Although law is normative and action-guiding, although it expresses itself properly in the modalities of the 'ought,' yet there are legal facts, and descriptions of the law can be genuinely factual. (Thus they can be factual even when false, that is, they can be false. If not, could a lawyer ever be justly made liable for professional negligence through acting on a culpably false view of the law?) They are factual in that they state or purport to state institutional facts in the senses which we analyse and expound. Even if our analyses or expositions are erroneous, they seek to deal with a question which will not go away: is there here any truth or falsity, or merely greater or less persuasiveness of a rhetorical sort?

Institutional facts are not raw experiences, but experience read and interpreted through the medium of rules. This in turn implies that it is by a hermeneutic understanding of legal talk or discourse and of the way in which our action and judgment may be oriented to rules that we can comprehend the facticity of legal facts. This forces us to re-interpret the question, 'What is there?', asked as a philosophical question. It is not always a matter of brute existence, as though that were quite independent of humans and their discourse, but rather a question built into our discourses in various ways; within them, however, it has a very particular importance. Brute existence, indeed, seems to me (if less so to Weinberger) to be more problematic than institutional facticity. It is easier to lay hold of truths in which you can have solid confidence in the cultural world than in the world viewed (or aspirationally viewed) without cultural assumptions. Yet it seems as though it may be an ineluctable presupposition that beyond the world of our culture and experience, and in some way grounding or guaranteeing it, is a world which just exists as it exists. I see no way of avoiding the question whether such a presupposition is really as ineluctable as so often it seems. I do not advocate, nor does Weinberger, any absolutism of answers; only inevitability of the questions.

I conclude as I commenced. For us whose work is in English, there is all too real a risk of reflecting only on our own reflections. To smash the two-way mirror is to do more than merely jump through the looking-glass. We have much to learn in active dialogue with colleagues in other linguistic and philosophical traditions. My evidence, however, is by no means supportive of the view that what we cannot but learn is a radical antifoundationalism. I offer Alexy and Weinberger as co-witnesses, and I rest here the case for foundationalism, at any rate in a decent and moderate form.

NOTES

1 See Grondin's contribution to this volume, 46.

2 N. MacCormick, 'The Democratic Intellect and the Law,' *Legal Studies* **5** (1985) 172-82

3 George Davie, *The Democratic Intellect* (Edinburgh: Edinburgh University Press 1961). See now also his *The Crisis of the Democratic Intellect* (Edinburgh: Polygon Books 1986).

4 A. Hunt, 'Jurisprudence, Philosophy and Legal Education — Against Foundationalism,' *Legal Studies* **6** (1986) 292-302

5 As disclosed in *Philosophy and the Mirror of Nature* (Princeton, NJ: Princeton University Press 1979), and as discussed in the present volume by William M. Sullivan, to whose lucid account I am much indebted.

6 Mario Jori, *Saggi di Metagiurisprudenza* (Milan: Dott. A. Giuffré 1985)

7 Robert Alexy, *Theorie der juristischen Argumentation* (Frankfurt-am-Main: Suhrkamp 1978)

8 See N. MacCormick, *Legal Reasoning and Legal Theory* (Oxford: Oxford University Press 1978).

9 2nd edn., Frankfurt-am-Main, 1972

10 Discussed in Alexy, *Theorie*, 134-77; other references in this section may be gathered from the same work (178-218), or N. MacCormick, 'Legal Reasoning and Practical Reason,' *Midwest Studies in Philosophy* 7 (1982) 271-86.

11 R.M. Hare, *The Language of Morals* (Oxford: Oxford University Press 1952), *Freedom and Reason* (Oxford: Oxford University Press 1963), *Moral Thinking* (Oxford: Oxford University Press 1981)

12 S.E. Toulmin, *The Uses of Argument* (Cambridge: Cambridge University Press 1958), *The Place of Reason in Ethics* (Cambridge: Cambridge University Press 1950)

13 See Jürgen Habermas, 'Was heisst Universalpragmatik?', K.O. Apel, ed., *Sprachpragmatik und Philosophie* (Frankfurt-am-Main: Suhrkamp 1976) 174-272.

14 P. Amselek, ed., *Theorie des Actes de Langage, Ethique et Droit* (Paris: Presses Universitaires de France 1986)

15 See N. MacCormick, 'Legal Reasoning and Practical Reason'; the forthcoming translation of Alexy is by Ruth Adler (assisted by N. MacCormick) and will be published by Oxford University Press in 1988, under the (provisional) title *A Theory of Legal Reasoning*.

16 Alexy, *Theorie*, 271-3, 364; MacCormick, *Legal Reasoning and Legal Theory*, chapter 2

17 See Bickenbach, 222 below, and Ronald Dworkin, *Law's Empire* (Cambridge, MA: Harvard University Press 1986), chapters 1 & 2.

18 See Shiner, 243-5 below.

19 I owe this way of putting the point, and indeed a proper grasp of the point, to a seminar by Jerzy Wroblewski in Edinburgh, November 1987. See J. Wroblewski, 'Rational Law-Maker and Interpretative Choices,' *Rivista Internazionale di Filosofia del Diritto* 62 (1985) 129-47; 'Legal Language and Legal Interpretation,' *Law and Philosophy* 4 (1985) 239-55.

20 Berlin: Duncker und Humblot 1985

21 Dordrecht: D. Reidel 1986

22 N. MacCormick, 'Law as Institutional Fact,' *Law Quarterly Review* **90** (1974) 102-29; O. Weinberger, 'Das Recht als institutionelle Tatsache,' *Rechtstheorie* **11** (1980) 427-42, but also 'Die Norm als Gedanke und Realität,' *Österreichische Zeitschrift für öffentliches Recht* **20** (1970) 203-16, for his first statement of position on this.

Jerome E. Bickenbach

Legal Hermeneutics and the Possibility of Legal Critique

I

Hans-Georg Gadamer has claimed that 'hermeneutic philosophy is the heir of the older tradition of practical philosophy' which sought to 'justify this way of reason and defend practical and political reason against the domination of technology based on science.'[1] Gadamer's 'rediscovery of the fundamental hermeneutic problem' arose from the insight that the subdivisions of traditional hermeneutics – understanding, interpretation and application – are internally related, indeed fused elements of the single activity of understanding.[2] The 'inner fusion' of understanding and interpretation in effective-historical consciousness is perhaps Gadamer's major contribution to hermeneutics. Yet the claim that philosophical hermeneutics follows in the tradition of classical practical philosophy relies on the additional fusion of interpretative understanding and application. Gadamer derives this latter fusion from his understanding of Aristotle's analysis of *phronēsis* in Book VI of the *Nicomachean Ethics*, supplemented by a consideration of the 'exemplary significance of legal hermeneutics.'[3]

Gadamer's principal concern in *Truth and Method* is with the understanding and interpretation of historical texts, not ethics or law. Indeed he brings in Aristotle's ethics and legal hermeneutics only to shed light on the phenomenon of hermeneutical understanding and to support his claim that the human sciences (the *Geisteswissenschaften*) are practical disciplines which, at least since the Enlightenment, have been unduly influenced by the methodology of the natural sciences. Despite this emphasis, the application of philosophical hermeneutics to ethics and law is clear enough. In particular, if Gadamer is correct legal reasoning counts as something of a paradigm of the hermeneutic approach.

Although Continental scholars such as Emilio Betti, Karl Engisch and Karl Larenz have treated the hermeneutical aspects of legal theory extensively, few English-speaking philosophers of law are aware of this work or seem interested in applying it to current debates. A notable and, given his influence, significant exception is Ronald Dworkin, who in *Law's Empire* and elsewhere has reached into the hermeneutic tradition to restate his critique of positivistic and other 'semantic' accounts of legal reasoning.[4] As one reads through *Law's Empire* there is little doubt that Dworkin's appropriation of elements of the hermeneutic tradition has served him well. Other English-speaking philosophers of law will undoubtedly now follow his lead and introduce themselves to the Continental literature.

In general, it seems to me that philosophers of law have much to learn from the hermeneutical tradition. My first purpose here is to outline briefly what about Dworkin's recent work might be called 'hermeneutical' and to suggest why he is able to highlight the poverty of a prominent and popular style of legal philosophizing. It is definitely not my purpose to sift through the details of Dworkin's account of theoretical disagreement in law, nor directly to question the version of his 'rights thesis' that is developed in *Law's Empire*. Rather, my initial purpose is merely to use Dworkin as an example of the value in bringing the insights and perspective of philosophical hermeneutics to the problems and debates of Anglo-American philosophy of law.

But I also wish to advise caution. Philosophers of law should be aware of a feature of Gadamerian hermeneutics which may be unwelcome. Dworkin is content to employ only those aspects of the hermeneutical approach that serve his specific jurisprudential interests. As a result he merely finesses a problematic aspect of philosophical hermeneutics. The difficulty concerns whether legal critique, and therefore reforming political praxis, can be accommodated within philosophical hermeneutics. This worry will become clear only when we pursue Gadamer's claim that hermeneutics is a successor to traditional practical philosophy.

II

What of positive value can we learn from Dworkin's approach? Although Dworkin somewhat bluntly manipulates hermeneutic insights for the purposes of his own agenda, the thrust of his approach is fully within that tradition. It seems to me, moreover, that his hermeneutically-inspired approach might help to show why much of the current debate between positivist and non-positivist accounts of law and legal reasoning is unproductive. I will mention three features of Dworkin's approach that are particularly instructive, and then, in the next section, isolate the particular muddle implicit in many current accounts of legal reasoning which Dworkin may have managed to avoid.

Dworkin opens with the claim that to understand legal disagreement one must take up the internal or participant's point of view. Legal disagreement is a matter of social practices, as lived by those whose practices they are, and accounts of law – philosophical, sociological or historical – that purport to stand back, or above, actual practice are impoverished and defective.[5] Initially, we can understand law because it is our law, and we can make sense of legal reasoning because it is the kind of reasoning which practitioners of our law engage in. To be sure, the historical or sociological perspectives are important; but these contribute to understanding only in so far as they include the participant's point of view: a social practice like legal adjudication can not coherently be claimed to be *really* the result of economic pressures or class struggle or *really* the working out of a legal logic, unless it could plausibly be understood that way by someone who actually participates in the practice.

By insisting on the internal point of view, Dworkin is in effect introducing as a methodological premise the inevitability of the 'hermeneutical situation,' the interpreter's pre-given awareness, what one brings to the task of making sense of a text or practice.[6] As interpreters seeking to understand, we come to a text or practice historically and traditionally situated; we come with our point of view, a perspective that is determined in part by our social practices, our forms of life. As a consequence, philosophical accounts of law that attempt to 'reconstruct' social practices in order to disclose hidden rules which explain the logical, although not the experienced, operation of a legal system are of little value. So too accounts of the logical structure of legal systems per se: they have little chance of explaining the phenomenon of legal disagreement as it actually exists. There is, in short, no special, neutral or privileged *philosophical perspective* on social practices. Only participation in those practices, or a hermeneutical understanding of that participation, can provide a useful perspective.

Dworkin's second hermeneutically-inspired move is to reject the basis for what he terms 'semantic' theories of law. These theories presume that we can only sensibly argue about what is the law on a particular question if we accept and follow criteria for deciding when something is a law.[7] Thus, according to Dworkin, all forms of legal positivism insist that what the law is, at any point in time, can only be determined by a set of factual criteria, however complex, specifying causal antecedents of established, recognized, or otherwise accepted authority. To know what the law is is either to trace a putative proposition of law back to its authoritative source – legislature, convention, or judicial pronouncement – or else, if one happens oneself to be an authoritative source, to identify in the exercise of one's authority that proposition's legality.

Here Dworkin is appropriating a fundamental hermeneutical insight, although it is one not unfamiliar to readers of Quine and Putnam.[8] The insight is simply that in order to understand a complex social practice, such as those bound up in the various institutions of the law, one cannot presume that there exists a collection of facts or rules, detached from the practices and independent of participation in these practices, that somehow speak directly to the investigator. Social practices are composed of an integrated field of human actions, but these are not brute data that can be neutrally identified and subjected to generalization. Rather, one must strive to disclose the purpose and point of these actions for those who are part of the practice: the reality of social practices can only be described in terms of their meaning for participants, and the discovery of this meaning is a complex and interactive affair.[9]

Dworkin's remedy for the fascination of 'semantic' theories of law is his third and most important, hermeneutically-inspired premise. He argues that when lawyers seek to identify the law, when judges weigh the submissions of counsels, and when non-experts debate the law, they are all engaged in a process of interpretation. Law itself is,

Dworkin claims, an interpretative concept. To make sense of legal controversy, and to understand law itself, the legal philosopher must realize that participants are essentially engaged in a process of imposing meaning on their practices. These practices are not mere givens in participants' lives; they have a value which is tied to the point these practices have for them.

Thus when lawyers debate with one another over the proper interpretation of a statute, the weight to be given to a precedent, or the force of a line of cases which appear to be leading from one understanding of a right or obligation to another, they are attempting to make sense of this legal material in terms of overall purposes and goals. That is, legal interpretation presumes a consensus embodied in the moral and political traditions, indeed the very culture, shared by participants. Without at least a rough consensus about the assumptions of a practice, its aims and purposes, it would be wholly mysterious, and no dispute could meaningfully exist. Against the background of a legal tradition, however, disputants can begin the process of interpretation: granting the aims and purposes of a common law doctrine or statutory regime, lawyers can then debate the extent to which these aims and purposes are furthered by the actual techniques settled on by legislatures or courts.

Dworkin argues further that the interpretative character of a complex of practices such as the law presupposes a central conception of the purpose of those practices. This central rationale allows lawyers to structure their arguments, for, given an overall point to law it is possible to situate particular disputes, to see these as elements of a more general, and presumptively coherent, tradition. Dworkin's central claim in *Law's Empire* is, following on his earlier work, that this central rationale is the rights thesis. Granting that governments have goals — prosperity, power, eminence, continuity — and use the collective force they monopolize to further these ends, the most abstract and fundamental point of legal practice is to guide and constrain this state power. Thus:

> Law insists that force not be used or withheld, no matter how useful that would be to ends in view, no matter how beneficial or noble these ends, except as licensed or required by individual rights and responsibilities flowing from past political decisions about when collective force is justified.[10]

III

The rights thesis, and other aspects of Dworkin's theory of law and legal reasoning, are familiar enough, but Dworkin's appropriation of hermeneutics enables him to restate these jurisprudential claims more forcefully. He has captured and used for his own purposes a hermeneutic characterization of practical reasoning as it would be employed in the law. Doing so, he suggests a way of extricating English-speaking philosophy of law from a muddle that has infected most accounts of legal reasoning.

The muddle arises from the presumption that legal reasoning must always fit into standard deductive categories, or at least be logically determinate: it must count as a justification.[11] It is claimed that a justification is a sound piece of reasoning only if it shows why a legal decision involves the direct application, to a particular fact situation, of legal rules embodied in statute, regulation, or precedent. Yet even a casual reading of actual judicial reasons discloses that generally accepted rules of reasoning (say, modus ponens) are rarely productive of answers to legal questions. Instances where it is a simple matter to apply in deductive fashion a general rule to a particular case are not unknown, of course. Yet arguably these cases do not involve *legal* reasoning at all. In interesting cases, judges seem to have recourse to a wide leeway of choice in how to understand and employ the rules embodied in precedents or how to interpret the words of a statute. Moreover, in certain 'hard' cases, it appears that judges are relying on extra-legal considerations, considerations of public policy or principle that are vaguely stated and do not determinately point in one direction rather than another. Thus, though it is claimed that legal reasoning must employ a deductivist canon of reasoning to count as legitimate, actual practice shows that it rarely does so.

From this muddle a variety of conclusions have been drawn: that legal reasoning is mere window-dressing for the subjective opinions or ideologically-loaded preferences of judges; that in many cases judicial reasoning involves the exercise of a discretion which sanctions judges to reach legal decisions on non-legal grounds; that the object of philosophical jurisprudence is to attempt to 'reconstruct' legal reasoning so that it becomes logically acceptable; or that legal reasoning, being non-logical, ought to be viewed as an example of authoritative persuasion. Whatever the conclusion, philosophers of law — should they be motivated to rescue the legal process from charges of ideological manipulation, political bias, or irrationality — seek to legitimate a process of justifying legal normative judgment which, by their own lights, must be denied the status of reasoning.

The hermeneutic tradition Dworkin relies upon was founded on the view that the general attempt to apply the methods of the natural sciences to human affairs is distorting and, in the end, can only lead to scepticism. Their solution is to return to the classical notion of practical reasonableness viewed as a process of interpretative understanding and to set aside the model of reasoning that treats as paradigmatic the subsumption of particular case to general rule. In the end, therefore, it is Gadamer's claim that hermeneutics is the heir of practical philosophy which should draw the attention of legal philosophers. A return to that tradition, and a fresh understanding of practical reasoning, holds out the prospect of productive and revitalized research into the problems with which philosophers of law have long struggled.

IV

There is, however, a danger in the hermeneutic approach which philosophers of law ought to be mindful of should they look to it for guidance. This difficulty has been the subject of considerable debate amongst hermeneuticians and seems particularly to affect Gadamer's work. The problem is that the claim of hermeneutics to have revitalized the tradition of practical philosophy relies on an understanding of practical reasoning which may preempt the possibility of hermeneutical critique. This fact is particularly vexing for legal philosophers who conceive of their role as offering constructive reassessments of substantive law and recommendations for change in actual legal regimes.

To situate this potential difficulty for legal hermeneutics we should remind ourselves of how Gadamer proposes to reintegrate understanding and application, why he relies on Aristotle's analysis of *phronēsis*, and why he feels that legal hermeneutics is the 'true model' of philosophical hermeneutics.[12]

When we deliberate about practical matters and moral conduct we must rely upon an understanding of ourselves and our ends. This necessarily involves us in the process of interpretation. We must interpret ourselves because our choices reflect pre-judgments and pre-understandings about our identity and our social relations. The products of the interaction between this self-understanding and the object of our deliberation are reasons which warrant practical action. These reasons have always to do with the application of general moral claims, values, or ideals to concrete situations.

With the question of application before his mind Gadamer notes that the hermeneutical problem of understanding a text and the kind of problem at issue in moral deliberation are analogous. In both cases we must acquire an understanding of a particular (an interpretation of a text) as the application of something universal (the text) to a particular situation. The hermeneutical approach suggests that understanding requires an interaction of interpreter and object of interpretation in which each is altered by the act of interpretation. To understand a text is always to understand it differently. But how can this relation between the universal and the concrete particular be characterized?

The relevance of moral deliberation and Aristotle's account of *phronēsis* is clear at this juncture. Aristotle wished to characterize a form of reasoning and knowledge that could mediate between the universal and the particular. Since we always encounter the good in the specific form of the particular practical situation, the object of moral knowledge must be to see in the concrete situation what morality requires of us in general. Moral knowledge that cannot be applied to the concrete case is not only of no use to the moral agent, it would also undermine moral agency. It is among the characteristics of morality that the person acting must know and decide and cannot let some external rule or method remove that responsibility. Thus *phronēsis*, the capacity of practical wisdom, determines what the person with this capacity, the *phronimos*, becomes. Reasoning well about what good conduct is in particular situations develops the habit of acting in accordance with that reasoning. So too, Gadamer argues, the interpreter and the object of interpretative understanding are co-determined by the act of understanding.

Gadamer is also concerned to appropriate Aristotle's distinction between *phronēsis* and the other 'intellectual virtues' of *epistēmē* (scientific, especially mathematical knowledge) and *technē* (technical know-how). *Epistēmē* provides knowledge of universals, of what exists of necessity. *Phronēsis*, unlike *epistēmē*, has as its object self-understanding and practical conduct, not general metaphysical or theoretical propositions. Moreover, since *technē* supplies us with skills that produce particular things while the end of moral knowledge is virtue as displayed in a lifetime of action, *phronēsis* and *technē* are essentially different. As Aristotle argues, *phronēsis* must provide moral knowledge for the sake of the moral agent, knowledge of oneself which is thereby directed to moral judgment. So too the interpreter striving to understand a text must seek to apply it to his or her own situation. The text must be understood as a universal (as itself, the text), but only insofar as the universal is related to the particular hermeneutical situation of the interpreter.

Gadamer concludes that hermeneutical understanding, like *phronēsis*, yields practical knowledge, knowledge that actually shapes our practice. This is neither the understanding of the scientist nor the technician. It is rather an understanding which incorporates and mediates our own hermeneutical situation – our own collection of prejudices and pre-understandings – with what we are seeking to interpret. Moreover, we do not come to understand by applying a given universal to a concrete case. It is the actual understanding of the universal itself that the given case constitutes for us.[13]

If Aristotle's analysis of *phronēsis* is for Gadamer 'a kind of model of the problems of hermeneutics,'[14] legal hermeneutics appears to him to be a paradigm of the hermeneutic approach. For legal reasoning embodies all of the essential elements of philosophical hermeneutics: it is essentially interpretative, it presupposes a tradition that must be applied to particular cases, and it requires that the legal reasoner creatively interact with that tradition in order to discover valid legal meaning and make it concrete through application.

Legal reasoning is essentially interpretative because, as Gadamer puts it, the distance between the legal 'universal' embodied in the tradition of a legal culture and the concrete legal situation in a particular case is essentially indissoluble.[15] Even in clear cases, the application of the law to a concrete case can not be the logical process of the subsumption of the individual under the universal. Interpretation is always required since each application of the law is a 'productive supplementation' of the legal tradition. Like morality, Gadamer notes, the law is constantly being developed through the 'fecundity of the individual case.' In light of the interaction between tradition, an interpreter in that tradition, and the concrete case, each legal judgment is a judgment about a special case: '... the evaluation of the case does not merely apply the measure of the universal principle according to which it is judged, but itself co-determines it, supplements and corrects it.'[16]

Legal reasoning presupposes a legal tradition because the possibility of legal validity and meaning flows from its tradition. The tradition transmits both legal authority and the grounding of the attitudes and behaviour which constitute legal practices. Our own legal tradition has developed from common law, legislative, constitutional and customary sources. But it is from the concretization of these materials that the content of our tradition arises. Moreover, in application, the legal tradition 'fully penetrates reality.' As participants in our legal tradition, jurists come to the law with an 'immediate expectation of meaning,' and it is by means of hermeneutic understanding that that meaning is realized in the particular case.

Finally, legal reasoning is only possible if the reasoners creatively interact with their legal tradition. The meaningful application of the law to particular cases is presumed, and the task is to discover the valid legal meaning in application. Although Gadamer is aware that the authoritative act of productively supplementing the law is one which our legal tradition reserved to legally constituted authorities such as judges, he insists that anyone who has immersed oneself in the tradition is capable of understanding the legal validity of a judicial decision. It is part of our conception of a legal order that the judge's decision does not proceed from an arbitrary or unpredictable reasoning, but rather is constituted by a legally valid interpretation. That is, it is possible to know, in principle, what the legal answer in each case is. 'Every lawyer and every counsel is able, in principle, to give correct advice, i.e., he is able to predict accurately the judge's decision on the basis of the existing laws.'[17]

V

Although Gadamer appears to agree with Dworkin's contentious claim that there is, for each legal question, a 'right answer,' there are also important differences between them, which suggest that the hermeneutic approach, as a form of practical reasoning, may preempt the possibility of direct legal criticism.

Gadamer argues that the precondition for legal hermeneutics is the existence of a legal tradition which ensures that the law is binding on all the members of the community in the same way. Where this is not the case — where, for example, the law is the manifestation of the will of an absolute ruler — there can be no question of interpreting the law to show that the particular case was decided according to the idea of law. There is a need for understanding and interpretation only when something is enacted in such a way that it is, as enacted, irremovable and binding.[18]

Thus, it appears that Gadamer would agree with Dworkin's well-known objections to strong judicial discretion,[19] although for different reasons. If, faced with a 'hard case,' a judge were granted strong discretion by the legal tradition to step outside of that tradition and decide the case on extra-legal grounds, then, Gadamer claims, that decision would not display legal validity. The decision, in short, would not be open to an interpretation which could uncover a legal understanding.

Gadamer is here developing a theme for which hermeneutics is noted, namely that understanding requires a hermeneutical situation given by the pre-understandings of a tradition. As interpreters we are limited by our own historicity. This theme is, of course, the basis for the hermeneutic critique of objectivism and foundationalism, views which presume that it is possible to stand outside of our historical situation. But if we are thus tied to our traditions, how may we criticize them? Gadamer insists elsewhere that 'it is a grave misunderstanding to assume that emphasis on the essential factor of tradition which enters into all understanding implies an uncritical acceptance of tradition and socio-political conservatism ... .'[20] Yet inasmuch as the standards, criteria, and norms we appeal to in order to criticize aspects of our tradition, or our present situation, have themselves been handed down to us from tradition, internal criticism of that tradition remains problematic.

The difficulty seems to undercut the prospects of practical philosophy itself. Practical philosophy in the Aristotelean tradition relies not only on *phronēsis*, it also seems to require a community of shared values and universal principles, perhaps on the model of Aristotle's *polis*. Yet we ourselves appear to be living in a time in which many of the universal principles and norms of practical conduct are not shared: our own hermeneutic situation is marked by general breakdown in the conditions required for the exercise of *phronēsis*.[21] If what is required is political praxis aimed at reinstating, or creating, the kind of community needed for both *phronēsis* and practical philosophy, how can hermeneutics help?

More particularly, in the absence of a community of shared values, how are we to understand our legal traditions in a way which makes plausible not only legal certainty, but also the possibility of subjecting existing features of the law and legal institutions to criticism? Can laws and legal institutions be criticized from within our legal tradition? If our own hermeneutical situation with respect to law reveals a growing lack of consensus over basic values, and if this lack of consensus has produced a 'pluralistic society' the nature of which undermines just that capacity of judgment which makes practical philosophy possible, is legal hermeneutics possible at all?

As I mentioned above, Dworkin has finessed this problem. For him legal interpretation has three phases: a pre-interpretative stage, in which the rules and standards that provide the tentative content of a law or other social practice are identified; an interpretative stage, where the interpreter settles on some general justification for the basic features of the law or practice; and a post-interpretative or reforming stage, at which the interpreter adjusts his or her sense of what the law or practice really requires.[22] At this last and obviously crucial stage, appeal may ultimately be made to the overall rationale of the law, namely the rights thesis. The aim of this stage is to engage in 'creative' and 'constructive' interpretation, the imposition of purpose on the law or practice in order to make of it the best possible example of its kind.

At the stage of post-interpretation, legal critique is possible because the rights thesis offers a sufficiently determinative standard by which all legal controversies and 'hard cases' can, in the end, be resolved; or so Dworkin believes. From the perspective of philosophical hermeneutics, however, at least as it has been propounded by Gadamer,[23] it is not at all clear whether a post-interpretative stage is possible. Rather it appears that philosophical hermeneutics must advise that our hermeneutic situation gives us legal certainty at the cost of being unable to submit elements of the tradition to internal critique, or to respond constructively to the breakdown of the conditions of practical reasoning in our culture.

Perhaps what philosophical hermeneutics really teaches us is that the basis for legal critique and political praxis lies beyond hermeneutics itself.[24] The hermeneutical perspective is essential for an understanding of law and legal reasoning, and thus philosophers of law have much to learn from this tradition. As well, critique itself presupposes understanding. If our ultimate aim is to go beyond understanding to critique proper, however, we seem to be led away from the lessons of hermeneutics. We must then enage in political praxis that aims to make concrete in our own time the conditions for practical philosophy.

NOTES

1 Hans-Georg Gadamer, 'Hermeneutics and Social Science,' *Cultural Hermeneutics* **2** (1975), 316

2 Hans-Georg Gadamer, *Truth and Method* (New York: Crossroad 1984), 274-8

3 Ibid., 278-305

4 See Ronald Dworkin, *Law's Empire* (Cambridge, MA: Harvard University Press 1986), and his earlier articles, 'Law as Interpretation' and 'My Reply to Stanley Fish (and Walter Benn Michaels): Please Don't Talk about Objectivity Any More,' in W.J.T. Mitchell, ed., *The Politics of Interpretation* (Chicago: University of Chicago Press 1983).

5 Dworkin, *Law's Empire*, 13-15

6 Ibid., 268 ff.

7 Ibid., 31-7

8 See W.O. Quine's discussion of 'radical translation' in Chapter II of *Word and Object* (Cambridge, MA: MIT Press 1960); and Hilary Putnam, *Meaning and the Moral Sciences* (London: Routledge and Kegan Paul 1978). The theme is explored extensively in Richard Rorty, *Philosophy and the Mirror of Nature* (Princeton, NJ: Princeton University Press 1979).

9 For this general argument against behavioural and empiricist approaches to the study of social reality see Charles Taylor, 'Interpretation and the Sciences of Man,' reprinted in his *Philosophical Papers*, Vol. 2 (Cambridge: Cambridge University Press 1985).

10 Dworkin, *Law's Empire*, 93

11 An example of the approach to legal reasoning that I am characterizing here is clearly presented in Martin P. Golding's *Legal Reasoning* (New York: Knopf 1984).

12 Gadamer's treatment of the question of application is found in *Truth and Method*, 274-305. I have found helpful discussions by Richard J. Bernstein, 'From Hermeneutics to Praxis,' in Robert Hollinger, ed., *Hermeneutics and Praxis* (Notre Dame, IN: University of Notre Dame Press 1985), and Ronald Beiner, *Political Judgment* (Chicago: University of Chicago Press 1983), 19-25 and Chapter Four.

13 Gadamer, *Truth and Method*, 305

14 Ibid., 289

15 Ibid., 471

16 Ibid., 37

17 Ibid., 294

18 Ibid., 294

19 See Ronald Dworkin, *Taking Rights Seriously*, revised ed. (Cambridge, MA: Harvard University Press 1978), chapters 2-4, 13, and 'No Right Answer?', in P.M.S. Hacker and J. Raz, eds., *Law, Morality and Society* (Oxford: Clarendon Press 1977), Chapter 3.

20 Hans-Georg Gadamer, 'The Problem of Historical Consciousness,' in P. Rabinow and W.M. Sullivan, eds., *Interpretative Social Science: A Reader* (Berkeley: University of California Press 1979), 108

21 Richard Bernstein makes this point in 'From Hermeneutics to Praxis,' 286.

22 Dworkin, *Law's Empire*, 65-8

23 Dworkin appears himself to be relying more on Habermas's than Gadamer's account of hermeneutics. See *Law's Empire*, 419-21.

24 Richard Bernstein has suggested this as the solution to Gadamer's problem in 'From Hermeneutics to Praxis,' 290.

Roger A. Shiner

The Hermeneutics of Adjudication

I

Knowledge for humans is typically expressible in language. A sentence
will express certain or foundational knowledge only if its meaning
is clear. But if sentences and texts are such that their meanings are
never clear, if discernment of meaning is always a matter of interpretation, then no sentence in a language could express foundational
knowledge. Thus do anti-foundationalist strategies and strategies which
give great weight to the concept of interpretation serve together in
a common philosophical cause.

Law as a social enterprise seems to require legal certainty. If laws
are not clearly and antecedently promulgated, then citizens cannot
autonomously plan their lives free from anxiety about unpredictable
official intervention. Texts, however, are integral to the legal enterprise – charters, constitutions, bills, statutes, all are fundamental legal stuff; modern common law is inconceivable without the practice
of reporting the opinions of judges and the decisions of courts. Unless those texts bear certain meanings, the legal enterprise is threatened
at its foundations. Analysis of the role of interpretation in adjudication is therefore a central task in legal philosophy.

I do not here attempt that task, but something more modest and
preliminary. Law is not the only social enterprise centrally dependent
on texts. The enterprise of the creation, enjoyment, and criticism of
works of literature is equally so dependent. Legal philosophers whose
aim is to advance understanding of law and the legal order may therefore quite plausibly turn to comparing law and literature, in the expectation that the comparison will be illuminating. Several have
recently done so, focussing especially on the fact that legal materials,

like literature, typically require interpretation. Perhaps the most well-known is Ronald Dworkin, whose views are discussed by Jerry Bickenbach in the article above. I shall argue here that the similarity between law and literature is largely superficial, and that the differences between law and literature are more striking and significant than the similarities. While it is clearly not false to assert that appellate adjudication is a matter of interpreting a text, the nature of appellate adjudication is more obscured than illumined if it is regarded as analogous to the creation and criticism of a work of literature. No threats to legal certainty come straightforwardly from the reliance of law on interpretation.

Aesthetic theorists frequently claim that Interpretation as a mode of thought is distinct both from Description and Evaluation. One can describe a poem as written in hexameters; one can evaluate it as the finest English epic of the eighteenth century; but one must interpret it as expressing a profound vision of the perfectibility of man. It is a commonplace in the practice of law itself that constitutions, statutes, and judicial rulings require interpretation. It is not difficult, therefore, to motivate the thought that adjudication may profitably be construed as Interpretation in some technical sense borrowed from aesthetic theory. The three traditional approaches to legal theory — legal positivism, natural law, and legal realism — all seem to deploy exclusively the categories of Description and Evaluation. The legal positivist thinks that those 'core' propositions of law which describe social facts of the positivist's preferred kind are descriptive, while those 'penumbral' propositions of law which are not in the same way descriptive of social fact are merely evaluative, merely expressions of judicial opinion. The natural law theorist thinks that all propositions of law are descriptive. They are descriptive, however, not of social fact but of 'natural fact.' Alternatively, one may think of the natural law theorist as claiming that all propositions of law are evaluative (at least, that is how positivism is wont to represent natural law theory). The realist, rule-sceptic, or critical legal scholar thinks that no propositions of law describe, for a proposition of law is true only if there are legal facts which make it true and there are no such legal facts. Since propositions of law do not describe, they must merely evaluate, merely be expressions of the judge's personal opinion. Theorists have the sense that insofar as legal theory oscillates endlessly between these traditional positions it is an exercise in futility. To reject this reliance on Description and Evaluation, and to espouse instead the cause of Interpretation seems to offer the chance of progress.

It is important to remember that while 'description,' 'evaluation,' and 'interpretation' have standard meanings outside technical philosophical contexts (meanings recoverable from any decent dictionary), inside philosophy the terms have no established theory-independent meaning at all. To 'interpret' may be pre-analytically to 'expound the meaning of,' to 'explain,' to 'render clear and explicit.' However, what counts as 'rendering clear and explicit' or 'explaining' for some given enterprise, and even whether clarity and explanation are available at all within that enterprise, are themselves typical philosophical questions about such enterprises as law, literary criticism, biblical studies, logic, science, and history. In and of itself, to assert that propositions of law are interpretive rather than descriptive or evaluative does little more than register a repudiation of naive or extreme versions of standard theories. I shall attempt here to characterize the enterprises of law and literature in terms which are as far as it is possible for them to be plain and theory-neutral. I do so in the service of explaining the thought that law and literature are indeed instances of interpretive enterprises, but in the knowledge that the content of that thought is given by the characterizations themselves rather than by the epithet 'interpretive.'

II

Law and literature are both enterprises concerned with 'texts.' Are they concerned with 'texts' that are 'texts' in the same sense? Are they concerned in the same way in each case with 'texts,' whatever the meaning of 'text'?

The 'black-letter text' of a poem or novel is fundamentally a fixed and determinate series of inscriptions in a language. There is a text of 'The Whitsun Weddings' or David Copperfield in an anthology or on a wall or between two covers only if there is in such a place one particular set of inscriptions rather than another. This remark is a slight exaggeration. Authors typically produce different drafts of literary works, and there may be historical reasons for controversy over which is the 'genuine' or 'authentic' text. But such controversies exist for specialized purposes and at the peripheries. They will not secure the claim that what I have on p.49 of *The Oxbridge Book of Modern English Verse* is a version of 'To His Coy Mistress,' or that next to *Nicholas Nickleby* and *The Old Curiosity Shop* is really, despite appearances, a copy of *Slaughterhouse Five*. Even those literary theorists who deny the existence of texts in classes nonetheless reconstruct the notion of 'text' in their preferred sense of, for example, *Paradise Lost* so that it is still a different 'text' from 'The Whitsun Weddings' or *David Copperfield*. Whatever the preferred theory of textuality, it is accepted as a constraint on the theory that these differences of identity are preserved, however strenuous the debate over what it is for each literary work to be the particular 'text' that it is.

In the case of law, there are legal texts that are fixed in very much the same kind of way. The Canadian Charter of Rights and Freedoms and the U.S. Constitution are each one particular set of 'black-letter' inscriptions rather than another. Again, one can imagine controversy about the exact details of the text (suppose, for instance, the version published in an official Gazette is marginally different from the version presented to a legislature for approval), but these controversies will be in the nature of the case exceptional. Moreover, although legal theorists may, and indeed do, dispute over just what it is for the U.S. Constitution to be the particular 'text' or 'document' that it is, it is an accepted constraint on the adequacy of any such theory that the difference of identity between the U.S. Constitution and the Canadian Charter of Rights and Freedoms is preserved. Much the same may also be said of statutes. One has on one's desk a copy of a particular Act of Congress or parliamentary Bill only if there is on one's desk one particular set of 'black-letter' inscriptions rather than another. And so on.

So far, then, there are similarities between law and literature – but only so far, and that is not very far. Let us begin to chart the differences.

III

(1) In the first place, the kind of fixed 'text' so far referred to exhausts the 'black-letter' materials in literature. Even the debate as to whether the notes to 'The Wasteland' are part of the poem is a debate over the extent of the 'black-letter' text, not over whether materials other than the black-letter text are part of the poem. (Mallarmé's famous remark about the white spaces on the page being the most important part of the poem is important in part because it is *paradoxical*.) However, fixed black-letter texts of this kind do not exhaust legal materials. In addition to charters (in jurisdictions that have them), constitutions, and statutes, there is (in common law jurisdictions, at least) the common law itself. The common law is spoken of as 'black-letter law,' but one must be careful about what that remark can mean. A statute is embodied in the words of its text. The words do not report the existence and content of the statute; they are the statute. The role of black-letter inscriptions in the case of the common law is different. Law Reports are genuinely reports. They report cases; sets of material facts, arguments by counsel, and adjudicative opinions by judges. Judges do characteristically formulate in words the ratio decidendi of the case before the court when rendering a decision; they state the rule for which they take the case to stand. It is a commonplace, however, that, unlike a charter, constitution, or statute, the words used in the statement of a ratio by a judge have no canonical status. The material facts of a common law case, rather than anything that might straightforwardly be called a 'text,' ultimately determine for what the case stands as an authority. The common law is thus not a matter of fixed texts, and in the end a matter of fact-situations, not a matter of texts at all. Insofar as the law contains the common law, it contains something for which there is no analogue at all in literature.[1]

It is a mistake, then, to represent law and literature as alike in that both have exclusively to do with fixed texts. In central and important ways, law does not have to do with fixed 'texts' at all, despite the importance to law of charters, constitutions, and statutes.

(2) Second, the ways in which a 'text' in literature and a 'text' in law are 'fixed' are themselves importantly different. The fixedness of a literary work is a permanent fixedness. The identity of a literary

work is traceable to a particular act of creation or particular series of continuous connected acts by a particular artist. At least, this is the usual case. There are works picked up and worked on for a while, dropped, picked up again, and so forth; works which form a series; works finished off posthumously by the author's best friend; works of joint authorship. These do not conform to the paradigm. However, we make sense of the artistic identity and integrity these works may have in terms of the paradigm of single artist and creative act or connected series of acts. The text of a poem is fixed as *that* set of inscriptions because *that* set of inscriptions is what *this* artist *then* wrote. More complex problems of identity arise when an author releases several different versions of a poem, say, at several different times. There is a real problem of identity here because the standard paradigm is under strain. Such a problem throws into relief, but does not dislodge, the paradigm case.

Law is again very different. It is true that, because of the nature of laws as norms of an institutionalized system, a statute or a common law ratio comes into existence at a datable time and place. Its existence as a text for the period of its life is determined by that institutional act. But legal texts are in the nature of the case vulnerable to deliberate modification and destruction. A statute can be repealed and replaced by another. A common law precedent is not always followed; it can be distinguished or even overruled. Works of literature could not play the role that they play in human life if they were subject to evanescence in this way. It is no coincidence that the test of time is a test of value for works of literature. The law, however, could not play the social role that it plays unless it were capable of change and evolution, and that means that laws themselves cannot be fixed and immune from change. Laws as texts are inherently transitory while works of literature are inherently enduring.

It might be thought that change and evolution imply fixedness. Suppose a constitution is amended. Then the 'old,' unamended constitution is a fixed text that has to be replaced. This example shows how the issue of the identity of laws is complex and controversial in a way that the identity of works of literature is not. Why should we say that the 'new' amended constitution is one legal text and the 'old' one another? Why should we not say that there is one constitution which has been amended? There is a genuine question here for theorists to debate. Moreover, as Joseph Raz has pointed out, laws do not come primarily as individuated texts, but come in systems of laws.[2] One command pronounced by one sovereign does not make a law. A particular statute is the particular statute that it is in part because it belongs to a particular system of laws; its apparent dependence upon the one dateable law-making act which created it is therefore misleading. However, once the systemic character of laws is taken into account, problems of the identity of laws arise. For example, section 7(3) of the Criminal Code of Canada explicitly preserves the validity of all the common law defenses to criminal charges. The plethora of sections which follow define all manner of criminal offences, to each of which section 7(3) applies. Is section 7(3) to be counted as one law and each of the offence-defining sections as one more law? Or is the section on assault, for instance, to be coupled with section 7(3) in order to be regarded as one law concerning assault? Are subsections defining sub-offences (if it may be put that way) each one law, or each parts of one major law? This is not the place to try to resolve these questions, even supposing they can be resolved. The point is that it is in the nature of laws to be part of systems, to interlock with each other in various complicated ways. Thus, while it may be true in some very broad sense that laws are texts, it is not possible to see how one particular law is a fixed and unique text in the way that one particular poem or novel is a fixed and unique text.

(3) Third, while there is a line of thought in theory of criticism which defends the view that there should be only one possible interpretation of a work of literature, this is a much-attacked position. It is attacked for two reasons. First, it fails to correspond to the phenomenology of the appreciation of literature, missing the fact that works of literature often stand many different interpretations, each of which seems to bring powerful illumination of the work and satisfaction to the appreciator. Second, that line of thought can find no room for the highly plausible idea that a work of literature is a great work just because and insofar as it can sustain a rich plurality of interpretations. My point is not that the 'one single interpretation' position is theoretically mistaken, although I believe it is. My point is that there is a genuine normative issue to be debated in the case of literary artworks.

In the case of law there is no such debatable issue. It would be a failure of legal drafting if every section of a statute supported a rich variety of equally valid interpretations of its meaning. The whole art of drafting is the art of eliminating as far as possible ambiguities of meaning in the texts of statutes and opinions. Of course, complete elimination cannot be attained. As Hart has put it, we suffer congenitally from relative ignorance of fact and relative indeterminacy of aim.[3] A system of laws must balance the need for certainty against the need to accommodate an uncertain and changing world. However this is to be done, and there are many sensible options here by way of institutional design, it is uncontroversial that to pass laws which possess quite deliberately multiple meaning is not one of these options. It is true that a statute may contain a deliberately vague phrase, such as 'fair and reasonable grounds,' as a way of delegating to an administrative tribunal a discretionary power. The expectation is nonetheless that the statute clearly so delegates, and clearly indicates what the delegation brings within the jurisdiction of the tribunal and what it does not.

The art of the literary artist is to combine fixedness of text with multiplicity of meaning. The art of the legal draftsperson is to combine transitoriness of text with elimination of multiplicity of meaning. To say that each of these persons is alike in that they are both composers of texts is to obscure these crucial differences.

(4) Fourth, there is in literature a considerable difference between the position of the artist as creator of the work and the position of the critic as the interpreter of the work. As Sparshott has emphasized, works of art are essentially *performances*, coming about as the products of intelligent agency.[4] The critic has to determine what the artist did in producing the particular work. This does not mean that the critic has to determine what the artist intended to do; the emphasis on performance does not constitute a form of intentionalism. Rather, it is a way of underlining the difference between the artist as performer and the critic as interpreter of the performance. 'Performance' is a term of the art of criticism, not of the art of artistry. The 'performances' of the critic begin where the performances of the artist end. This is true even if one regards the intentions of the artist as the appropriate standard for critical judgment.

When we turn to law, the situation is different. Law seems to be in this respect most like literature in the case where a court is faced with the task of interpreting a constitutional provision or a statute. Given the separation of powers, the court no more created the legal text in question than the critic created the poem or novel. The court seems to be faced with the task of interpreting someone else's performance (the legislature's). Such a thought is appropriate as far as it goes. The disanalogy comes in when one tries to find that in which the performance consists in each case. Larkin's performance in writing 'The Whitsun Weddings' is constituted exactly by the production of that set of inscriptions which is 'The Whitsun Weddings.' The legislature's performance in enacting section 1(1) of the Criminal Damage Act 1971 is not at all something constituted exactly by the enactment of that set of inscriptions which constitute that section. The difference is a manifestation of the status of the legal text as a text within an institutionalized system. The set of inscriptions constituting that section of that act is a legal text in part because the legislature have the legal authority to enact such performances. This is true, no matter what one's favourite theory as to that in which the possession of such authority consists. Moreover, not merely judicial interpretation but also judicial review of legislation is indicative of the institutionalized and systematic nature of law. That being so, the performances of legislatures and the performances of courts are interlocked. They are not distinct in the way that the performances of artists and of critics are distinct.

If one turns from constitutional and statute law to common law adjudication, the distinction between the judge as artist and the judge as critic (as it may be put) becomes harder, and arguably impossible to draw. The common law is not for nothing known as 'judge-made law.' In the common law, the legal materials are no more and no less than those that result from the decisions of courts. The judge in creative mode provides the material which the judge in critical mode interprets. One might say that one can imagine cases where artists are also critics — Eliot or Spender might be palmary recent examples — so that, if judges are also artists and critics, there seems to be no disanalogy. This impression is illusory. It is not part of the 'office' of the artist (if we may extend the use of that term, and it *is* an extension) also to be a critic, or part of the office of a critic also to be an artist.

It is however part of, even constitutive of, the office of the common law judge both to create and to interpret the law when adjudicating common law cases.

(5) The literary and the legal enterprises come closest together in the case of the development of literary genres. In an important sense the notion of 'genre' is a critic's notion. A group of writers may have a sense of belonging to a single school by virtue of sharing common artistic goals and a common conception of the techniques for reaching those goals. In this connection one might think of the Symbolists, the Imagists, or the Vorticists as examples. Alternatively, a contemporary writer might quite self-consciously see himself or herself as recreating a past style. Examples might be neo-Romanticism or neo-Classicism. The critic, however, while taking such biographical matters into account, chiefly declares a body of work to constitute a genre for reasons of similarities and analogies in the literary works themselves, independently of whether the authors believe the works should be grouped together. Moreover, the notion of a genre is an essentially retrospective notion. A critic can predict the emergence of a genre, but there is an unseemly arrogance in an artist's setting out to anticipate or create one. The critic surveys a body of literature that has grown up out of influences, conscious and unconscious, and sees the works as having similarities which make them more like each other than any one of them is like other works. The critic, in classifying a set of works as a genre, and in working out the principles of membership in the genre, is operating at a level of abstraction well above the detailed examination of particular literary texts. The critic sees patterns and notices resemblances within a wide range of material. However, after the critic has plausibly introduced the notion of a particular genre, writers may become more self-conscious about writing within it, and may have their own effect on its literary development.

In somewhat the same way, the judge when interpreting a legal text, even if following a narrow theory of statutory interpretation which searches simply for the ordinary meaning of the term but especially if following any wider theory, does not simply consider the minutiae of a single sentence but surveys a wider body of material. The judge also operates strictly retrospectively, seeing patterns in a number of past decisions and resemblances between the case in question and these decided cases. Landmark cases are decided by the recognition of a pattern that has emerged in a group of cases.[5] General concepts in law grow and develop in much the same way as genres grow and develop. They do so by judges' alternation between the quasi-critical role of discerning the pattern and the quasi-artistic role of identifying with it and seeking to decide future cases in its light.

It is therefore possible to identify an aspect of the literary enterprise and an aspect of the legal enterprise in respect of which the two enterprises are structured in a very similar way. However, this close analogy exists between the two enterprises only at a high level of abstraction. The structural analogy is one the theorist sees as embodied in the results of the interpretation of texts. It does not exist at the level on which the participant in each enterprise interprets the texts of that enterprise and in the way that the texts of the enterprise are texts. The recognition of a genre by a critic and the recognition of a legal concept by a judge are not similar because critics and judges interpret similar kinds of text in a similar way. The similarities I have indicated presuppose only that the critic does whatever he or she does qua critic, and the judge does whatever he or she does qua judge, and that there are certain similarities in the results of these respective operations. That each interprets similar texts in the same kind of way, and even that what each does is interpret texts, are matters which would have to be shown, if they can be shown, independently of the parallelism I have just described.

IV

(1) In short, a detailed examination of the two realms of law and literature reveals considerable differences in the position of the critic relative to 'black-letter' literary materials and the position of the judge in relation to 'black-letter' legal materials. Two things therefore follow. First, any slogan of the form 'law is like literature' is likely to be true, if at all, at a superficial level and in a simple-minded way. One may say, for example, that nothing in the above recitation of plain facts shows it to be false that both the legal and the literary enterprises consist in the interpretation of texts. I have acknowledged that, at a superficial level, it would be a mistake to deny that. But

I have also shown that the sense in which it is true that both law and literature involve the interpretation of texts is a sense too feeble to say anything significant about the kind of institution law is or the kind of interpretation that legal interpretation is. Second, the differences I have charted rule out the possibility of any direct inference from premisses stating features of the interpretation of literary texts to conclusions about the nature of adjudication and law. Although both the literary and the legal enterprises involve the interpretation of texts, it does not follow simply from the fact that literary interpretation has certain properties that legal interpretation also has those properties. It is impossible to make sensible claims about the status of the legal enterprise as an interpretive enterprise without carefully considering the process of adjudication in itself. The nature of legal interpretation will be determined far more by idiosyncratic features of legal reasoning and legal decision-making than by any high-level similarities between interpretation in law and interpretation in literature.

In a well-known passage, Hart sets out what he calls some 'pairs of contrasting facts.' Despite the absence of a single method for determining the content of an authority, the case-report's headnote is 'usually correct enough.' Even though there is no single authoritative formulation of a rule, there is 'often very general agreement ... that a given formulation is adequate.' Even though courts may act 'creatively' by narrowing or widening rules, the 'vast number' of common law rules 'are as determinate as any statutory rule.[6] I believe Hart's 'facts' are indeed facts. Their obtaining produces legal certainty, and is also quite compatible with adjudication being in a natural sense interpretation. Those who wish to decry legal certainty in the name of interpretation must confront these 'facts' on their own merits, and not suppose it possible to decide what law is like by deciding what literature is like.

(2) What does all the above have to do with *practical reasoning*, and in particular with the kind of approach to legal argumentation represented by Robert Alexy and promoted by Neil MacCormick?[7] The implications, broadly put, are the following.

I want to say again that my argument is not designed to show that adjudication is not interpretation. It is designed to show that, pace Dworkin and others, law is *not very much* like literature. The claim,

'Adjudication is Interpretation,' unsupported by a detailed examination of actual adjudication and how it is similar to and different from other modes of argumentation and criticism is likely to be a philosophically feeble claim. Consideration of a theory like Alexy's, however, shows why it is philosophically valuable to insist that 'adjudication is interpretation' (and even, perhaps, that law *is* like literature!). As described by MacCormick, Alexy offers a set of principles for the justification of legal decisions at an enormously high level of abstraction, far removed from anything that goes on even in the highest tribunal in the land. Alexy's theory of practical reasoning is as far removed from what adjudication is actually about as a theory of literary criticism would be if it mentioned not one single literary artwork or piece of literary criticism. It is difficult to see how one can say anything illuminating about the specific practice of adjudication at such a high level of generality. To insist that adjudication is interpretation (and even, perhaps, that law is like literature) fulfils the valuable function of focussing attention on the need to take seriously in the legal enterprise concrete individual persons, their decisions, actions, and material situations, for the literary enterprise is paradigmatically the enterprise of concrete unique entities.[8]

NOTES

1 Customary law, in the sense of customs of the realm having legal force, is even more distinct. Such customs are by definition not present in black-letter law. However, customary law is an increasingly vestigial aspect of contemporary legal systems, and so no argumentative weight is placed upon it in this essay.

2 Joseph Raz, 'Legal Principles and the Limits of Law,' *Yale Law Journal* **81** (1972) 823-54, at 825-9

3 H.L.A. Hart, *The Concept of Law* (Oxford: Clarendon Press 1961)

4 Francis Sparshott, *The Theory of the Arts* (Princeton, NJ: Princeton University Press 1982), 38-43:

> A performance ... is whatever is performed by a performer as such
> in and by the performing of it, and can be defined as the imputed
> end of any action conceived as intelligently intended to achieve just
> that end. More briefly, a performance is anything made or done,
> as one conceives it when one attends strictly to the making and do-
> ing. (41-2)

In 'treating something as a performance [one] assumes intelligent agency' (42); the 'singling out' of something as a performance is the 'specific
operation of teleological intelligence, whether on the part of agents
or of observers' (40).

5 Think here of the role of *Donoghue v Stevenson* or *McPherson v Buick
Motors* in the development of tort law, and the way that in the former
Lord Atkin claimed to find his ground-breaking 'neighbour principle'
already embodied in decided cases.

6 Hart, *Concept of Law*, 131-2

7 Neil MacCormick, 'Legal Reasoning and Practical Reason,' *Midwest
Studies in Philosophy* **7** (1982) 271-86

8 I should like to thank Annette Barnes for many valuable discussions
about interpretation in literature, and for helpful comments on an earlier version of this essay. Her own study of interpretation in art criticism, *On Interpretation*, is forthcoming (Oxford: Basil Blackwell 1987).
The present essay is based on research supported by the Social Sciences
and Humanities Research Council of Canada. This support is grate-
fully acknowledged.

Notes on Contributors

Barry Allen studied philosophy at the University of Lethbridge and at Princeton. Since completing a dissertation on Wittgenstein in 1986 he has worked on studies in contemporary Continental philosophy, regularly teaching in this area at McMaster.

Jerome E. Bickenbach is Associate Professor of Philosophy and Lecturer in Law, Queen's University. He writes in legal theory and law, focussing on criminal and constitutional jurisprudence, and is the author, with C.I. Kyer, of *The Fiercest Debate: Caesar Wright, the Benchers, and Legal Education in Ontario.*

Robert Burch is Assistant Professor of Philosophy, University of Alberta, and has taught previously at Haverford College, PA. His writings have focused on the philosophy of technology and pedagogy, and on more general topics in continental philosophy. He is an Editor of *Canadian Philosophical Reviews*, an Associate Editor of *Phenomenology and Pedagogy*, and on the Board of Referees, *Canadian Journal of Philosophy.*

Rebecca Comay studied philosophy at Toronto, Near Eastern studies in Jerusalem, and Egyptology and Assyriology at Yale. She now teaches continental philosophy at the University of Toronto. She has recently written a book on Hegel and Heidegger, tentatively titled *'Beyond' Aufhebung: Reflections on the Bad Infinite*, forthcoming shortly in the 'Intersections' series of SUNY Press.

Jean Grondin, Professor of German and Contemporary Philosophy at Laval University, Québec. Book publications: *Hermenuetische Wahrheit? Zum Wahrheitsbegriff Hans-Georg Gadamers* (Königstein: Forum Academicum 1982); *Le tournant dans la pensée de Martin Heidegger* (Paris: PUF, collection Epiméthée 1987).

David Hitchcock, Associate Professor of Philosophy at McMaster University, is the author of *Critical Thinking* (Methuen 1983) and of articles and addresses on Plato's conception of the good, Aristotle's treatment of future singular statements, Stoic propositional logic, the deduction-induction distinction, and enthymematic arguments.

Neil MacCormick is Regius Professor of Public Law and the Law of Nature and Nations in the University of Edinburgh, where he is also currently Dean of the Faculty of Law. His principal publications are *Legal Reasoning and Legal Theory* (1978), *H L A Hart* (1981), *Legal Right and Social Democracy* (1982) and (with Ota Weinberger) *An Institutional Theory of Law* (1986).

G.B. Madison is Professor of Philosophy at McMaster University and Professor of Philosophy in the Graduate Faculty of the University of Toronto. He is the author of *The Phenomenology of Merleau-Ponty*, *Understanding: A Phenomenological-Pragmatic Analysis*, *The Logic of Liberty*, and *Figures and Themes in the Hermeneutics of Postmodernity* (forthcoming). He has published numerous articles in English, French, and German. Professor Madison is coordinator of the Canadian Society for Hermeneutics and Postmodern Thought.

Peter McCormick is Professor of Philosophy and English Literature at the University of Ottawa. The editor of several collections on Husserl and Ingarden, he is also the editor of *The Reasons of Art* and the author of *Heidegger and the Language of the World*, and the forthcoming *Fictions, Philosophies, and the Problems of Poetics*.

Dieter Misgeld has taught in Canada at Laurentian University and, since 1973, at Ontario Institute for Studies in Education. He is cross-appointed to the Department of Philosophy (Graduate faculty), University of Toronto. His publications are on hermeneutics and critical theory, hermeneutics and social science, critical theory and sociology, critical theory and education. He is co-editor (together with Volker Meja and Nico Stehr) of *Modern German Sociology* (New York: Columbia University Press 1987)

Jeff Mitscherling is Assistant Professor of Philosophy at the University of Guelph. His areas of specialization include Greek philosophy, aesthetics, phenomenology, and hermeneutics. He has published in several journals, including *Kant-Studien*, *Philosophy and Phenomenological Research*, *Classical Quarterly*, *Apeiron*, and *The British Journal of Aesthetics*. He is currently completing a lengthy study entitled *The Image of a Second Sun: Plato's View of Poetry*.

Kai Nielsen is Professor and Head of the Department of Philosophy at the University of Calgary. He has previously taught at Amherst College, New York University, Brooklyn College, the Graduate Center of the City University of New York, and the University of Ottawa. He is past president of the Canadian Philosophical Association and an Executive Editor of the *Canadian Journal of Philosophy*. His most recent book is *Equality and Liberty: A Defense of Radical Egalitarianism* (Rowman and Allanheld 1985).

Douglas Odegard teaches philosophy at the University of Guelph. He is the author of *Knowledge and Scepticism* (1982) and has published several journal articles on knowledge.

Roger A. Shiner is Professor of Philosophy at the University of Alberta. He has published numerous articles on philosophy of law in both philosophy journals and law journals. He also writes in aesthetics, and is a former Secretary-Treasurer of the Canadian Society for Aesthetics and former Trustee of the American Society for Aesthetics.

Index of Names

Index of Subjects

action, 16, 24, 38-9, 55, 59-74
agency, 16, 26-7
anti-foundationalism, 1-2, 4-8, 11, 17-18, 23, 27, 34, 80, 92, 139, 150, 165, 173, 179, 190-1, 202, 204-5, 211-12, 214, 223, 233; *see also* foundationalism, non-foundationalism, post-foundationalism

certainty, 2, 8-9, 18, 41, 54, 106, 113, 150, 152, 174, 188, 203-4, 228-9, 233-4, 240, 244
coherence, 51, 137, 139, 145-6, 150, 188
consensus, 2, 121, 138, 147, 158-60, 175, 184, 189; rational, 2-3, 22-5, 158, 173-5, 188
conversation, 1, 6, 8, 10-11, 31, 41, 56, 79-81, 85-97, 99-102, 108-17, 122-33, 204-5, 207; distinguished from dialogue, 81, 128-9, 132; as ghettoization, 102; as persuasion, 96; rational, 10-11; and universal human community, 16, 56, 115; *see also* dialogue
critical theory, 30, 144-5, 155-9, 165-70, 174-8
criticism/critique, 11, 89, 92-3, 95, 109-10, 112-13, 130-1, 133, 197-8, 218, 227-9, 233-4, 245; legal, 198, 227-9; negative, 10, 179; *see also* critical theory, social criticism

deduction/deductivism, 9-10, 196, 209-10, 222
dialogue, 10, 18, 55-6, 81, 128-32; as critical inquiry, 130; rebels against foundations, 55; *see also* conversation, language

epistemology, 2, 4, 6, 8, 10, 18, 22, 29, 80, 111, 123-5, 137, 184, 188, 203-4

facts, 8, 24, 29, 39, 212-3, 234, 244
foundationalism, 1-2, 4-5, 7, 9-10, 15-16, 21, 23-4, 27-8, 30, 34, 36, 79-80, 104-5, 109, 111, 180, 184-6, 188, 195, 199, 203, 205, 211, 227; moderate/modest, 137, 196-7, 205, 211, 214
foundations, 1, 3, 4, 6, 8, 11, 54, 84, 125, 197, 203, 211, 233

hermeneutics, 9-11, 18, 30, 35, 45, 48-56, 81, 111-12, 121-6, 130-1, 198, 209, 217-29; critical potential of, 130-1, 218, 223, 227-9
hermeneutical circle, 35, 49, 95, 152, 159, 183
historicity, 46, 49, 130, 132, 227; of inquiry, 130; of validity claims, 16; as enemy of foundations, 6, 49
historicism, 1, 5, 10, 28-9, 49, 90, 94-5

incommensurability, 18, 27, 157, 159-60, 188-90
inquiry, 11, 130, 183, 187
interpretation, 8-9, 11, 35, 37, 40-1, 49, 51, 197-8, 208-10, 220-1, 223-5, 233-45
interpretive dialectics, 17, 37, 40, 42

justification, 2, 3, 31, 138, 145, 147, 151, 187, 189, 198, 210, 222

253